Read SAP PRESS online also

With booksonline we offer you online access to leading SAP experts'
knowledge. Whether you use it as a beneficial supplement or as an
alternative to the printed book – with booksonline you can:

• Access any book at any time
• Quickly look up and find what you need
• Compile your own SAP library

Your advantage as the reader of this book

Register your book on our website and obtain an exclusive and free test
access to its online version. You're convinced you like the online book?
Then you can purchase it at a preferential price!

And here's how to make use of your advantage

1. Visit www.sap-press.com
2. Click on the link for SAP PRESS booksonline
3. Enter your free trial license key
4. Test-drive your online book with full access for a limited time!

Your personal **license key** for your test
access including the preferential offer

edfc-xzma-unsw-jt39

Maximize Your Warehouse Operations with SAP® ERP

 PRESS

SAP PRESS is a joint initiative of SAP and Galileo Press. The know-how offered by SAP specialists combined with the expertise of the Galileo Press publishing house offers the reader expert books in the field. SAP PRESS features first-hand information and expert advice, and provides useful skills for professional decision-making.

SAP PRESS offers a variety of books on technical and business related topics for the SAP user. For further information, please visit our website: *www.sap-press.com*.

Martin Murray
SAP Warehouse Management: Functionality and Technical Configuration
2008, 504 pp.
978-1-59229-133-5

Othmar Gau
Transportation Management with SAP LES
2008, 574 pp.
978-1-59229-169-4

Varun Uppuleti
Customizing Extended Warehouse Management with SAP ERP
2010, 226 pp.
978-1-59229-286-8

Srivathsan Narayanan
Optimizing Reverse Logistics with SAP ERP
2010, app 315 pp.
978-1-59229-325-4

Martin Murray

Maximize Your Warehouse Operations with SAP® ERP

Galileo Press

Bonn • Boston

Galileo Press is named after the Italian physicist, mathematician and philosopher Galileo Galilei (1564–1642). He is known as one of the founders of modern science and an advocate of our contemporary, heliocentric worldview. His words *Eppur se muove* (And yet it moves) have become legendary. The Galileo Press logo depicts Jupiter orbited by the four Galilean moons, which were discovered by Galileo in 1610.

Editor Meg Dunkerley
Copyeditor Ruth Saavedra
Cover Design Jill Winitzer
Photo Credit Image Copyright cofkocof. Used inder license from Shutterstock.com.
Layout Design Vera Brauner
Production Editor Kelly O'Callaghan
Assistant Production Editor Graham Geary
Typesetting Publishers' Design and Production Services, Inc.
Printed and bound in Canada

ISBN 978-1-59229-309-4

© 2010 by Galileo Press Inc., Boston (MA)
1st Edition 2010

Library of Congress Cataloging-in-Publication Data
Murray, Martin, 1964–
  Maximize your warehouse operations with SAP ERP / Martin Murray. ± 1st ed.
      p. cm.
  Includes bibliographical references and index.
  ISBN-13: 978-1-59229-309-4 (alk. paper)
  ISBN-10: 1-59229-309-3 (alk. paper)
  1. Warehouses — Management — Computer programs   2. Inventory control — Computer programs.
  3. Business logistics — Computer programs.   4. SAP ERP.   I. Title.
      HF5485.M87 2010
      658.7'85028553 — dc22

                                                                          2009042514

Contents at a Glance

Contents

Acknowledgments

The author would like to thank Meg Dunkerley of SAP PRESS for her faith in him and her patient, tireless efforts in ensuring this book was completed. Thanks also to Ruth Saavedra for her editing of the final draft.

Preface

In writing this book I have addressed the needs of the Warehouse Management professional that wishes to maximize the warehouse management functionality in SAP ERP to provide successful solutions to complex warehouse problems.

I have examined warehouse processes that cover the breadth of the warehouse management functionality in SAP ERP. In doing this, I have explained the business and technical functions that need to be combined to produce a successful solution.

This book describes the efficiencies that can be obtained by maximizing the warehouse management functionality in SAP ERP. To illustrate the points made, I include real-world examples in each chapter that will provide you with insight to help you transform your own warehouse operations.

Who This Book Is For

This book is for the Warehouse Management consultant using SAP ERP or supply chain analyst whose company is implementing or has implemented warehouse management in SAP ERP. It is especially useful for professionals who want to understand warehouse management functionality, and how they can use it to transform their warehouse operations. We assume readers have a basic understanding of warehouse management functionality in SAP ERP, but require additional knowledge to use the solution to improve the operation of their companies' warehouse operation.

This book examines all warehouse processes from incoming product to shipment completion, and it looks at the challenges and opportunities at each key processing point in both technical and operational terms. Throughout the book readers will find success stories, best practices, and explanations of the warehouse management tools in SAP ERP to achieve results with a minimum amount of time and expense.

Organization of This Book

This book is examines the full breadth of operations in the warehouse. It discusses how, by maximizing the use of the warehouse management functionality, you can successfully implement complex procedures. So let's take a look at how the book is organized.

Chapter 1 – Introduction

This chapter is for the readers to refamiliarize themselves with the importance of warehouse operations and the basic organization and master data in warehouse management in SAP ERP. The introduction explains the purpose of the book and gives the reader an overview of the warehouse management functionality in SAP ERP.

Chapter 2 – Effective Inbound Execution

This chapter examines the elements of the inbound delivery process. It discusses the advanced shipping notice and how it is important in the creation of inbound deliveries. The chapter goes on to discuss receipt at the warehouse and how handling units and automatic putaway can streamline storage in the warehouse.

Chapter 3 – Enhancing Your Managed Putaway and Quality Inspection Processes

This chapter reviews the managed putaway and quality inspection processing in the warehouse. The chapter describes processes such as fixed bin, open storage, next empty bin, and addition to stock strategies that can be used to efficiently put away material in the warehouse.

Chapter 4 – Improving Internal Warehouse Operations

This chapter covers general activities that take place inside the warehouse. The chapter examines general warehouse goods movements, such as the transfer requirements and transfer orders that are used to move materials and posting changes that amend the status of materials. Throughout the chapter we'll examine various processes and strategies to show how to make internal warehouse movements more efficient.

Chapter 5 – Effective Picking Operations and Storage Unit Management

This chapter discusses the different picking strategies, such as FIFO, LIFO, partial quantity, and fixed bin, which are used in the warehouse and can improve the warehouse operation. The chapter also examines the efficiencies of storage unit management when it is implemented in the warehouse.

Chapter 6 – Efficient Shipment Completion

This chapter reviews the steps required to complete a shipment, including the creation and monitoring of outbound deliveries. We'll see a variety of procedures that can increase efficiencies in the shipment process.

Chapter 7 – Maximizing Returns Processing

In this chapter we'll review the complete returns process, from the initial call from the customer to the restocking of materials in the warehouse. The chapter also examines the role of different departments in the process and discusses how reverse logistics can create a new revenue stream for your company.

Chapter 8 – Efficient Physical Inventory

This chapter discusses the inventory procedures that clients use to maximize the efficiency of their inventory accuracy. These include cycle counting and continuous inventory, which are becoming more common as companies move away from traditional annual physical inventories.

Chapter 9 – Successful Cross-Docking

This chapter examines reasons why your company may want to introduce cross-docking and how to implement cross-docking in your warehouse. Cross-docking is an important aspect to many companies, especially retail-orientated businesses. It is an efficient way that can help your company improve deliveries to customers while reducing warehouse resources.

Chapter 10 – Working with Hazardous Materials

In this chapter we'll discuss the subject of hazardous materials, which are used in the production of finished goods in thousands of companies every day. The storage and management of these materials is extremely important to the safe operation of the warehouse.

Chapter 11 – Using Radio Frequency Identification Effectively

The use of RFID is increasing, and this chapter examines how you can use the SAP Auto-ID Infrastructure application to implement a successful RFID process. The chapter also discusses the successful uses of radio frequency in the warehouse.

Chapter 12 – Effective Use of Warehouse Data and Reporting

In this chapter we'll examine several key standard warehouse management reports in SAP ERP that can enhance your staff's ability to create efficiencies in warehouse processes. The chapter also reviews the warehouse activity monitor, which is crucial in the operation of an efficient warehouse.

Chapter 13 – Conclusion

This chapter summarizes the elements discussed in the book and examines how the concepts can be adopted to produce successful warehouse processes based on maximizing the use warehouse management in SAP ERP.

I hope this book gives you the information that will help you maximize the use of the warehouse management functionality in SAP ERP. I hope you can use the knowledge you gain from reading this book to develop your skills to help your company benefit from using SAP ERP.

Martin Murray

In warehouse management in SAP ERP, the warehouse is divided into several components. Storage types, storage sections, and storage bins are unique locations where an item has been stored, and these coordinates allow items to be located.

1 Introduction

Warehouses have been around for hundreds of years, but today the warehouse is a key component of the any company's supply chain. Technological advances in computer-based warehouse management systems (WMSs) have made it possible for the operation of the modern warehouse to be its most efficient, reducing delivery times to the customer and reducing the cost of warehouse operation to a minimum and maximize company profits.

The modern warehouse faces significant challenges. Increasingly complex customer and consumer demands must be balanced against pressures to improve cost control and squeeze maximum accuracy and productivity from a dynamic workforce. SAP provides a variety of tools to address these issues, including the warehouse management functionality in SAP ERP, which provides a solid foundation for effective warehouse management. However, many companies that have implemented this functionality underuse it and are not aware of the underlying effective warehousing principles.

SAP provides tools for the warehouse

In the first section of this chapter, we'll look at the important warehouse operations that can be found in the modern warehouse.

1.1 The Importance of Warehouse Operations

In the past the warehouse was considered a storage facility where items are placed once they were manufactured. Companies often followed a make-to-stock strategy where finished goods were manufactured to a forecast rather than a customer's requirement. When a sales order was received from a customer, the order was fulfilled from inventory. This meant the customer didn't have to wait for the item to be manufactured, but it required companies to closely manage their inventory.

In the past warehouses were just storage facilities

Value-added warehouse operations

Although some companies saw warehousing as a necessary but unwanted part of doing business, some businesses began to see the importance of warehouses as facilities that offer value-added operations beyond just storage. The introduction of regional distribution centers saw companies use these super warehouses as locations that offer a number of efficiencies.

1.1.1 Transport Consolidation

Reduced shipping costs with transport consolidation

Regional distribution centers were able to consolidate items that were sent from smaller warehouses. The smaller shipments from the individual warehouses didn't allow for full truckloads, so items were moved using less-than-truckload (LTL) carriers, which is a more expensive method of shipping to a customer. The cost saving was gained by the regional distribution center because it allows customers to receive one large shipment of materials by shipping with full truckloads (TLs) instead of receiving a number of smaller shipments from multiple warehouses. Figure 1.1 shows the consolidation of transported items to the customer.

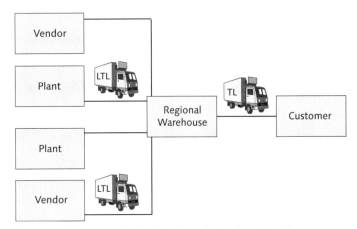

Figure 1.1 Transportation Cost Savings of a Regional Warehouse

1.1.2 Product Mixing

Product mixing can improve customer service

The regional warehouses could also produce a value-added service to both customers and the business by combining a variety of materials into single shipments to customers and to the company's production facilities. A regional distribution center could fulfill a sales order for several items faster than individual warehouses could. If a sales order was sent to an individual plant, the onsite warehouse might contain only some of the items needed, and the other items would have to be shipped from other warehouses to fulfill the order. If a regional warehouse received items from a number of plants, then the sales order could be fulfilled faster because all of the items would be available in the single location. This value-added process is called product mixing. Figure 1.2 shows that one plant supplies the regional warehouse with product A, whereas another plant sends product B. When a customer sends a sales order for products A and B, the regional warehouse can fulfill the order faster than the individual plants.

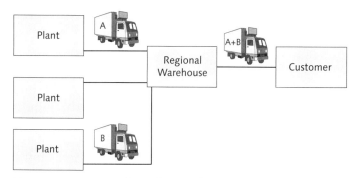

Figure 1.2 Customer Sales Order Is Fulfilled by the Regional Warehouse

The process is equally efficient for inbound deliveries to a production facility. If suppliers send items to the regional warehouse rather than to the individual production facilities, the plants need less space for storing raw materials and don't have to wait for items to arrive from multiple suppliers. Figure 1.3 shows items C and D being sent to the regional warehouse, which in turn supplies them to the production plant when a requirement occurs.

Combining raw materials for production

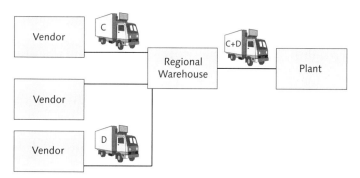

Figure 1.3 Raw Materials Sent to Fulfill an Order at the Production Plant

1.1.3   Process Improvements

The introduction of supply chain methodologies and just-in-time philosophies made the warehouse an important element in the supply chain. The warehouse is an active contributor to the efficiency of the supply chain. Operations within the warehouse have become increasingly efficient, because items are required to move through the warehouse and to the customer even faster. Items no longer spend weeks and months in the warehouse, but move from production to customer in a matter of days or hours.

To improve profitability and service to the customer, companies required the shortest possible time between the end of the production line and delivery to the customer. To achieve this, businesses began to increase the efficiencies of processes throughout their supply chains, including warehouse operations. To improve warehouse processes, companies redesigned warehouses, developed layout methodologies, and implemented picking and placement strategies along with automation and warehouse-specific software.

In the 1990s many software companies began to develop WMS packages that assisted companies with achieving more efficient warehouse operations. These warehouse-specific software suites allowed the staff to more efficiently place items in the warehouse and locate items for picking. However, standalone warehouse systems need interfaces to pass data to and from other systems.

The advent of enterprise resource planning (ERP) packages, such as SAP ERP, has reduced the need for standalone warehouse systems. The warehouse management functionality in SAP ERP includes the functions found in the stand-alone systems with extended transportation and distribution capabilities.

So let's review the organizational structure for warehouse management in SAP ERP.

1.2   Understanding Warehouse Management in SAP ERP

The warehouse management functionality in SAP ERP is part of logistics execution in SAP, along with transportation and direct delivery applications. The warehouse management functionality is a necessary element for companies that have true warehouse operations. However, some companies refer to their managed warehouse, but it is sometimes no more than a building where their materials are stored in a haphazard fashion. In these cases the company has a warehouse where item location is not formalized and materials are stored in a random fashion. In a goods receipt situation, the warehouse staff receives and moves items to the first open space that is found. When materials are to be moved to production or shipped to a customer, finding a specific item in the warehouse is time-consuming.

However, some companies don't require the warehouse management functionality in SAP ERP. For businesses that don't have a wide range of products and whose products are not necessarily batch managed or don't have a shelf life limitation, simple storage solutions using materials management with SAP ERP Operations may be sufficient. So to begin, let's look at the organizational structure that a business will use when implementing warehouse management in SAP ERP, beginning with the company code.

1.2.1 Company Code

The U.S. Census Bureau in 2002 defined a company as follows:

> *A company comprises all the establishments that operate under the ownership or control of a single organization. A company may be a business, service, or membership organization; it may consist of one or several establishments and operate at one or several locations. It includes all subsidiary organizations, all establishments that are majority-owned by the company or any subsidiary, and all the establishments that can be directed or managed by the company or any subsidiary.*

Defining a company code

In SAP systems, the company code is defined as the smallest organizational unit for which a complete self-contained set of accounts can be drawn up. This provides data for generating balance sheets and profit-and-loss statements. The company code represents legally independent companies. Using more than one company code allows a business to manage the financial data for different independent companies at the same time. When a customer is deciding on its organizational structure, it can use one or more company codes. Figure 1.4 shows the organizational components a company needs to be considered when implementing an SAP system.

The company code represents legally independent companies

Figure 1.4 shows company 1000, which has two plants associated with the company code. Plant 1000 has two storage locations, 1001 and 1002, whereas storage location 2001 has only one storage location assigned,

2001. Two warehouses are defined within the company structure: 100 and 200. Warehouse 100 is within the plant 1000 structure and linked directly to storage location 1001. Warehouse 200 is part of the plant 2000 structure and linked to storage location 2001.

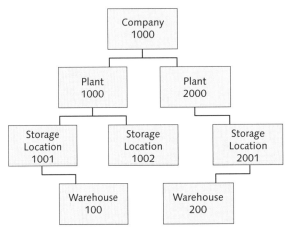

Figure 1.4 Organizational Structure in an SAP System

> **Example**
>
> A logistics management company offers transportation, warehousing, and consulting as part of their overall business. To ensure that each part of the company is able to provide independent financial reports, the three business lines are created as three separate company codes in the SAP implementation.

You can create the company code using Transaction OX02. The menu path is IMG • Enterprise Structure • Definition • Financial Accounting • Define, Copy, Delete, Check Company Code. The field is defined as a four-character alphanumeric string. In Transaction OX02, it is possible to copy from an existing company code and change the name, city, and country to your company details. This transaction will update table T001. Figure 1.5 shows the creation of a company code.

After creating the company code, you'll need to maintain the company code address. To do this, use Transaction OBY6. This transaction will update table SADR.

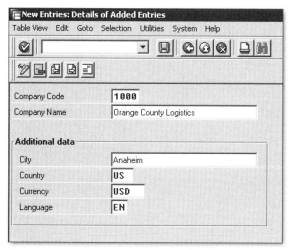

Figure 1.5 Creating a Company Code

Now that we've reviewed the company code structure within the SAP system, let's move on to plants.

1.2.2 Plant

The definition of a plant can vary greatly from business to business and industry to industry. A general definition of plant is a location that holds valuated stock or an organizational unit that is central to production planning. Some companies define a plant as a location that contains customer service or maintenance facilities. The definition of a plant varies depending on the customer's needs when implementing their SAP system.

> A plant is a location that holds valuated stock

When you create a plant in your SAP system, you have to enter a certain amount of information, including name, address, tax jurisdiction information, and the factory calendar that is used at the plant.

A four-character string defines the plant field. You can configure it using Transaction OX10. Follow the menu path IMG • ENTERPRISE STRUCTURE • DEFINITION • LOGISTICS – GENERAL • DEFINE, COPY, DELETE, CHECK PLANT.

Figure 1.6 shows the information that is added for the plant.

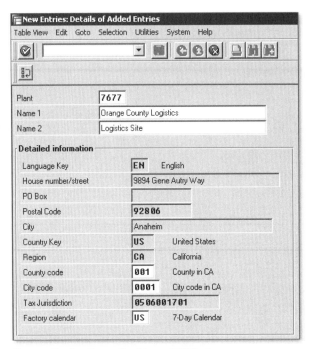

Figure 1.6 Creating a Plant in an SAP System

The organizational structure within SAP systems, allows you to assign one or more plants to a single company code.

> **Example**
>
> A logistics management company offers transportation, warehousing, and consulting as part of their overall business. Each of the businesses has been given its own company code. The transportation business has five locations across the U.S. and Canada. These locations can be created as plants and linked to the one company code.

You assign a company code to the plant so that all plant transactions can be attributed to a single legal entity, that is, a company code. You can achieve this in Transaction OX18 or via the menu path IMG • ENTERPRISE STRUCTURE • ASSIGNMENT • LOGISTICS – GENERAL • ASSIGN PLANT TO COMPANY CODE.

The plant is assigned to one company code

A plant is assigned to one company code, but a company code can have more than one plant assigned to it. Figure 1.7 shows five plants assigned to a single company code.

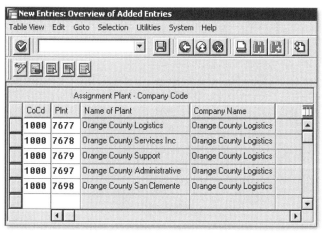

Figure 1.7 Assignment of Plants to a Company Code

In the next section, we'll look at the components of the plant by examining storage locations.

1.2.3 Storage Location

In the plant there are areas where materials are stored. These areas can be physically defined, for example, where materials are stored in different rooms or racking systems, or can be as simple as lines drawn on the floor. The storage location can be a logical location, which is defined in the system but doesn't have any physical location.

SAP defines a storage location as a place where stock is physically kept within a plant. At least one storage location is always defined for one plant. It is the lowest level of location definition within the materials management functionality in SAP ERP.

The storage location is where stock is physically kept

In an SAP system you can define a storage location with a four-character string which you can configure using Transaction OX09. The menu path is IMG • Enterprise Structure • Definition • Materials Management • Maintain Storage Location.

Figure 1.8 shows the creation of three storage locations (SLoc) for Plant 7677. After you enter the storage locations, you'll be directed to another screen to enter secondary information such as address and telephone number.

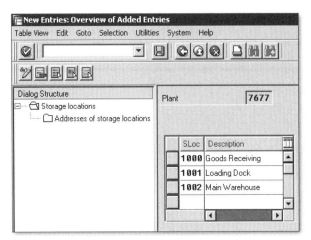

Figure 1.8   Creation of Storage Locations

Although the storage location is the lowest storage level in materials management, it is not the lowest level in the SAP system. Depending on the customer's requirements, the number of materials that are stored, the number of unique locations, and the sophistication of the customer's current inventory system, you may need to implement the warehouse management functionality in SAP ERP. This provides the opportunity to manage inventory at a bin level.

When warehouse management in SAP ERP has been implemented, you make the storage location the link to the warehouse management functionality by assigning a warehouse to a storage location. So let's move on to discuss the warehouse.

1.2.4   Warehouse

Depending on the complexity of the operations in a facility, an SAP customer has to decide whether to implement the warehouse management functionality. Basic storage location functionality within materials management is not enough for the modern warehouse, and as warehouse processes become ever more complex, the decision to implement warehouse management in SAP ERP becomes easier to make.

The warehouse contains storage types

The warehouse is made up of a number of distinct areas called storage types. These can then be subdivided into storage sections, and at the lowest level is the storage bin. Because the warehouse management functionality in SAP ERP can be operated as a stand-alone, decentralized system, independent of the rest of the SAP system, it is different from other SAP solutions such as sales and distribution and production planning.

The warehouse structure relates directly to a storage location in materials management. A warehouse can be created in configuration but doesn't have a physical address attached to it when configuration takes place. The warehouse only relates to a physical entity when it is assigned to a storage location.

The warehouse is defined by a three-character string. You can find the transaction for creating a warehouse number by following the menu path IMG • Enterprise Structure • Definition • Logistics Execution • Define, Copy, Delete, Check Warehouse Number.

First, the warehouse number has to be created as shown in Figure 1.9.

Figure 1.9 Creating the Warehouse

After you define the warehouse, you need to assign it to a plant and storage location. The warehouse may often be assigned to just one storage location, but depending on how the storage locations have been defined in materials management, the warehouse may have to be assigned to more than one storage location.

The warehouse is assigned to a plant and storage location

You can find the transaction for assigning a warehouse to a plant and storage location combination via the menu path IMG • Enterprise Structure • Assignment • Logistics Execution • Assign Warehouse Number to Plant/Storage Location.

Figure 1.10 shows the assignment of a warehouse to a specific storage location.

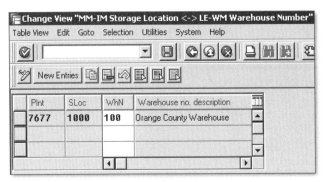

Figure 1.10 Assignment of a Warehouse to a Storage Location

The warehouse is divided into several smaller areas called storage types, which we'll discuss next.

1.2.5 Storage Type

Definition of a storage type

Within the warehouse are areas where items are stored, which are identified in the SAP system. These storage areas are called storage types. When a warehouse is initially designed, the layout of the warehouse is analyzed based on a number of objectives including:

- To provide the most efficient handling of the stored materials
- To provide the maximum flexibility to meet any changes in warehousing that the company may require
- To get maximum use out of the space inside the warehouse
- To provide the most economic warehousing procedures based on layout

You access the transaction for creating a storage type via the menu path IMG • LOGISTICS EXECUTION • WAREHOUSE MANAGEMENT • MASTER DATA • DEFINE STORAGE TYPE.

Figure 1.11 shows the details of Storage type 005 at Warehouse 100.

Each storage type has attributes that can be assigned to it, as shown in Figure 1.11. These attributes are used for stock placement and stock removal, and will be discussed in later chapters.

The storage type can be subdivided into more specific sections that refer to areas within the physical location. These are called storage sections, and we'll discuss them in the next section.

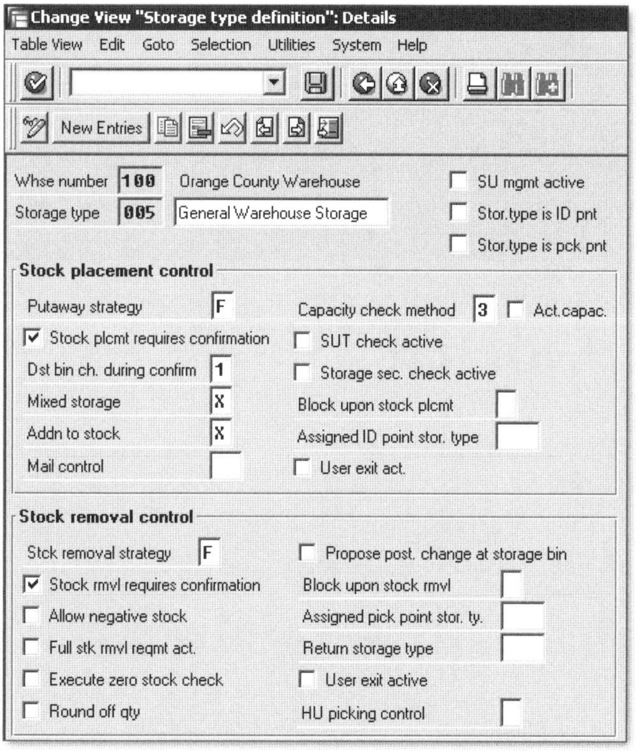

Figure 1.11 Definition of a Storage Type

1.2.6   Storage Section

The storage type can be divided into areas called storage sections. The storage section contains the storage bins where the materials are stored. Many storage types have only one storage section, because there is no requirement to break the storage type into further distinct areas. There is a requirement that at least one storage section must be defined for each storage type.

> A storage type consists of at least one storage section

You can find the transaction for creating a storage section via the menu path IMG • Logistics Execution • Warehouse Management • Master Data • Define Storage Sections.

Figure 1.12 shows that two storage sections have been created for storage type 005. The two sections distinguish between slow-moving and faster-moving stock in the storage type.

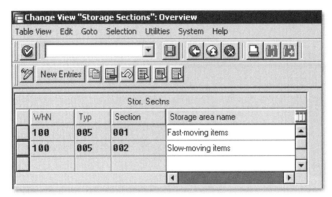

Figure 1.12 Creation of Storage Sections

When the materials are placed into storage in the warehouse, it is placed in the storage bin, and this is what we'll examine in the next section.

1.2.7 Storage Bin

The storage bin is the smallest unit of storage in the warehouse. There is no set size for a storage bin, and it can vary between companies, warehouses, and even in the same storage type.

A storage bin can be a location on a shelf, a location on a carousel, or a plastic tub in a rack. No matter what the shape or size of the physical bin, every material in the warehouse is stored in a storage bin.

Storage bins can be created manually or automatically. You create a storage bin manually using Transaction LS01N, which you can access via the menu path SAP • Logistics • Logistics Execution • Warehouse Management • Master Data • Storage Bin • Create • Manually.

To create the storage bin, you enter the warehouse number, storage type, and storage bin number, as shown in Figure 1.13. Once you've filled in these fields, the other field to fill in to create the storage bin is the storage section number. The other fields on the entry screen, such as picking area and maximum weight, are optional.

We've now reviewed the organizational structure of warehouse management in SAP ERP. Let's move on to the make-up of the physical warehouse.

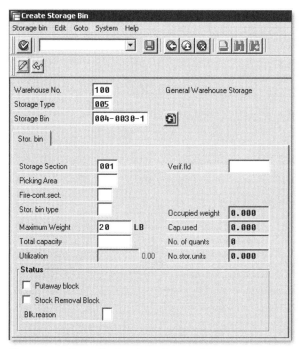

Figure 1.13 Manually Creating a Storage Bin

1.3 Understanding the Physical Warehouse

The internal organization of a warehouse directly relates to the nature of a company's business. For example, a large retailer with distribution centers would consider warehousing to be a primary function, whereas a company that manufactures custom mechanical equipment may only use warehousing for maintenance and spare parts. Between these two extremes, businesses use warehousing as part of their normal supply chain.

Warehousing as part of the normal supply chain

When we look at the functions of the physical warehouse, some are directly related to the warehouse, and some perform support functions for the warehouse. Functions that are directly related include receiving, sorting, and transportation, whereas quality and sales offer supporting functions.

1.3.1 Receiving, Shipping, and Storage

The basic functions of any warehouse include the receipt of goods, the storage of those items in the warehouse, and the shipment of items to customers, production facilities, or other company locations.

1.3.2 Inventory Accuracy

The accuracy of inventory levels is important to any business. If the inventory levels are not accurate, materials may not be available for customer orders, and this will negatively affect customer satisfaction. Similarly, if items are not available for production, this can delay manufactured finished goods and subsequently affect customer satisfaction. Inventory accuracy can also affect the storage of inbound materials. Items arriving at the warehouse are allocated empty storage bins, and if the bins are full due to inventory inaccuracies, this wastes time and resources.

1.3.3 Value-Added Processes

Some processes performed in the warehouse can add value and in turn increase customer satisfaction with a minimum expenditure of resources. An important value-added process performed within the warehouse is the repackaging of items from bulk packaging to smaller single packages suitable for delivery to customers. Many warehouses perform finishing processes on items before they are shipped to customers. When items are received from production, they may require some minor customization that is specific to a customer, such as applying price labels or special packaging. The process is performed in the warehouse just prior to delivery.

1.3.4 Warehouse Safety

The warehouse can be a dangerous place, but the storage of hazardous materials requires additional safeguards to ensure materials are stored and handled correctly. The physical warehouse requires significant safety features that need to meet the requirements of regulatory agencies such as the EPA and OSHA. Special safety features can include:

▶ High-pressure foam sprinkler system
▶ Fire and theft system that is constantly monitored
▶ Primary and secondary containment system
▶ HAZMAT certification for drivers
▶ Special OSHA training for warehouse staff

1.3.5 Delivery Process

The warehouse function interfaces with the transport department to ensure that customer deliveries leave the facility at the correct time. The transport department arranges carriers to be at the facility at an exact time, and the warehouse staff prepares each delivery to be at the dock at the precise time the carrier arrives.

1.3.6 Inspection and Quality Process

As part of the receiving and shipping process, the warehouse can be required to perform inspection and quality procedures. On the receipt of material from a vendor, the warehouse staff can perform a visual inspection, and depending on the complexity of material, staff can carry out some quality testing. This doesn't replace detailed quality testing, but inspections by warehouse staff can quickly identify problems, and items can be returned to the vendor. On outbound shipments, warehouse staff can inspect items before they are shipped to the customer to ensure that there are no obvious quality issues. This simple process can improve customer satisfaction while reducing costs.

Inspection prior to shipping can help customer service

Now that we've looked at the processes that can be found in the physical warehouse, we'll review the importance of the physical layout of the warehouse.

1.4 Defining the Warehouse Layout

Creating a design for a warehouse is a project that follows a number of design principles. These include the use of a single-story facility, the use of simple single-line flow of materials in the warehouse, the use of the most efficient materials-handling equipment, and the maximum use of space.

Design principles are key to warehouse layout

1.4.1 Design Principles for Warehouse Layout

The design principles for the warehouse layout are straightforward and use common sense. You should follow several principles of warehouse layout.

Use a Single-Story Facility

A single-story facility is preferred for a warehouse because it's easier to construct, and materials handling is straightforward. A second story produces complications in materials flow, but for locations where land is at a premium, a two-story facility may be the only option.

Direct Flow of Goods

A warehouse design should allow the material flow to be as direct as possible. Creating a straight line between the areas from receiving to shipping, minimizes the travel time between areas. A layout that has a nonlinear design can create backtracking paths that reduce efficiency. Figure 1.14 shows the direct flow principle.

Figure 1.14 Direct Flow of Goods through the Warehouse

Efficient Materials Handling

The use of efficient materials-handling equipment can improve the efficiency of moving materials in the warehouse. Equipment such as forklifts is commonplace in warehouses, but other materials-handling equipment can also be used. Conveyor systems can move materials from one area to another with great efficiency and are found in many order picking systems. Picker-to-part systems and parts-to-picker systems can increase efficiencies, but there is an initial cost to consider.

Effective Storage Plan

Maximizing the space in the warehouse is important to ensure that all of the available space is used. However, as much as it is important to maximize storage, the layout of the space has to make placement and picking as efficient as possible.

Minimize Aisles, Maximize Height

The aisle width determines the overall capacity of the warehouse. The storage capacity can be significantly reduced if the aisles are too wide. The aisle width should be minimized but to a width at which the materials-handling equipment can still operate safely. Equipment with a small turning radius can reduce aisles further and increase warehouse capacity. The height of the warehouse can be exploited to further increase warehouse capacity. Raising the height of the racking increases the storage capacity of the warehouse.

Minimizing aisle width can increase storage capacity

1.4.2 Warehouse Layout Objectives

When designing the layout of a warehouse, you should consider a number of fundamental objectives. These include maximization of the warehouse capacity, efficiency of warehouse movements, and maximization of productivity.

Maximizing Warehouse Capacity

The key objective is to maximize the capacity of the warehouse because this reduces the cost of storing material. Having large storage areas with limited access can increase storage capacity, but limited access is only appropriate with stock that has a low turnover. If you have a warehouse with items with a high turnover, the access to storage areas needs to be as easy as possible for quick access.

Increased capacity can reduce storage costs

Efficiency of Warehouse Movements

Each warehouse movement needs to be as efficient as possible. The layout of the warehouse needs to minimize movements between areas so that as few resources are expended as possible. By reducing the length of each movement, you can increase the number of movements performed by each resource per hour.

Maximizing Productivity

Reducing the time of each material movement can increase productivity; however, additional improvements can be made to increase productivity. Increasing the use of efficient materials-handling equipment can increase productivity. Over time, the key to increasing productivity is to introduce

Warehouse management can improve productivity

several performance metrics. The warehouse management functionality in SAP ERP offers a number of reports that can assist in this area. These are monitored to identify where the improvements in the warehouse should be made.

The layout of the warehouse is important in maximizing the storage capacity, efficiency, and productivity. The warehouse management functionality in SAP ERP can help warehouse management produce an efficient and productive warehouse.

1.5 How This Book Is Organized

We wrote this book to address the many complex challenges of modern warehouse management using SAP ERP. It teaches users how to use the solution without the addition of third-party software and the additional costs and challenges that create. Readers will learn how to seamlessly integrate and customize warehouse management in SAP ERP to meet their own business processes and needs. As discussed in the preface, the chapters in this book cover the key elements of the warehouse management functionality in SAP ERP.

1.6 Summary

This chapter started by reviewing efficient warehouse operations that can be found in the modern warehouse, such as transport consolidation and product mixing. We then moved on to discuss the overall warehouse structure with regard to the physical layout of the warehouse. You learned about how the configuration of the warehouse, its assignment to a storage location, and the creation of storage types are all part of the initial warehouse design. The importance of this initial design work cannot be overstated. The physical warehouse has to be represented in the SAP system.

Understanding the design principles of warehouse layout is very important, and we hope that after examining a number of them, this chapter has given you a solid start to the topic. You should understand the day-to-day functions of warehouse operations.

In the next chapter, we'll discuss the goods receipt process, and you'll learn how to efficiently carry out receiving with SAP.

Vendors fulfill purchase orders by sending deliveries. Using the inbound delivery process allows your company to manage incoming deliveries to make the most of your warehouse resources.

2   Effective Inbound Execution

The receiving of materials into a facility should be an efficient process that is accurate, streamlined, and rapid. When performed correctly, the receiving process should produce an effective use of your warehouse space and resources.

The goods receipt process is the movement of materials into the warehouse from an external source, which could be a vendor, or from the production facility. A receipt process checks the accuracy of both the materials and the quantity. You can check the materials for quality and quarantine if needed. If the quality is satisfactory, the process moves the materials into the warehouse and increases the stock levels of the materials received.

The goods receipt is an important point in the movement of materials. Accepting the items triggers the ownership and financial liability. The receipt of the materials is also the starting point of the tracking of those materials in the facility.

Several processes can trigger inbound deliveries. In the first section of this chapter, we'll review these with respect to the inbound delivery functionality.

2.1   Inbound Delivery Process

The inbound delivery should describe exactly what materials can be received on what date and at what time. The advantages of the inbound delivery function when receiving materials into the warehouse are that you can complete several processes in advance of the materials arriving because the supplier has sent the necessary information to the plant ahead of time using an *advanced shipping notice*, commonly known as an ASN. First, let's look at the elements that make up the inbound delivery process.

Inbound delivery details date and time the items are expected

The inbound delivery process starts when the items are staged at the vendor for pickup by the shipper. The items are made ready for shipment by placing them on a pallet or shipping container at the vendor's shipping area. The items are loaded on to the shipper's vehicle and transported to the ship-to location. The process is completed when the items are received at the ship-to party and a goods receipt transaction is processed. We'll highlight the elements of the inbound delivery process below.

2.1.1 Create a Purchase Order or Scheduling Agreement

Purchase from vendor can be part of a scheduling agreement

When you require items for production or resale, you purchase them from a vendor. If you have a scheduling agreement in place with a vendor, deliveries will occur at regular intervals. If no scheduling agreement exists, you can create a purchase order using Transaction ME21N. You can access the transaction via the menu path SAP • LOGISTICS • MATERIALS MANAGEMENT • PURCHASING • PURCHASE ORDER • CREATE • VENDOR/ SUPPLYING PLANT KNOWN. Figure 2.1 shows an example of a purchase order for five drill presses that have been ordered from Dremel Industries to be delivered on October 22, 2009.

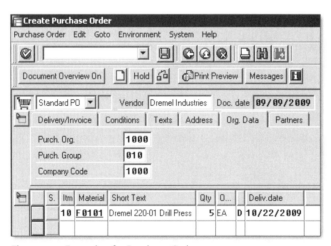

Figure 2.1 Example of a Purchase Order

2.1.2 Determine the Goods Receiving Point

The goods receiving point determines where items arrive

You determine the goods receiving point based on a configuration that has been entered in the IMG. For an inbound delivery, you assign the goods receiving point based on the receiving plant and storage location that was entered into the purchase order. You can find the configuration using the menu path IMG • LOGISTICS EXECUTION • SHIPPING • BASIC SHIPPING FUNCTIONS • SHIPPING POINT AND GOODS RECEIVING POINT DETERMINATION • ASSIGN GOODS RECEIVING POINTS FOR INBOUND DELIVERIES.

Figure 2.2 shows the configuration that allows you to determine a goods receiving point based on the receiving plant and storage location. For Plant 1000 and Storage Location 1000, Shipping Point 0034 is assigned as the goods receiving point.

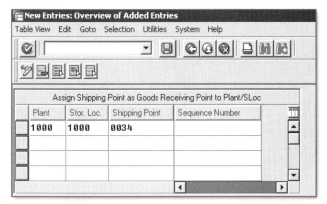

Figure 2.2 Configuration for Goods Receiving Point

2.1.3   Create a Manual Inbound Delivery for a Purchase Order

The inbound delivery can be created either manually or automatically if your vendor sends an advanced shipping notice via electronic data interchange (EDI). In this section, we'll look at the manual creation of an inbound delivery for a purchase order.

Inbound delivery can be manually created

You can create a manual inbound delivery using Transaction VL31N or by going to SAP • LOGISTICS • LOGISTICS EXECUTION • INBOUND PROCESS • GOODS RECEIPT FOR INBOUND DELIVERY • INBOUND DELIVERY • CREATE • SINGLE DOCUMENTS.

Figure 2.3 shows the manual creation of an inbound delivery for purchase order 4500000079.

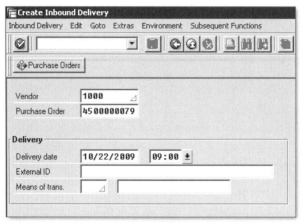

Figure 2.3 Manually Creating an Inbound Delivery

After you've entered the purchase order number and vendor number, the inbound delivery transaction will show the line item transposed from the purchase order 4500000079. Then, you just need to check the item quantity, delivery date, and time for accuracy. If the vendor has identified any specific changes, you can make these to the line item before creating the inbound delivery. Figure 2.4 shows the line item detail for the inbound delivery.

Figure 2.4 Item Detail for the Inbound Delivery

After the item details have been approved, you can save the transaction, and an inbound delivery is created.

2.1.4 Create an Inbound Delivery for a Purchase Order Using EDI

An inbound delivery can be created automatically for a purchase order via EDI. The SAP system must be configured to allow the generation of an inbound delivery for an incoming shipping notification. In addition, the purchase order must be annotated with the correct confirmation information for an inbound delivery to be created.

An inbound delivery can be created via the shipping notice

Inbound EDI Process

The inbound process receives an EDI document, in this case a shipping notification from a vendor. The EDI-specific headers and trailers are removed from the EDI document and it is converted into an IDoc format suitable for SAP applications. The IDoc is stored as a text file, and an inbound program reads the IDoc file and creates an IDoc so it can be processed. A posting program processes the IDoc and creates an application document, in this case a shipping notification, which is then used to create an inbound delivery.

A shipping notice can be called an advance ship notice

Definition of an IDoc

An IDoc is a document that facilitates data exchange between SAP R/3 and non-R/3 systems. An IDoc acts as intermediate storage of information, which can be sent bi-directionally.

An IDoc is made up of three distinct parts

An IDoc is made up of the three parts:

- **Control record**
  This section contains control information regarding the IDoc. It contains the name of the sender, the name of the receiver, the message type, and the IDoc type. There is always a single control record, and it is always the first record in the set.

- **Data record**
  This part consists of a header that contains the identity of the IDoc. It contains a sequential segment number, a segment type description, and a field containing the actual data of the segment. There can be more than one data record.

▸ **Status record**

This shows the information regarding the already processed stages and remaining processing stages of the IDoc. Several status records can be attached to an IDoc. At every processing stage, a status code, date, and time stamp are assigned.

Configuration for Inbound Delivery via EDI

You can only create the inbound delivery for a purchase order if several configuration steps have been completed. A confirmation has to have been received from the vendor, and certain configuration steps should be entered.

First, the shipping notices received from vendors should be configured to allow you to create an inbound delivery. When a vendor sends a shipping notice or a confirmation, the details confirm the delivery dates and quantities of the materials entered in the scheduling agreement release or purchase order sent to the vendor.

To ensure that an inbound delivery can be created from the vendor's confirmation, you must ensure that the confirmation control key is set by going to IMG • MATERIALS MANAGEMENT • PURCHASING • CONFIRMATIONS • SET UP CONFIRMATION CONTROL.

Figure 2.5 shows the configuration of the shipping notification, confirmation control key 0004, to allow an inbound delivery to be created.

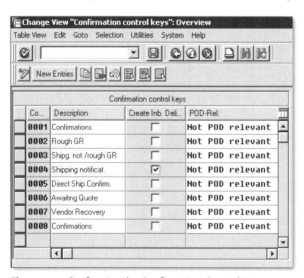

Figure 2.5 Configuring the Confirmation Control Key

Although the configuration shown in Figure 2.5 will allow you to create inbound deliveries for a purchase order, if you want the shipment to go to a specific plant and storage location, you must take an additional configuration step. Follow the configuration menu path IMG • LOGISTICS EXECUTION • SHIPPING • DELIVERIES • DEFINE ORDER CONFIRMATIONS FOR INBOUND DELIVERIES.

Figure 2.6 shows the configuration that will ensure that an inbound delivery is created for confirmations such as shipping notifications. The configuration is specific for category, order type, plant, and storage location. In Figure 2.6 the first line shows that for order type NB, which refers to a purchase order, plant 1000 and storage location 1000, an inbound delivery will automatically be created for confirmation 0004, which is a shipping notification.

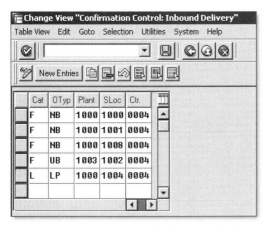

Figure 2.6 Inbound Delivery Configuration for Plant and Storage Location

On the fourth line in Figure 2.6 the configuration is shown for order type UB, a stock transport order, and LP, a scheduling agreement. In this case a shipping notification can be received via EDI for plant 1003 and storage location 1002.

To create an inbound delivery for a transmitted confirmation from a vendor, you must first update the purchase order with the correct confirmation key. When creating a purchase order, the purchaser can add the confirmation key to the purchase order line item, as shown in Figure 2.7. The confirmation control key (Conf.Ctrl) field shows that the confirmation expected is a shipping notification, and the current status is pending, because the purchase order has not yet been created.

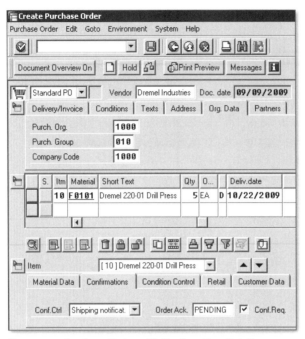

Figure 2.7 Purchase Order with Confirmation Details

Partner profiles
must be
maintained for
vendors using EDI

To receive a confirmation from a vendor via EDI, you have to maintain the partner profiles of the IDoc interface for those vendors. You must fill in several fields in the partner profile. You can find the configuration using Transaction WE20 or the menu path IMG • Logistics • Materials Management • Purchasing • Messages • EDI • Set Up Partner Profile. Figure 2.8 shows the configuration for the partner profile.

With inbound parameters, you specify the conditions for inbound EDI processing. Via the process code entered, you specify how the data is to be processed further in the application. You can also specify who should carry out the necessary reprocessing in the event of an error.

The inbound options allow you to enter a message type that normally relates to the United Nations (UN) EDIFACT standard. In this case the shipping notification is an inbound message from the vendor and is identified by the DESADV message type.

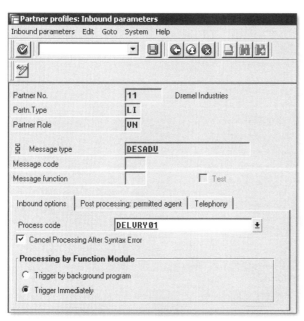

Figure 2.8 Configuration for Partner Profile

You can enter a process code that the IDoc interface uses to find the business process that controls the conversion of the IDoc into an SAP document.

Process codes convert IDocs to SAP documents

Creating a Manual IDoc

You can test the IDoc by using the test tool in SAP to manually generate an IDoc and send the IDoc for inbound processing. You can access the test tool via Transaction code WE19.

Figure 2.9 shows the initial screen for creating a manual IDoc using the test tool. To create a manual IDoc, you enter the message type for a shipping notification, which in this case is DESADV. This may not be the message type used at your company, so check with your EDI team.

The next screen (shown in Figure 2.10) in Transaction WE19 shows the fields that can be manually entered for IDocs.

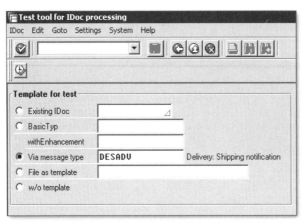

Figure 2.9 Test Tool for IDoc Processing

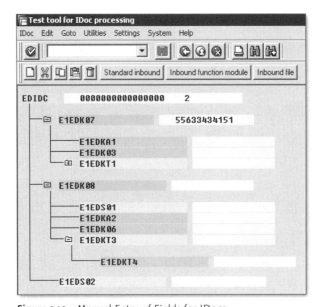

Figure 2.10 Manual Entry of Fields for IDocs

Figure 2.10 shows the fields that you can add manually to create the IDoc. Once the document is saved, the IDoc is treated like it was sent by an external system. The IDoc can then be converted to an inbound delivery document.

2.1.5 Repacking the Inbound Delivery

When an inbound delivery arrives at the warehouse, the items can arrive in a variety of configurations. Sometimes items arrive shrink-wrapped on pallets and can moved directly into the warehouse without anyone having to break down the pallet or repack the items. This can save considerable time and warehouse resources. As part of the purchasing contract with a vendor, it may be possible for your purchasing department to negotiate that the vendor prepares the items to be automatically be placed in storage. If the items on the inbound delivery are not prepared for the warehouse, they may need to be repacked on pallets or in storage containers so they can be safely stored in the warehouse. If items are not packed correctly, damage to the items or spoilage may occur.

Repacking inbound deliveries may be necessary for efficient storage

> **Example**
>
> When items are received that need to be placed in cold storage, the packaging from the vendor may only be suitable for short-term storage. In this case the items need to be repacked in containers certified for the cold storage area.

Some vendors send items to a third-party shipper who combines the items on a single pallet before they arrive at your warehouse. When the inbound delivery arrives, it needs to be broken down so the items can be either repacked in a container suitable for the warehouse or combined on a pallet with the same material from other deliveries. A more detailed examination of the packing process for inbound deliveries can be found in the Section 2.2.

Items on an inbound delivery may arrive combined on one pallet

Repacking is important when you receive returns from customers. When items are returned, they need to be separated from other items in the delivery and packed in an appropriate container so that it can be clearly identified as a return. We'll examine the returns process in greater detail in Chapter 7.

2.1.6 Automatic Putaway for Inbound Deliveries

The putaway process for an inbound delivery includes the search for an appropriate storage bin in the warehouse based on the configuration of the storage type search strategy.

Automatic putaway can save time finding suitable locations

Each item line of the inbound delivery has a putaway status that allows the warehouse supervisor to monitor the progress of the putaway. The status is set depending on what putaway process has been completed.

There are four putaway statuses for line items on an inbound delivery, as shown in Figure 2.11:

▸ Not relevant

▸ Not yet processed

▸ Partially processed

▸ Completely processed

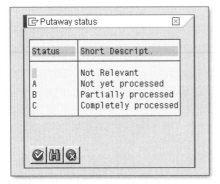

Figure 2.11 Putaway Statuses for an Inbound Delivery

When an inbound delivery is set up for automatic putaway, the SAP system creates the transfer orders that need to be completed. The automatic putaway is determined by an output type called WMTA, which must be assigned to the inbound delivery.

You can set up the WMTA output type in your system by following several configuration steps. First, create the output type WMTA by following the menu path IMG • Logistics Execution • Shipping • Basic Shipping Functions • Output Control • Output Determination • Maintain Output Determination for Inbound Deliveries • Define Output Types for Inbound Delivery.

This transaction allows you to enter the new output type, WMTA. On the initial screen click on the New Entries button, shown in Figure 2.12.

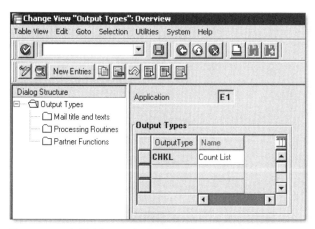

Figure 2.12 Initial Screen to Create a New Output Type

The new entry is for the output type WMTA. The data required for this output type should be assigned to access sequence 0001. You add this new data on the General data tab, as shown in Figure 2.13.

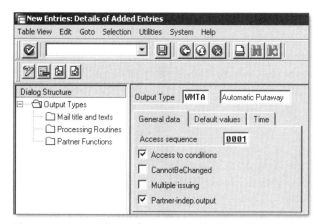

Figure 2.13 General Data for Output Type WMTA

The output type requires that two fields are selected: one to allow access to the conditions and the other to define partner-independent output. After you enter this data, the next step is to access the processing routines.

Figure 2.14 shows the configuration for the processing routine for output type WMTA. Select Special function in the Transm. Medium field and assign program RLAUTA20.

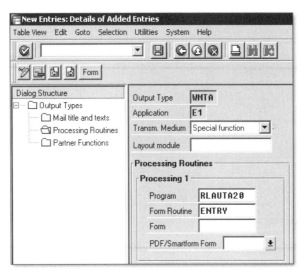

Figure 2.14 Processing Routines for Output Type WMTA

After you've entered all of the configuration for WMTA, save the output type.

The next step of the configuration is to add the output type to a procedure. To maintain the output determination procedures, follow the navigation menu IMG • Logistics Execution • Shipping • Basic Shipping Functions • Output Control • Output Determination • Maintain Output Determination for Inbound Deliveries • Define Output Types for Inbound Delivery.

The standard SAP output determination procedure is E00001. If you want to create a new procedure, use the data standards in place at your company. In this case we've created a new procedure called Z00001, shown in Figure 2.15.

The usage field determines for which area the condition is used, in this case B for output conditions. The application field further breaks down the condition. In this instance, E1 refers to the inbound delivery, so the procedure (Z00001) we're adding is for inbound delivery output.

The next step is to enter the control data for the new procedure. Select your new procedure and click on the Control Data tab in the dialog structure. Figure 2.16 shows the one entry for the procedure that is the output type WMTA.

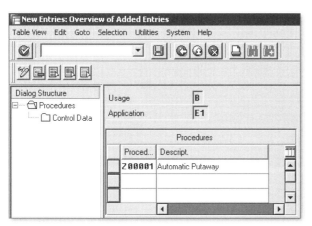

Figure 2.15 Creation of a New Output Determination Procedure

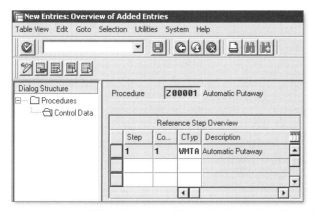

Figure 2.16 Add Control Data for Output Determination Procedure

After entering the output type into the procedure, save it and then assigned it to the delivery type. To complete this task, you can either use Transaction VNE7 or follow the menu path IMG • Logistics Execution • Shipping • Basic Shipping Functions • Output Control • Output Determination • Maintain Output Determination for Inbound Deliveries • Assign Output Determination Procedures.

Figure 2.17 shows final configuration step, where the inbound delivery type, EL, is linked to the new output determination procedure, Z00001, and the output type WMTA. This pulls in the Z00001 procedure for each inbound delivery.

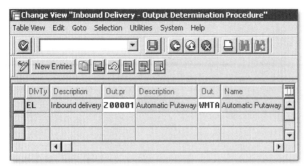

Figure 2.17 Assignment of Output Determination Procedure

After you complete the configuration, you must create the condition records for the inbound delivery. You can use Transaction MN24 to enter the condition records or go to SAP • Logistics • Materials Management • Purchasing • Master Data • Messages • Inbound Delivery • Create.

Figure 2.18 shows the condition record for the inbound delivery. The delivery type entered is EL, which represents the inbound delivery. The other information required for the condition record is the message transmission medium, which should be entered as a special function represented by the number 8. You use this because no output is being created; in this case the system automatically creates transfer orders for the items on the inbound delivery.

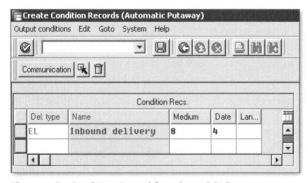

Figure 2.18 Condition Record for Inbound Delivery

The other field you need to fill in on the inbound delivery condition record, shown in Figure 2.18, is the date or dispatch time field. For the inbound delivery the output should be created immediately, represented by the number 4.

After you've entered the condition record for inbound delivery, the system automatically creates the transfer orders to put away the items on the inbound delivery.

In the next section, we'll review the packing process of the inbound delivery, as well as the use of handling units in the inbound delivery process.

2.2   Packing Items for Inbound Deliveries

Packing can be part of the inbound delivery process. It's not a necessary part of the delivery, but many businesses have to use the packing function to prepare the items from an inbound delivery for storage in the warehouse.

Packing items may be necessary for storage materials

When an inbound delivery arrives at the warehouse, the items can be moved into the warehouse. Sometimes different materials arrive lose or shrink-wrapped on pallets, and it is necessary to break down the contents of the pallet and pack the items in suitable containers for storage in the warehouse to ensure the safety of not only warehouse personnel, but also the product being stored.

2.2.1   Using Handling Units

When packing materials for an inbound delivery, you need to use *handling units*. The handling unit is a physical unit in the SAP system that consists of a packaging material, which could be a box or a container, and the materials that are stored within the packaging. A handling unit can be stored within another handling unit, which is called *nesting*.

Handling units are used in inventory management

> **Example**
>
> A retailer receives inbound deliveries of clothing from their manufacturers in China. The items arrive from the manufacturer in boxes on a pallet, but each pallet contains boxes of different sizes. In their warehouse, the retailer requires that the items be stored in one storage bin that is all the same size clothing. This requires each pallet on the inbound delivery to be broken down and the boxes sorted so that boxes containing the same size are combined together. Because the packaging from the manufacturer is not suitable for storage in the warehouse, the warehouse uses a larger packaging container or handling unit that holds four boxes. These larger containers are then stored six to a pallet, another handling unit, shrink-wrapped, and placed in the warehouse.

A unique number is assigned to the handling unit so it can be tracked. This means that all relevant information regarding the materials is contained in the handling unit, so that batch or serial numbers are not lost and are still available to other processes.

2.2.2 Creating a Handling Unit

A handling unit consists of packaging materials

The packing of material can be achieved within the inbound delivery transaction. You can create the handling unit during the packing process.

You can access the inbound delivery using Transaction VL32N or by following the menu path SAP • LOGISTICS • LOGISTICS EXECUTION • INBOUND PROCESS • GOODS RECEIPT FOR INBOUND DELIVERY • INBOUND DELIVERY • CHANGE • SINGLE DOCUMENT.

On the initial screen of the inbound delivery, you should highlight the line item of the inbound delivery that you want to pack and select the menu option EDIT • PACK.

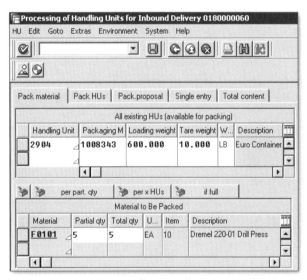

Figure 2.19 Creating a Handling Unit for an Inbound Delivery

In Figure 2.19 the handling unit is created by entering the packaging material, the maximum loading weight of the materials that will placed in the handling unit, and the tare weight of the packaging material. The number of the handling unit is unique, and the system creates it when the packaging material is added and the transaction is saved.

2.2.3 Packing Materials in a Handling Unit

After the handling unit has been created, the material can be packed into handling unit. The material can be packed into the handling unit using the Single entry tab, shown in Figure 2.20.

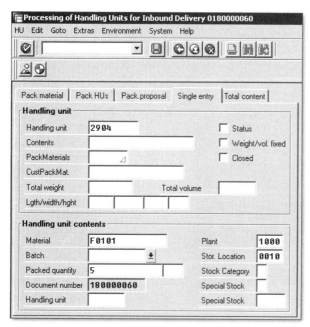

Figure 2.20 Packing the Handling Unit

You can see in Figure 2.20 that it's possible to manually add the material to the handling unit. The unique number of the handling unit is added, along with the material and the quantity to pack. Once the items are completed, the transaction can be saved and the handling unit is then packed.

If you want to see the contents of the handling unit, simply select the Total content tab. Figure 2.21 shows the details of the Total content tab. The handling unit, with the handling unit number 2904, is shown, and the packaging material number 1008343. The contents of the handling unit are shown as material F0101 with a quantity of 5.

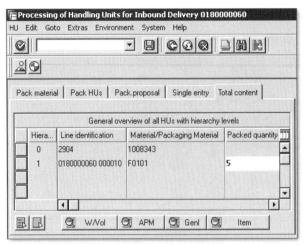

Figure 2.21 Total Content of the Handling Unit

2.2.4 Nesting Handling Units

A handling unit can be stored within another handling unit

When items have been packed into a handling unit, the situation could arise where the handling unit needs to be placed inside another handling unit. For example, a packaging box containing the items from inbound delivery may need to be packed into a storage crate to be stored in the warehouse. In this case the packaging box and the storage crate are both created as handling units in the SAP system.

The method of packing a handling unit in another handling unit is similar to packing any materials using the inbound delivery. You can access the inbound delivery using Transaction VL32N or by following the menu path SAP • LOGISTICS • LOGISTICS EXECUTION • INBOUND PROCESS • GOODS RECEIPT FOR INBOUND DELIVERY • INBOUND DELIVERY • CHANGE • SINGLE DOCUMENT.

On the initial screen of the inbound delivery, highlight the line item of the inbound delivery you want to pack and then select the menu option EDIT • PACK.

Figure 2.22 shows that another handling unit has been added to the inbound delivery. On this occasion, handling unit 2905 has been created and is comprised of the packaging material BO61. Notice that there are no longer any materials to pack because they are already contained in the handling unit 2904.

It's now possible to pack handling unit 2904, which contains material F0101, in the new handling unit, 2905, by selecting the Single entry tab.

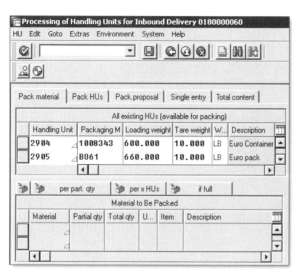

Figure 2.22 Entering a Second Handling Unit in the Inbound Delivery

Figure 2.23 shows handling unit 2905 and the contents for that handling unit, which are handling unit 2904.

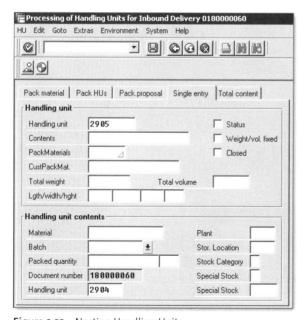

Figure 2.23 Nesting Handling Units

After the packing has been completed, you can view an overview of the packing hierarchy in the Total content tab.

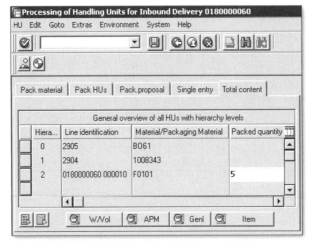

Figure 2.24 Packing Hierarchy in the Inbound Delivery

Figure 2.24 shows the handling units 2904 and 2905, with 2905 being the highest level in the hierarchy (the container that is being moved in the warehouse). That container contains another handling unit, 2904, which in turn contains material F0101, which was received as part of the inbound delivery.

2.2.5 Unpacking a Handling Unit

If there has been an error in the packing of the inbound delivery items, they can be removed from the handling unit in which they were packed. You can perform this operation within the Inbound Delivery Transaction VL32N.

> **Example**
>
> An inbound delivery from an automotive spare parts manufacturer contained 400 packs of sparks plugs. The packs were loose in the shipping carrier's packaging, so the 400 packs were placed in a storage container suitable for racks in the warehouse. Before placing the container in the warehouse, the supervisor decided to move other incoming materials into the racking, so the packs of spark plugs needed to be unpacked from the storage container and placed in a large plastic tote in an open storage area.

When you want to unpack a handling unit, you can access the packing area in Transaction VL32N and then select the menu option EDIT • PACK.

From here, click on the Total content tab to display the handling unit hierarchy. Then you can select the handling unit to unpack, as shown in Figure 2.24.

After deciding which handling unit to unpack, you can highlight the items to be unpacked and select EDIT • UNPACK from the menu. You can also do this by using the function keys `Shift` + `F7`. The screen will return with a message saying the items are unpacked, and the line item will no longer be on the screen. If you click on the Pack material tab, the items will be packed again.

After the materials are placed in the correct handling unit for the warehouse, the putaway process can be completed, which we'll discuss further in Chapter 3.

In the next section, we'll move on to examine an important tool for the warehouse manager, the inbound delivery monitor.

2.3 Inbound Delivery Monitor

Warehouse management can use the inbound delivery monitor to process open deliveries and display those that have already been completed. This is useful because, using the inbound delivery monitor, the warehouse staff can review inbound deliveries with different statuses in a single list and then perform any further necessary processing.

The inbound delivery monitor allows efficient use of resources

2.3.1 Basic Functionality of the Inbound Delivery Monitor

You can access the inbound delivery monitor, shown in Figure 2.25, via Transaction VL06I or the menu path SAP • LOGISTICS • LOGISTICS EXECUTION • INBOUND PROCESS • GOODS RECEIPT FOR INBOUND DELIVERY • INBOUND DELIVERY • LISTS • INBOUND DELIVERY MONITOR.

Figure 2.25 shows the options that are available for the inbound delivery monitor. Each option offers you a work list that you can create based on selection criteria. In addition, you can execute each option with a variant. The inbound delivery monitor has the standard variant selected for the initial status, but you can change this when you chose the option or when you select the Display Variants button. Figure 2.26 shows the inbound delivery monitor options with the variants that are currently assigned.

Create variants for efficient monitoring

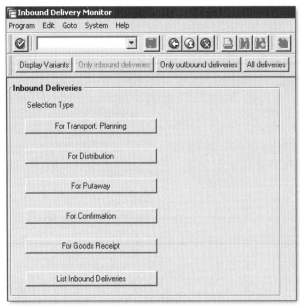

Figure 2.25 Inbound Delivery Monitor

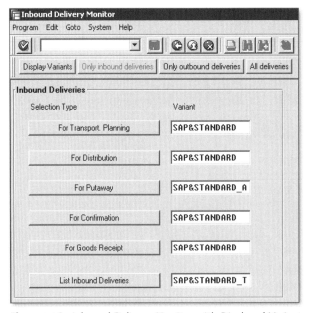

Figure 2.26 Inbound Delivery Monitor with Displayed Variants

The inbound delivery monitor can be a more productive tool for your warehouse staff because they are able to develop more relevant variants for the range of options that can ultimately reduce data entry repetition.

2.3.2   List Inbound Deliveries

When your warehouse staff needs to know what inbound deliveries are due, you can use the inbound delivery monitor, and select the List Inbound Deliveries button. Figure 2.27 shows the next screen, which is the selection screen for the option. In this case a date range has been entered to select inbound deliveries.

Frequent monitoring of deliveries is vital for efficiency

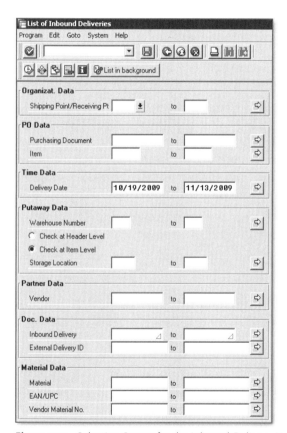

Figure 2.27   Selection Screen for the Inbound Delivery Monitor

After you execute the selection screen with the required input, the results screen is displayed that shows all inbound deliveries that meet the criteria, illustrated in Figure 2.28.

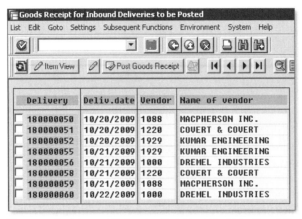

Figure 2.28 Inbound Deliveries that Meet the Selection Criteria

Monitoring can quickly identify problems
Warehouse management should review the inbound delivery monitor during each shift as new deliveries arrive. If, for whatever reason, inbound deliveries are delayed, this can affect production.

Figure 2.28 shows the relevant inbound deliveries for the date range entered. You then have a range of subsequent functions that you can perform on the deliveries. By selecting Subsequent Functions from the menu, you can change the details of the inbound delivery, create any relevant transfer orders, or post the goods issue.

In the next section, we'll review an example of how a business has created an efficient inbound delivery process.

2.4   Business Examples – Efficient Inbound Deliveries

Using all elements of your SAP system's functionality can maximize efficiencies
In the past companies relied on their vendors ensure that deliveries arrived with the correct quantity and on the correct day as agreed upon in the purchase orders. However, vendors may have manufacturing or transportation problems, and inbound deliveries can be late or incorrect without any notice. These inaccuracies and delays can affect the production schedule and deliveries to customers. Despite the introduction of products like SAP ERP, vendors still have problems, and deliveries are delayed or incomplete.

This section looks at how businesses use the functionality of their SAP systems and their own business methods to create an efficient inbound delivery process.

2.4.1   Purchasing Process

An efficient inbound delivery process begins with purchasing. Having a good relationship with a supplier is the first step to efficient inbound deliveries. Large companies constantly review their vendors and reward those who provide the most accurate deliveries. Accurate and on-time deliveries ensure that production schedules are met and deliveries to customers are on time. If you can rely on your vendors to always provide on-time deliveries, then you can realize efficiencies in the production process.

Excellent vendor relationships can improve efficiencies

> **Example**
>
> A large U.S. electronics manufacturer relies on deliveries of electronic components from China, Taiwan, and Japan. Despite the distance between the vendors in Asia and the U.S. manufacturing site, the company expects 98.5% of its inbound deliveries to arrive on or before the due date with 100% accuracy. These figures are due to a number of procedures the purchasing department has put in place. The company implemented a complete suite of EDI transactions. Purchase orders are created in the SAP system and sent to vendors, who are then required to send an acknowledgement and an advanced shipping notice (ASN) when the delivery is shipped. In addition to the EDI, the purchasing department follows up on orders to ensure the delivery will arrive on the promised date.

2.4.2   Inbound Deliveries

Creating an inbound delivery automatically using EDI means that information is immediately available to the warehouse staff. The earlier the inbound delivery information is available, the more efficiency it can bring into the process. Constant monitoring of the inbound deliveries ensures that resources are assigned to deliveries in the most efficient manner.

Inbound delivery details the date and time the items are expected

> **Example**
>
> A multinational clothing retailer purchases complete items from manufacturers in China and Vietnam. To avoid potential problems with delivery dates, the retailer insists that any vendor they deal with is fully compliant with their EDI requirements. Part of the requirement is that an advance shipping notice is transmitted so that an automatic inbound delivery can be created in the SAP system at the earliest opportunity. As the retailer receives over 200 deliveries a day, the warehouse staff uses the inbound delivery monitor to keep on top of the delivery pipeline. By knowing when every delivery is due to arrive, the retailer can efficiently move resources to unload waiting vehicles.

2.4.3   Automatic Putaway

SAP ERP can automatically generate transfer orders for the items

When an inbound delivery is received, the system can be configured so that it automatically generates transfer orders for the warehouse. The transfer orders inform the warehouse staff where to take the items to be stored. Automatic putaway can save time and resources as the system finds a suitable location for the incoming materials. If the system is configured correctly, including warehouse layout and putaway strategies, the automatic putaway process can significantly increase the efficiency of the warehouse.

> **Example**
>
> A Canadian footwear retailer uses a central distribution center for its North American operation. The warehouse is attached to the distribution center and receives deliveries from overseas manufacturers in shipping containers several times a day. In each container the products are shrink-wrapped on pallets, and the vendors are required to place items with the same material number on each pallet. The retailer doesn't need to break the pallets down when they arrive, and they can be moved directly into the warehouse. To make the process as efficient as possible, the company implemented automatic putaway so that the system generates the relevant transfer orders when the pallet is retrieved from the shipping container.

Automatic putaway may not be suitable for all SAP customers

Automatic putaway may not be suitable for all SAP customers, but when it is suitable, the automatic putaway process can create a significant savings of time and resources in the warehouse.

2.4.4   Use of Handling Units

Handling units contain packaging material used to store items

Each day that a material is stored in the warehouse is a cost that a business will want to minimize. Warehouse costs include the rent of the warehouse, utilities, personnel, equipment, and insurance. Warehousing costs can be reduced not only by minimizing the time an item is stored in the warehouse, but by ensuring that the warehouse is operating at peak efficiency. Handling units are an efficient way to store items in the warehouse. Using as few sizes of container as possible in the warehouse, allows materials to be stored in the maximum number of locations.

> **Example**
>
> A German automotive company has a distribution center in Mexico. The warehouse at the distribution center is fitted with racks that are of all sizes. In addition to the racks, they have two storage carousels for small items that hold one size of container. They decided to implement the rack configuration so items could be placed in a container and then stored in any location in the warehouse. The distribution center receives over 30 container loads of automotive parts a day, and the line items on the inbound deliveries are usually mixed on a pallet with other line items. To deal with this issue, the warehouse staff reviews each incoming delivery and ensures that there were enough storage containers at the receiving area. Each pallet that arrives is broken down, and materials are packed into the waiting storage containers. The container or handling unit information is then recorded in the inbound delivery. The storage containers are then moved into the racking. The smaller items are stored in carousel containers and moved to the carousel at least once an hour.

The inbound delivery process in the warehouse management functionality in SAP ERP allows companies to maximize the use of their resources because the delivery information is available in a more timely fashion. Companies that use all of the available functionality such as inbound deliveries and handling units gain efficiencies that they otherwise would not realize.

Inbound delivery allows maximization of resources

2.5 Summary

In this chapter we examined the elements of inbound delivery processes. There are several distinct components to the process. Beginning with an effective purchasing strategy, vendors receive orders vendors and return advanced shipping notices returned so inbound deliveries can be created and monitored. On receipt at the warehouse, the deliveries are dealt with in the most efficient manner, and the use of handling units and automatic putaway streamlines storage in the warehouse. Efficient movements of inbound materials are critical when a business is operating with low inventory or operating within a just-in-time environment.

In the next chapter, we'll build on what we discussed here and examine how a company can maximize the putaway and quality inspection process in the warehouse.

Putaway strategies can help maximize the efficiencies of warehouse operations by minimizing the input from warehouse staff.

3 Enhancing Your Managed Putaway and Quality Inspection Processes

In this chapter we'll discuss the putaway process in the warehouse and the associated quality inspection. The materials to be put away in the warehouse arrive as part of an inbound delivery, which relates back to an original purchase order sent to the vendor. The putaway process should allow materials to be placed into the warehouse with the minimum of intervention, so decisions need to be made about where certain types of materials are stored depending on the layout of your warehouse.

Some companies believe it isn't necessary to manage the putaway strategies for materials entering the warehouse and use a manual putaway process so that a storage bin is assigned at the time of the transfer order process. But if a company wants to use the warehouse management functionality available in SAP ERP to achieve warehouse efficiency, it's important that the putaway process include the necessary putaway strategies.

The putaway strategy ensures that the appropriate storage bin is assigned for the most efficient storage of the inbound materials. Using a putaway strategy may not be necessary, but adopting system-generated putaway removes unnecessary intervention by warehouse staff and speeds up the material putaway process.

3.1 Managing the Putaway Process

Companies that are identified as having world-class warehousing have similar characteristics in as much as they are proponents of maximizing the functionality of their enterprise resource planning (ERP) or warehousing systems. Luckily for you, SAP customers are fortunate to have implemented

SAP offers a number of putaway strategies

a business solution that offers a wide range of putaway strategies. In this section we'll examine each of the putaway strategies so that you can identify which of the strategies are applicable to your warehouse operations.

3.1.1 Putaway Strategies

Putaway strategy helps propose storage bin

A putaway strategy allows a material to be automatically proposed for putaway in a storage bin within an identified storage type. The assignment of the storage bin depends on the configuration of the storage type and the storage strategies defined in the material master record. For some materials, it may not be possible to allow the automatic assignment of a storage bin, and manual putaway is necessary. In this case no putaway strategy would be defined in the material master. The most common reason for a company to use a manual assignment of a storage type is if the material is being placed into mixed storage. For example, materials that are irregularly shaped and not suitable for storage in the warehouse, may be placed in mixed storage types that are oversized and contain other materials with similar characteristics.

There is one strategy per storage type

Several putaway strategies are available to be assigned to a storage type. The strategy tells the system how to select the optimum storage bin within the selected storage type. To ensure that a material is assigned the optimum bin, it's important to identify the correct putaway strategy for the storage types in the warehouse.

There are several putaway strategies that you can assign to a storage type.

► Fixed bin storage

► Open storage

► Next empty storage bin

► Addition to existing stock

In the next section, we'll look at the first of these putaway strategies, fixed bin storage.

3.1.2 Fixed Bin Storage Strategy

Materials can have one fixed bin per storage type

You assign the fixed bin storage strategy to a storage type where a material is placed in a fixed bin. This means the system can automatically create a transfer order to place materials into their designated storage bins in the warehouse. A storage bin can be defined for each storage type in the material master record.

First, let's examine the configuration for the fixed bin strategy. The strategy is assigned to the storage type and can be defined by following the menu path IMG • LOGISTICS EXECUTION • WAREHOUSE MANAGEMENT • STRATE-GIES • PUTAWAY STRATEGIES • DEFINE STRATEGY FOR FIXED BINS.

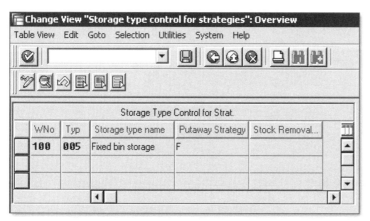

Figure 3.1 Fixed Bin Strategy Assigned to Storage Type 005

Figure 3.1 shows the assignment of the fixed bin strategy to storage type 005. The strategy is indicated by the letter F.

The fixed storage bin for a material is entered in the material master for each storage type where a fixed bin is applicable. The fixed storage bin field can be found in the warehouse management screens, depending on the version of SAP system your company has implemented.

Fixed storage bin is entered in the material master

Figure 3.2 shows the warehouse management data in the material master record for material 700000066. This data is specific to warehouse 001 and storage type 005. The data shows that the material is assigned to storage bin 095-01-420 when the material is placed in storage type 005.

For example, when a transfer order is automatically created and storage type 005 has been selected, the transfer order will reflect the fixed storage bin in the material master, that is, 095-01-420.

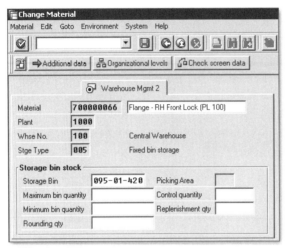

Figure 3.2 Fixed Storage Bin Entered in the Material Master Record

3.1.3 Open Storage Strategy

Open storage is used where there are no racks

Some warehouses are extremely simple. Instead of racks and shelving, the warehouse may just consist of open areas that are not well defined. Although this type of warehouse layout is not suitable for every company, open storage is useful for oversized, awkward, and heavy items that cannot be stored on racks. Open storage is also used when a company is transitioning from one warehouse layout to another or when damage to the warehouse requires materials to be moved into one holding area.

The configuration for open storage is assigned to the storage type and can be defined by following the menu path IMG • LOGISTICS EXECUTION • WAREHOUSE MANAGEMENT • STRATEGIES • PUTAWAY STRATEGIES • DEFINE STRATEGY FOR OPEN STORAGE.

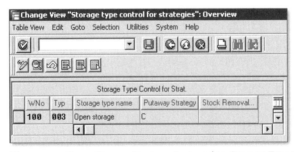

Figure 3.3 Open Storage Strategy Assigned to Storage Type 003

Figure 3.3 shows that storage type 003 has been designated as open storage. The strategy is indicated by the letter C. When configuring the storage type for open storage, the Mixed storage and Addn to stock checkboxes must be selected so that different materials can be entered into the one storage bin. This configuration is shown in Figure 3.4.

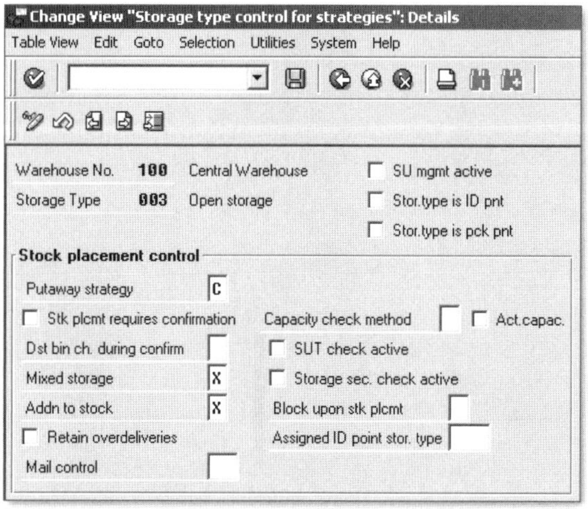

Figure 3.4 Configuration for Open Storage Strategy

A storage type that has been identified as being subject to the open storage putaway strategy will only have one storage bin for each storage section that is created for the storage type.

Open storage has one storage bin per storage section

> **Example**
>
> In warehouse 001, storage type 003 has been designated as open storage because physically, it's an area behind the racking where oversized and overweight materials are stored. Although it's one open area, the height of the area varies, so it is decided to create two storage sections, 001 and 002, for the one storage type. For each of the storage sections, a storage bin is created: 003-001-01 for storage section 001 and 003-002-01 for storage section 002.

When a transfer order is automatically created for an inbound delivery and storage type 003 has been selected, the transfer order will reflect the storage bin associated with the storage sections defined for the storage type. If only one storage section is defined for the open storage type, then the same storage bin will be selected for all transfer orders created for storage type 003.

3.1.4 Next Empty Storage Bin Strategy

Next empty bin is suitable for random storage

In some warehouses a structure has been created where random storage is acceptable, meaning materials can be stored in any bin within the storage type. This depends on the nature of the materials stored in the warehouse. For example, different materials may all be stored in the same size container. If this is the case, then the putaway strategy used can be configured so that the system will select the next empty storage bin.

Many warehouses that the operate carousel systems use the next empty storage bin strategy because the bin locations on the carousel systems are the same size. Also, access to any location on the carousel is the same because the bin is brought to the operator.

> **Example**
>
> Many warehouses operate automated storage and retrieval systems (ASRSs). These can be horizontal carousels, vertical carousels, or vertical lift modules (VLMs). These storage machines utilize chain and track linkages that rotate box-structure shelving modules in a vertical or horizontal plane. Carousels are available in a variety of load-carrying capacities, shelf module dimensions, and heights. When activated, the shelves rotate to bring the requested bin location to the operator. Carousels are integrated with SAP systems so that the machines operate with SAP ERP.

The configuration for next empty storage bin is assigned to the storage type and can be defined by following the menu path IMG • LOGISTICS EXECUTION • WAREHOUSE MANAGEMENT • STRATEGIES • PUTAWAY STRATEGIES • DEFINE STRATEGY FOR EMPTY STORAGE BIN.

Figure 3.5 shows that storage type 001, high rack storage, has been designated as next empty storage bin. The strategy is indicated by the letter L.

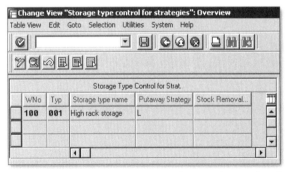

Figure 3.5 Next Empty Storage Bin Strategy Assigned to Storage Type 001

A warehouse has a vertical storage carousel where all of the storage bins are the same size. The carousel is identified in the SAP system as one storage type and configured with the next empty storage bin putaway strategy. When a transfer order is automatically created for an inbound delivery, the material is assigned to the carousel, and the next empty storage bin is assigned.

3.1.5 Addition to Existing Stock Strategy

When you assign the addition to existing stock strategy to a storage type, an automatically created transfer order for the storage type adds material to a storage bin that already contains a quantity of the same material.

Materials can be added to a bin with existing stock

However, this strategy requires that the capacity of each storage bin be defined because the strategy only assigns materials to a storage bin that has sufficient capacity remaining. If no storage bins have available capacity to add material, the system searches for the next available empty storage bin.

This strategy is useful for businesses that operate their warehouse close to capacity because it maximizes the use of each storage bin in the warehouse. However, it's important to ensure that the capacity of each storage bin has been entered correctly.

The capacity of each bin must be known

You assign the configuration for the addition to existing stock strategy to the storage type and can define it via the menu path IMG • LOGISTICS EXECUTION • WAREHOUSE MANAGEMENT • STRATEGIES • PUTAWAY STRATEGIES • DEFINE STRATEGY FOR ADDITION TO EXISTING STOCK.

Figure 3.6 shows that storage type 001, shelf storage, has been designated as addition to existing stock. The strategy is indicated by the letter I.

You have to make an additional configuration to the storage type to ensure that the capacity check has been added and the storage type allows addition to stock. Because this strategy depends on the correct capacity of the storage bins being calculated, it's important to ensure that this configuration has been added.

Capacity calculation is used in this strategy

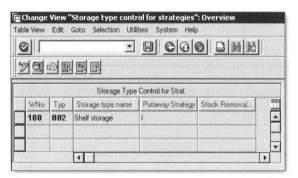

Figure 3.6 Addition to Existing Stock Strategy Assigned to Storage Type 002

Figure 3.7 shows that the configuration has been added to allow addition to stock. In addition, a value has been added for the capacity check method. In this instance a value of 1 has been entered, which means the system will check capacity based on the maximum weight defined for each storage bin. There are several other options for the capacity check method, which you can see in Figure 3.8.

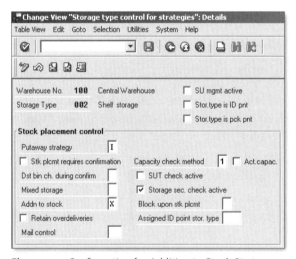

Figure 3.7 Configuration for Addition to Stock Strategy

Active capacity check can affect performance

The other element to the capacity check is the active capacity (Act. Capac) checkbox. If this is selected, the system will check each bin when a putaway into storage is proposed. Although this may be useful, the system performance can be significantly degraded when you choose this option. It's best not to use this option unless system performance is not an issue.

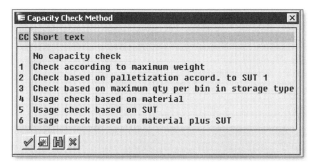

Figure 3.8 Capacity Check Methods for a Storage Type

Figure 3.8 shows the capacity check methods you can use in the configuration of the storage type. For the addition to stock putaway strategy, capacity check method 1 can be used because it calculated the capacity of each storage bin based on the maximum weight allowed in each bin and the weight of the material that is stored in the bin. You can also use capacity check method 3, because it determines the capacity of the bin based on the maximum number of items allowed per bin rather than weight.

Regardless of the capacity check that you use, the calculation can only be effective when the correct information is entered into each storage bin and for each material stored. If information is missing, the calculation is invalid, and incorrect putaway may occur.

Capacity errors can cause putaway problems

Material Master Data for Capacity Check

To ensure that the capacity check can operate successfully, you need to ensure that the correct information is entered in the material master record for each item stored in bins that are proposed based on capacity.

You can define the capacity of a bin by weight or volume. You determine the capacity calculation of a bin based on values entered in the warehouse management screens on the material master for the specific warehouse. The capacity calculation is only valid when the material master has the capacity information entered in the record.

Capacity depends on accurate material information

Figure 3.9 shows that the gross weight has been added for the material 700000066 that is stored in the warehouse 100. The gross weight entered here can be used to calculate whether or not the material can be added to a storage bin. In addition, a value has been added in the capacity usage field for this material. The capacity calculation can use this value when capacity check method 3 is used, which we looked at in Figure 3.8.

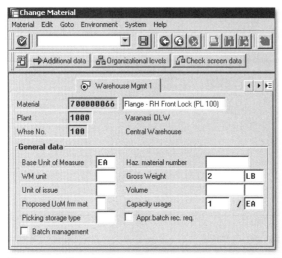

Figure 3.9 Capacity Information in the Material Master Record

Storage Bin Data for Capacity Check

Capacity can be based on weight or quantity

The storage bin has two fields for capacity checking that relate to the fields on the material master. The capacity of a storage bin can be determined by entering a value that is the maximum weight that the bin can accommodate or by a value that is entered that determines how many items can be placed in the bin. You can enter both these values when creating a storage bin, via Transaction LS01N, as shown in Figure 3.10.

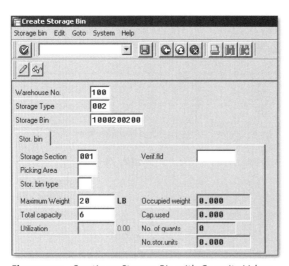

Figure 3.10 Creating a Storage Bin with Capacity Values

You fill in the Maximum Weight and the Total capacity fields for the storage bin, which the system uses to determine the available capacity of the storage bin. You can use the total capacity field when a transfer order into the storage bin is proposed. The system reviews the Total capacity and capacity currently used (Cap. used) fields to determine if a further transfer into the bin is possible.

> **Example**
>
> Storage bin 10-40-50 was created with a maximum weight capacity of 12 pounds. Currently, a total of four items are in the bin, each weighing 2.5 pounds, so the current occupied weight is 10 pounds. With 2 pounds of available capacity remaining, the system will not propose this storage bin for another transfer order because the available capacity is less than the weight of a single item.

The storage bin capacity checking functionality is an efficient way for you to automatically create transfer orders that are based on the actual situation in the warehouse. If you don't use capacity checks, the putaway may be delayed if there is not enough room in the storage bin. If this is the case, the warehouse operator has to spend time finding another suitable storage bin.

Capacity checking is efficient for automatic transfer orders

3.1.6 Using the Storage Type Search

When a material is to be put away, you can execute the storage type search to determine what storage type needs to be selected to find a suitable storage bin. A material is usually suitable to be stored in more than one storage type, and the storage type search allows you to determine the order in which storage types are selected to find a suitable storage bin.

> **Example**
>
> Material ABC123 can be stored in any of the racking that radiates from the goods receiving area. Each row of racking is identified as a unique storage type. To minimize travel time for putaway, the storage type search looks for an empty storage bin in the storage type closest to the goods receiving area. If none are available, the search moves on to the next closet storage type for an empty bin, and so on.

This search allows for the most efficient use of resources and is particularly useful if your warehouse has a large number of movements requiring maximum efficiency.

Storage type search allows for the most efficient use of resources

Material Master Data for Storage Type Search

The storage type search is based on the information entered in the material master record. When you create a material, the data entered for a warehouse should reflect how the material should be put away and picked. You achieve this by entering a storage type indicator, which the storage type search uses to find an available storage bin.

The warehouse data on the material master record contains the Storage Section Ind. (indicator) field, which is used in the storage type search. Figure 3.11 shows the warehouse data for the material.

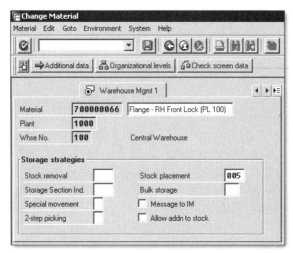

Figure 3.11 Stock Placement Information in the Material Master Record

The Stock placement field contains the storage type indicator that you can use in the storage type search. The storage type indicator is not a storage type, but is an indicator that allows a search of several related storage types.

Storage Type Indicator

You define the storage type indicator is defined during configuration, and it allows you to search the storage type to process several storage types, based on priority, to find a suitable storage bin.

To define the storage type indicator, follow the menu path IMG • Logistics Execution • Warehouse Management • Strategies • Activate Storage Type Search • Define.

Figure 3.12 shows the configuration of the storage type indicator. A unique storage type indicator is defined for each warehouse, and they are then used in the material master record and the storage type search.

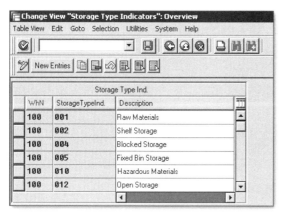

Figure 3.12   Configuring the Storage Type Indicator

Storage Type Search

The storage type search defines how you can search the system for a storage type based on the warehouse, the storage type indicator, and whether the search is for picking or putaway. In addition, there are a number of fields, such as the stock category and the special stock indicator, that you can define to make the storage type search more specific.

Figure 3.13 shows the configuration of the putaway storage type search for warehouse 100 and storage type indicator 005. The putaway is defined by the letter E, and picking is indicated by the letter A. For each unique selection the configuration allows a list of up to 30 storage types to be entered by priority. For example, in Figure 3.13 the storage type search for warehouse 100 and storage type indicator 005 will select the first storage type in the priority list, storage type 005. The system will determine if 005 has a suitable storage bin based on the putaway strategy assigned to the storage type. If no storage bins are available, the search will then proceed to the next storage type in the priority list and so on. This search is an effective way for you to select suitable storage bins without manual intervention.

To make the storage type search more specific, Figure 3.13 shows two other fields that can be defined. The Stock Cat. field reflects the status of a material as shown in Figure 3.14.

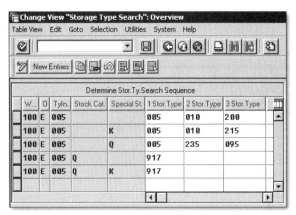

Figure 3.13 Configuration of the Storage Type Search

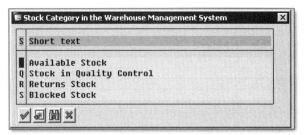

Figure 3.14 Stock Category in Storage Type Search

Search for quality, returns, and blocked stock

You can use the stock category in the search strategy so that a different storage type can be selected based on whether the material to be put away is in quality control, a returned material, or in a blocked status. Along with the stock category, you can further specify the storage type search by using the special stock indicator, as shown in Figure 3.15.

Figure 3.15 Special Stock Description for Storage Type Search

The special stock indicator allows a specific storage type search if you put away stock, such as project stock or consignment stock, in certain storage types. For example, vendor consignment stock may be put away in a storage type that is distinctly separate for company-owned inventory. The search strategy in Figure 3.13 shows the storage type search for special stocks (K), consignment stock, and project stock (Q).

Specific search for special stock like consignment or project

---

Example

Material ABC123 is stored in warehouse 001 and has been assigned storage type indicator 009 in the material master record. In the storage type search configuration, five storage types are in the priority list for warehouse 001 and storage type indicator 009. When a transfer order is created, the system accesses the storage type search to find a suitable storage bin. When the system selects the first storage type, it uses the putaway strategy configured for that storage type to find a suitable storage bin. If it doesn't find a suitable storage bin, the system then selects the next storage type and uses the putaway strategy configured to find a storage bin. This process continues until a suitable storage bin is found or all storage types are exhausted. If no suitable storage bin is available using the storage type search, the system will issue a message.

For complex warehouses that have configured more than one storage section per storage type, another specific search can be implemented, called the storage section search.

3.1.7 Storage Section Search

If a warehouse has storage types that are divided into several storage sections, then you can configure a storage section search to develop a more detailed storage bin search. The storage section search is used when the storage type search has selected a storage type. You configure the storage section search the same way as the storage type search, whereas you enter a storage section indicator in the material master that is used in conjunction with the warehouse to select a storage section based on a priority list of up to 30 storage sections. To define the storage section indicator, follow the menu path IMG • Logistics Execution • Warehouse Management • Strategies • Activate Storage Section Search. Figure 3.16 shows the storage section indicators that can be configured for a warehouse.

Searches can also be used for storage sections

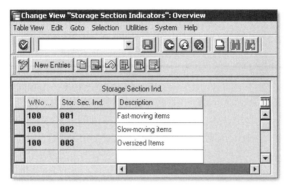

Figure 3.16 Configuration of the Storage Section Indicator

Figure 3.17 shows the storage section indicator on the material master record, which is valid for both putaway and picking strategies.

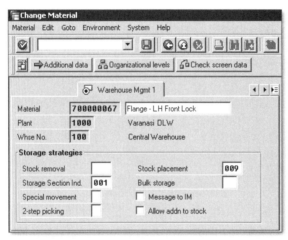

Figure 3.17 Storage Section Indicator in the Material Master Record

Using the storage section, you can search the warehouse, storage type, and storage section indicator. From there, you proceed to check the first storage section in the priority list to find a suitable storage bin. If you don't find a storage bin, the search then moves on to check the storage bins in the next storage section in the priority list.

Figure 3.18 shows the storage section search for warehouse 100 and storage type 001. There are three storage section indicators for the warehouse and storage type combination, each of which has a specific priority list of storage sections.

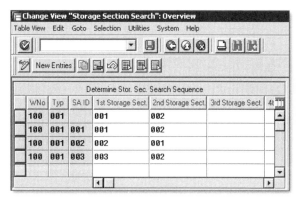

Figure 3.18 Storage Section Search

The storage section search is only effective if you've entered the correct priority for each storage section indicator. Please note that when the layout of a warehouse changes, you need to validate the configuration of both the storage type search and storage section search to ensure that the priority lists are still correct or if amendments need to be made.

3.2 Quality Inspection in the Warehouse

Quality is an important part of the supply chain, and the inspection of incoming materials is necessary for many companies. To make the inspection process work efficiently with the warehouse management processes, the quality management functionality allows the warehouse staff to monitor items that are being inspected. In quality management the term *inspection lot* is refers to the inspected material. The SAP system uses the inspection lot to record, process, and manage information for a quality inspection.

Quality inspection should be an efficient process

3.2.1 Interface Warehouse Management to Quality Management

To ensure that the warehouse management functions in SAP ERP are integrated with the quality management functionality, you need to complete a specific configuration step. You can define the two tools via the menu path IMG • LOGISTICS EXECUTION • WAREHOUSE MANAGEMENT • INTERFACES • DEFINE QUALITY MANAGEMENT.

The first part to defining quality management functions in warehouse management is to configure the QM Control indicator. You can use this in the storage type search table to activate the quality management interface

Warehouse and quality components need to be configured

and instruct the system how to handle inspection lots received into the warehouse.

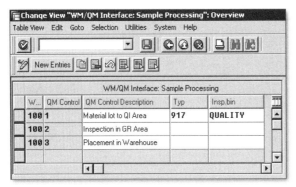

Figure 3.19 Defining the QM Control Indicator

Figure 3.19 shows the configuration of the QM Control indicator. In this case three indicators have been defined for warehouse 100. QM Control indicator 1 has also been configured to define the storage type and storage bin that should be used when an inspection lot is received into the warehouse. This can now be added to the storage type search configuration so the system can use the correct storage type and bin for an inspection lot.

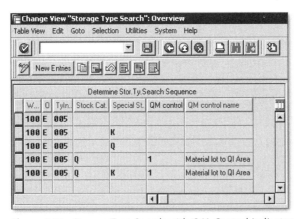

Figure 3.20 Storage Type Search with QM Control Indicator

Figure 3.20 shows the storage type search for warehouse 100 and storage type 005. However, the configuration has been amended to include the QM control indicator 1 for stock category Q, which is stock in quality control. Adding this QM control indicator to the storage search makes the search for a storage bin more efficient. From the search you can now determine that an item that is in quality control and is an inspection lot should be automatically transferred to storage type 917 and to the storage bin Quality.

3.2.2   Inspection Lots

The material master record contains the information that can allow the system to create an inspection lot when a goods receipt is posted for an inbound delivery. When the inspection lot is created, the inspection lot number is entered into the quant record. You can find the quant by using Transaction LS23 or following the menu path SAP • LOGISTICS • LOGISTICS EXECUTION • INTERNAL WAREHOUSE PROCESSES • BINS AND STOCK • DISPLAY • SINGLE DISPLAYS • QUANT.

The inspection lot is a group of items to be inspected

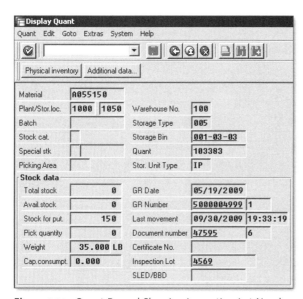

Figure 3.21   Quant Record Showing Inspection Lot Number

Figure 3.21 shows the data for quant 103383. This quant has an inspection lot number, 4569, assigned to it. The quality staff has to examine the inspection lot and decide whether the material can be moved to unrestricted stock or rejected. When this decision is made in the quality management component, the stock is moved, and to make the process efficient a transfer order is automatically created in the background.

3.2.3   Usage Decision

A usage decision
accepts or rejects
the received
material

The quality staff makes a usage decision can be made about an inspection lot using Transaction QA11 or by following the menu path SAP • Logistics • Quality Management • Quality Inspection • Inspection Lot • Usage Decision • Record.

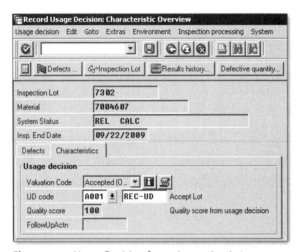

Figure 3.22   Usage Decision for an Inspection Lot

Figure 3.22 shows the usage decision, UD code, being made for inspection lot 7302. You can configure the usage decision to allow the quality department to define a range of decisions that reflect the items being inspected.

To configure the usage decisions, use Transaction QS51 or follow the menu path IMG • Quality Management • Quality Inspection • Inspection Lot Completion • Maintain Catalogs for Usage Decisions.

Figure 3.23 shows the usage decisions that you can make about an inspection lot. There are a number of usage decisions that can be used to accept an inspection lot and a number that can be used for rejection.

Usage decisions
result materials
movement within
the warehouse

When the quality department makes a usage decision, this results in materials being moved within the warehouse. For example, if an inspection lot is accepted and the materials can then be moved from quality to unrestricted use, a posting change notice signals the change in the status of the materials. You can use a transfer order to perform the status change.

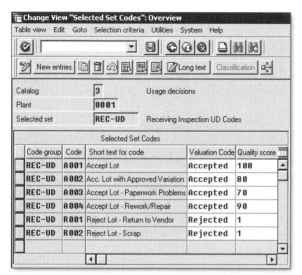

Figure 3.23 Configuration of Usage Decisions

If a usage decision is made that results in stock being rejected, the material can be returned to the vendor or scrapped, if that is the arrangement with the vendor. In this case the transfer order will remove the material from the warehouse.

3.2.4 Finding Inspection Lots in the Warehouse

You can find inspection lots in the warehouse by using the bin status report, Transaction LX03, via the menu path SAP • LOGISTICS • LOGISTICS EXECUTION • INTERNAL WAREHOUSE PROCESSES • BINS AND STOCK • DISPLAY • BIN STATUS REPORT.

Figure 3.24 shows the selection screen for the bin status report. To find the inspection lots, enter a Q in the Stock Category field for stock in quality control, as well as the appropriate warehouse number and storage types.

The results of the bin status report show a list of bins that have items in the quality status.

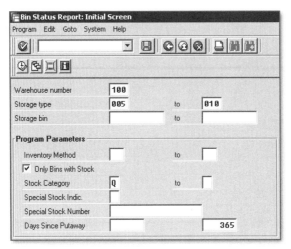

Figure 3.24 Selection Screen for Bin Status Report

Figure 3.25 shows the results of the bin status report. The report shows the bins where material is in quality control. If you click on the material on the line item, the system will show the quant with the inspection lot details, which is shown in Figure 3.21.

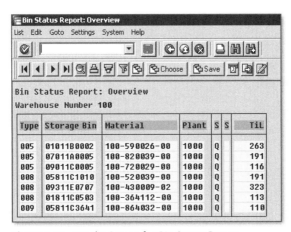

Figure 3.25 Results Screen for Bin Status Report

Quality inspection is important for the efficiency of the plant

The inspection of materials when they arrive at your warehouse is important for the efficiency of the plant. If items are stored in the warehouse prior to testing, they consume your resources in putaway and storage costs. If you administer quality inspection as soon as possible, then any material in the warehouse can be assumed to be usable. This is important to the production process, because delays in manufacturing due to defective components can affect customer delivery dates and increase production costs.

3.3   Business Example – Effective Putaway Strategies

If you're using warehouse management in SAP ERP, you have the ability to implement efficient putaway of materials in the warehouse. The warehouse management functionality within SAP ERP provides the ability to accurately place material in the warehouse with the minimum of resources consumed.

Putaway strategies are an important part of efficient warehouses. The strategies available in the warehouse management functionality in SAP ERP offer several options for companies that may have a variety of warehousing needs.

Putaway strategies are an important part of efficient warehouses

3.3.1   Fixed Bin Storage

Many companies require that a certain material must be stored in a particular storage bin for each of the storage types in the warehouse where it can be placed. Although this strategy doesn't use the flexibility of the warehouse management functionality, it does allow efficiency in the putaway of material.

> **Example**
>
> A U.S. automotive parts company has several regional distribution centers that replenish stores in those regions. Each distribution center receives thousands of items from U.S. and foreign parts manufacturers each day. The company constantly analyzes the replenishment orders from its stores and online sales to determine the sales volumes. Depending on this analysis, the company then decides where items should be stored to minimize travel time from the receiving bay to the storage bin. The company decided that by using fixed bin storage, they could minimize travel time to put away the fast-moving items and in picking the items for its replenishment orders.

The advantage of using fixed bin storage is that transfer orders can be prepared prior to the inbound delivery. In addition, fixed bin storage is a relatively simple strategy that doesn't adversely affect efficiencies in picking.

3.3.2 Open Storage

Open storage is not a complex putaway strategy

Open storage is the least complex strategy and doesn't offer the sophistication of other strategies. The strategy is common in simple warehouses without formal racking. Open storage is useful for oversized, awkward, and heavy items that cannot be stored to racks.

> **Example**
>
> A Canadian manufacturer of recyclable aluminum beverage cans receives aluminum coils from the manufacturer and requires these to be stored in the warehouse. The aluminum coils are significant in size and weight and are stored on pallets. The company evaluated the time it took a forklift operator to place the coils in the racking area compared with the time it took to place the coils in an open storage area. The results of the analysis were that it took on average four times longer to complete a transfer order for racking than open storage, owing to the number of maneuvers required. Despite initial concerns about the use of open storage, the company found it significantly increased efficiency.

3.3.3 Next Empty Storage Bin

Materials can be stored in any of the storage bins

The next empty storage bin strategy allows material to be placed in the next empty bin within a storage type. This is particularly useful when the materials being stored in the storage type can be stored in any of the storage bins. You would use this strategy when materials have to be stored in a separate storage bin rather than being added to existing stock.

> **Example**
>
> A U.S. leader in pharmaceutical distribution has several distribution centers that are licensed and inspected by federal and state government agencies. Each distribution center contains products from several thousand suppliers and delivers to retail drugstores, as well as hospital pharmacies and outpatient clinics. When pharmaceuticals arrive at each distribution center, the storage bins on the transfer orders are automatically defined using the next empty bin strategy. The company adopted this strategy because they require each new delivery of pharmaceuticals to be placed in its own storage bin. The primary reason behind this was so that pharmaceuticals with different expiration dates and lots were not mixed, which would occur with a strategy such as addition to existing stock. Although this method used significantly more storage than other strategies, the company ensured that each storage bin contained materials of only one lot number and expiry date.

3.3.4   Addition to Existing Stock

Companies use the addition to existing stock strategy to add materials to a storage bin that already contains some of the same material. The complexity involved in this strategy is that each bin requires a capacity to be defined, and each material needs capacity information added. If either of these elements is missing, the capacity calculation cannot be completed, and putaway efficiency will be compromised.

Materials can be added to materials already stored in a bin

> **Example**
>
> A Canadian manufacturer of railroad components used a warehouse for their maintenance, repair, and operations (MRO) parts. Prior to the implementation of their SAP system, the parts warehouse used stand-alone warehouse management software (WMS) that interfaced with a purchasing system. The legacy WMS told the warehouse staff where to put away items, but the WMS didn't have any size or capacity measurements for the storage bins. As a result, putaway was extremely inefficient because bins were often full when the operator tried to put away new materials. The operator would then have to contact the warehouse supervisor to select a new bin and then locate the new bin and try to put away the material again. As the number of empty bins fell, the putaway process became increasingly difficult, and the backlog of materials to put away became a bottleneck.
>
> When the implemented the SAP system, the warehouse managers decided that they needed to use the functionality to create a more efficient warehouse. The implementation was combined with a survey of the warehouse storage bins, and accurate measurements were taken along with a review of all materials in the MRO warehouse. The data collection project ran parallel to the SAP implementation, and as a result, the warehouse managers decided to use the addition to stock strategy to maximize the capacity of each storage bin. The new putaway process ensured that each transfer order performed by the warehouse staff would result in the material being placed in the correct bin without the operator needing to wait while another bin was selected owing to capacity problems.

The addition to stock strategy is useful for businesses that operate their warehouse close to capacity because it maximizes the use of each storage bin in the warehouse.

3.4   Summary

This chapter has examined the variety of ways that you can achieve efficiency in your company with your putaway process. There are a number of strategies that you can adopt that are suited to a variety of companies that implement warehouse management in SAP ERP. Fixed bin storage is a simple but effective strategy and is particularly useful for companies that have fast-moving stock. This strategy allows the material to be put away directly to a specific storage bin.

The open storage strategy is an efficient strategy in simple warehouses without formal racking. It can make for rapid putaway of heavy and awkward-sized materials so they don't impede movement within the warehouse.

The next empty storage bin strategy is an efficient strategy for warehouses that can allow materials to be stored in any of the storage bins within a storage type. This can create efficient putaway in warehouses where bin locations are of the same or similar properties.

Addition to stock strategies make efficient use of a warehouse. By allowing materials to be added to existing materials in a storage bin, the capacity of each bin can be maximized, but only when the capacity of each bin and that of the material to be put away are known.

Efficient putaway of materials is critical to warehouse operations. In a warehouse with hundreds or thousands of movements per hour, each movement must be accurate. If the operator finds that a storage bin is not suitable for the material to be put away, there is a waste of time and resources, plus the additional delay in the putaway of other waiting transfer orders.

The next chapter will build on what we have learned about efficient putaway strategies and examine the internal operations that occur in the warehouse.

After materials have been placed in the warehouse, you can move them or change the status. You can make improvements to these warehouse operations by maximizing the use of the warehouse management functionality in SAP ERP.

4 Improving Internal Warehouse Operations

In this chapter, we'll discuss the movements that occur in the warehouse and ways you can improve these movements. When materials are stored in the warehouse, sometimes you need to change their location or make an amendment to their status.

The integration between inventory management and warehouse management in SAP ERP means that a movement of materials in inventory management results in the same movement in the warehouse management functionality in SAP ERP. For example, a movement of materials into a storage location will result in two postings: one in inventory management and one in warehouse management in SAP ERP.

Inventory management movements include goods receipts, goods issues, and stock transfers, whereas for the warehouse management functionality in SAP ERP, the transfer requirement and transfer orders are used to plan and move materials. In addition, the posting change will amend the status of material, for example, changing quality inspection to unrestricted.

The movements of goods in the warehouse should require as little intervention by warehouse staff as possible, and this will effectively speed up the materials movement process. In this chapter, we'll explore the internal warehouse operations and what can be done to help you maximize efficiency. The first section looks at the materials movement concepts that are used in the warehouse.

4.1   Materials Movement Concepts

Inventory
management
can trigger a
movement in
warehouse
management

If your company has implemented warehouse management functionality in SAP ERP, you need to understand that movements in the inventory management functionality, part of materials management in SAP ERP Operations, trigger subsequent movements in the warehouse management functionality of SAP ERP. In this section, we'll examine the concepts of materials movement in the warehouse.

4.1.1   Integration Between Inventory Management and Warehouse Management in SAP ERP

A warehouse
is assigned to a
plant and storage
location

When deciding the structure of a plant, it is important to consider which storage locations are to be warehouse managed. The link between the two applications is configured in the IMG. You can find the transaction by following the menu path IMG • Enterprise Structure • Assignment • Logistics Execution • Assign Warehouse Number to Plant/Storage Location.

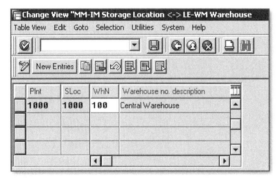

Figure 4.1   Assignment of Warehouse to Plant and Storage Location

Figure 4.1 shows the configuration where a warehouse is assigned to a plant and storage location combination. A warehouse can be assigned to a number of plant and storage location combinations. This configuration tells the SAP system that the storage location is managed by the warehouse management functionality in SAP ERP.

Further integration between the two areas is found in configuration. These specifications are required to ensure that the when materials are moved in the plant, between one storage location and another, the movement occurs in the correct storage types in the warehouse.

To find this configuration, follow the menu path IMG • Logistics Execu-tion • Warehouse Management • Interfaces • Inventory Manage-ment • Define Storage Location Control.

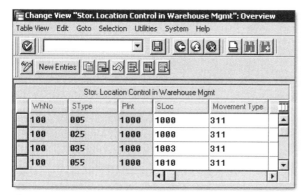

Figure 4.2 Storage Location Control in Warehouse Management

Figure 4.2 shows the configuration that assigns a storage type to a particu-lar plant and storage location combination. In this case storage types 005 and 025 correspond to plant 1000, storage location 1000, whereas storage type 035 corresponds to plant 1000 and storage location 1003. Therefore, an inventory management movement between storage locations 1000 and 1003 will trigger a movement in warehouse management functionality in SAP ERP between two storage types, either 005 and 035 or 025 and 035.

4.1.2 Interim Storage Types

The interim storage type is the conduit between the inventory manage-ment and warehouse management functionalities in SAP ERP. When a goods receipt is posted by the inventory management function into a stor-age location that is managed by warehouse management in SAP ERP, the quantity is initially posted into an interim storage type, which acts as a logical receiving area in the warehouse.

Interim storage type is the bridge between inventory management and warehouse management in SAP ERP

There should be at least four interim storage types:

- Goods receipt area
- Goods issue area
- Posting change area
- Inventory differences area

Depending on what transactions a company uses, they can create other interim storage types. These can include interim storage types for purchase orders and production orders.

Interim storage types are in the range between 900 and 999

You define interim storage types an SAP configuration the same way as other storage types, apart from the fact that interim storage types need to be defined in the range between 900 and 999. The transaction to configure the interim storage type can be found via the menu path IMG • LOGISTICS EXECUTION • WAREHOUSE MANAGEMENT • MASTER DATA • DEFINE STORAGE TYPE.

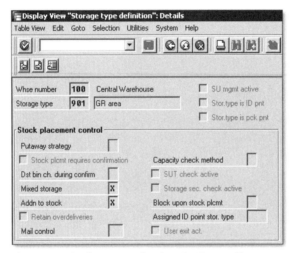

Figure 4.3 Configuration of an Interim Storage Type

Figure 4.3 shows the configuration for the interim storage type. Because the interim storage type incorporates several different materials from a variety of incoming goods receipts or outgoing goods issues, the storage type should be configured to allow mixed storage and be set for addition to stock.

After you've configured the interim storage types, you need to define the storage bins for each of them.

4.1.3 Interim Storage Bins

You can assign interim storage bins for interim storage types

The interim storage type can have storage bins that offer different information to the warehouse staff. The storage bins in an interim storage type can have either predefined coordinates, dynamic coordinates, or fixed coordinates. We'll examine each of these throughout this section.

Predefined Coordinates

When you create an interim storage type, it's possible to create one or more storage bins that have predefined coordinates. For example, in Figure 4.3, the interim storage type defined for the goods receipt area is 901, and several storage bins can be created such as INITIAL and WE-ZONE.

You create storage bins for interim storage types in the same manner as storage bins for other storage types, using Transaction LS01N or by following the menu path SAP • LOGISTICS • LOGISTICS EXECUTION • MASTER DATA • WAREHOUSE • STORAGE BIN • CREATE • MANUALLY.

You can predefine interim storage bins

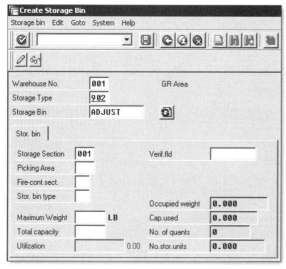

Figure 4.4 Storage Bin for an Interim Storage Type

Figure 4.4 shows the creation of a storage bin for interim storage type 902. Once you've created the storage bin, you can use it to determine logically where to place material in the interim storage type when a goods movement is posted. The goods movement uses a movement type, and the system uses the movement type to select which interim storage bin will receive the quantity of material in the interim storage type.

Each relevant movement type is configured with the required interim storage bin. You can configure the interim storage bin in the movement type by following the menu path IMG • LOGISTICS EXECUTION • WAREHOUSE MANAGEMENT • ACTIVITIES • TRANSFERS • DEFINE MOVEMENT TYPES.

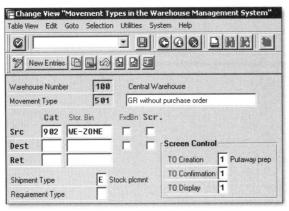

Figure 4.5 Interim Storage Bin Defined in a Movement Type

Figure 4.5 shows the configuration for movement type 501, where interim storage type 902 and interim storage bin WE-ZONE have been entered. This allows the interim storage bins to be predefined when transfer requirements are created for inbound and outbound movements of material.

To illustrate how this corresponds to an actual movement, Figure 4.6 shows a transfer requirement, 100500, that was generated by a 501 movement type. The document shows the source storage type as interim storage type 902 and the interim storage bin as WE-ZONE.

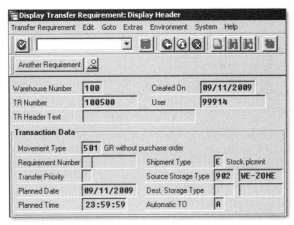

Figure 4.6 Transfer Requirement Showing Interim Storage Bin

If movement types have been annotated with interim storage bins that have yet to be created, the system can automatically create these missing storage bins using Transaction LX20. You can also access the transaction through the menu path SAP • Logistics • Logistics Execution • Master Data • Warehouse • Storage Bin • Create • For Interim Storage. The transaction shows the missing interim storage bins and gives the ability to create them.

Dynamic Coordinates

Using dynamic coordinates for interim storage bins can give greater visibility of the incoming or outgoing stock in the warehouse. The dynamic coordinate allows the document number that triggered the stock movement to be used as the coordinates for the interim storage bin.

Dynamic coordinates use the document number for a storage bin

You define the dynamic coordinate feature for the interim storage bin in the goods movement. You can configure each goods movement to allow predefined coordinates, as we saw previously in Figure 4.5, or dynamic coordinates, as shown in Figure 4.7.

To configure each movement type is that is configured for dynamic coordinates, follow the menu path IMG • Logistics Execution • Warehouse Management • Activities • Transfers • Define Movement Types.

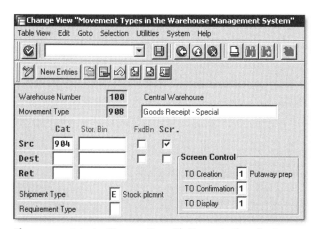

Figure 4.7 Interim Storage Bin with Dynamic Coordinates

Figure 4.7 shows movement type 908, for a goods receipt, and interim storage area 904 has been entered. No predetermined storage bin has been entered, but the Scr checkbox, which instructs the movement type to use dynamic coordinates, is selected. This allows a transfer requirement to record the document number as the interim storage bin. The document number can be the incoming purchase order number, cost center, delivery number, and so on. This means that each quant is individually identifiable by the document number. If you used predefined coordinates, were wouldn't bc thc casc.

To illustrate how the dynamic coordinate corresponds to an actual movement, Figure 4.8 shows a transfer requirement, 100505, that was generated by movement type 101. The document shows the source storage type as interim storage type 902 and the interim storage bin as 4500008128, which is the purchase order number.

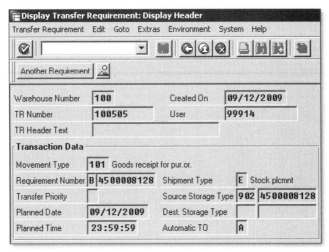

Figure 4.8 Transfer Requirement Showing Interim Storage Bin

Fixed Bin Coordinates

Fixed bins are defined in the material master record

The material master record can contain a fixed storage bin. If a material is received into a storage type that has a fixed bin assigned, it is then posted directly to the assigned fixed bin, without requiring an interim storage bin. For the goods receipt posting, the system therefore doesn't create a transfer requirement.

Figure 4.9 shows a material that has a fixed storage bin assigned for storage type 005. The fixed storage bin will be assigned when goods are received into the warehouse.

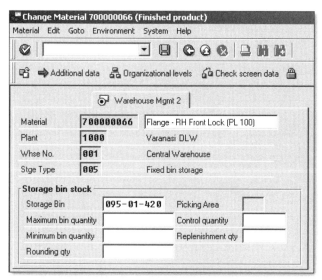

Figure 4.9 Fixed Storage Bin for Storage Type

4.1.4 Stock Comparison

Because the inventory of materials in the warehouse is reflected in the two SAP ERP functionalities, inventory management and warehouse management, the situation may arise where the inventory totals aren't synchronized. Although this event is not a common occurrence, there is a transaction that allows the inventory totals to be compared and corrected is necessary. Transaction LX23 allows a comparison between the plant and a warehouse, or at a lower level, the storage location stock against the stock in the warehouse. You can also access this transaction by going to SAP • Logistics • Logistics Execution • Internal Warehouse Processes • Physical Inventory • In Warehouse Management • Stock Comparison.

Inventory between inventory management and warehouse management functionality in SAP ERP should be reviewed regularly

Figure 4.10 shows the selection screen for the stock comparison. In this instance, you can see that the comparison is for the inventory management stock in storage location 1000 against the warehouse stock.

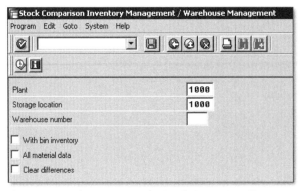

Figure 4.10 Selection Screen for Stock Comparison Transaction

Figure 4.11 shows the results of the stock comparison. The inventory management stock position shows a total of 266 for material 30545475 and 8640 for material 30545477. The warehouse management stock shows zero for both these materials, and the difference is shown. You can then review the variance between the inventory management and warehouse management stocks and clear it if necessary.

> **Note**
>
> You cannot use stock comparison with Transaction LX23 for handling unit managed storage locations.

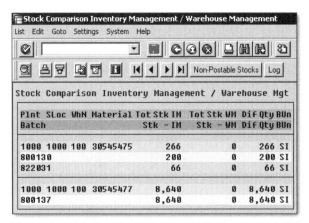

Figure 4.11 Results of the Inventory vs. Warehouse Stock Comparison

With the stock comparison transaction, your SAP system always assumes that the warehouse management stock is correct. Therefore, when there's a difference, the inventory management stock is adjusted to the warehouse management stock and not vice versa. This assumes that the stock in the warehouse management functionality in SAP ERP is more accurate because the inventory management stock is accumulated at the storage location level; the stock in warehouse management is accurate on the storage bin level.

The stock comparison transaction allows the differences to be cleared automatically if the Clear differences checkbox, shown in Figure 4.10, is selected. When the transaction finds differences, it creates a batch input session for the post differences transaction, MI10, in the physical inventory area. An automatic physical inventory is carried out during the processing that adjusts the inventory management stock to the warehouse management stock in SAP ERP.

If a physical review of the plant stock finds that the inventory management stock is correct and the warehouse stock is incorrect, then this situation should be corrected by a warehouse management physical inventory count.

The stock comparison report is an important tool for the warehouse manager. Stock figures need to be accurate in both the inventory management and warehouse management functionalities of SAP ERP, so this report should be executed on a regular basis.

In the next section we'll review the goods movements that are used in the warehouse.

4.2 Goods Movements in the Warehouse

After you take the configuration steps for the inventory management and warehouse management functions of SAP ERP, the movements triggered by the transactions in inventory management will be reflected in warehouse management functionality as transfer requirements, transfer orders, and posting changes. In this section we'll examine the transfer requirements and transfer orders triggered by goods receipts and goods issues in inventory management functionality in SAP ERP.

4.2.1 Transfer Requirement

When a goods movement is executed in the inventory management functionality in SAP ERP, a transfer requirement is created in warehouse management. The transfer requirement is the planning phase of the movement where material is planned to be moved from one location in the warehouse to another.

The transfer requirement is used to translate the information from the inventory management goods movement to a planned movement in the warehouse. The transfer requirement is automatically created so that the materials can be moved into the warehouse. You should use the information on the transfer requirement in conjunction with other transfer requirements so that warehouse managers can plan where to assign warehouse resources.

The transfer requirement is made up of a header and line items
The transfer requirement is comprised of header information and several item lines of materials to be moved in the warehouse.

The line items include information such as:

▶ The materials to be moved within the warehouse

▶ The quantity of the materials to be moved

▶ The date of when the materials should it be moved

▶ The transfer types such as a putaway, pick, or stock transfer

▶ A reason the materials have to be moved, for example, because of a production order or a purchase order

Transfer requirements can be either created automatically, triggered by a goods movement, or created manually.

Automatic Transfer Requirement

Automatic transfer requirements make materials movements extremely efficient
An automatic transfer requirement is created when a transaction for a goods movement is executed and the corresponding warehouse movement type is configured for the automatic creation of a transfer requirement. If you have automatically created transfer requirements, you remove the need for manual intervention and reduce the resources needed in transfers. Although initial configuration is required, the automatic creation of transfer requirements is an excellent example of how SAP ERP warehouse functionality can make materials movements extremely efficient.

You can configure the indicator to set for the automatic creation of a transfer requirement using the Transaction OMLR or via the menu path IMG • LOGISTICS EXECUTION • WAREHOUSE MANAGEMENT • INTERFACES • INVENTORY MANAGEMENT • DEFINE MOVEMENT TYPES.

Figure 4.12 shows the configuration for the warehouse management movement types. When you define a movement type, you can decide to configure the movement to automatically create a transfer requirement for the movement or leave the creation to be a manual process. There may be some movements where manual transfer requirements are required, and that may depend on the physical attributes of the materials your company is receiving or the specific layout of your warehouse. In general, maximizing the uses of the automatic creation of transfer requirements can create generate greater efficiencies in your warehouse.

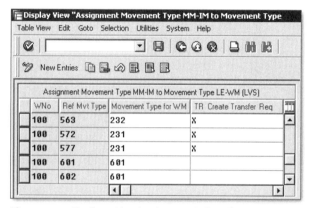

Figure 4.12 Configuration for Automatic Transfer Requirement

Manual Transfer Requirement

Although automatically created transfer requirements are efficient for warehouse operations, they may mean that you need to manually create a transfer requirement. This is common when you need to perform a goods issue to a cost center, which is often used when issuing materials to a salesman for samples.

Manual transfer requirements may be necessary in a warehouse

You must configure the warehouse movement type to allow manual transfer requirements to be created. To find the configuration, follow the menu path IMG • LOGISTICS EXECUTION • WAREHOUSE MANAGEMENT • ACTIVITIES • TRANSFERS • DEFINE MOVEMENT TYPES.

Figure 4.13 shows the configuration for warehouse movement type 909. Select the Manual TR creation allowed checkbox to allow manual transfer requirements to be created.

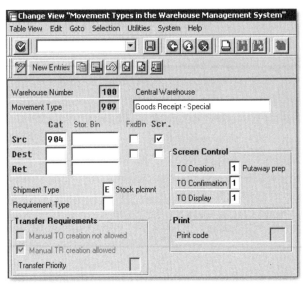

Figure 4.13 Configuration for Manual Transfer Requirements

You can create a manual transfer requirement with Transaction LB01 or via SAP • LOGISTICS • LOGISTICS EXECUTION • INTERNAL WAREHOUSE PROCESSES • TRANSFER REQUIREMENT • CREATE • WITHOUT REFERENCE.

> **Note**
>
> When trying to create a manual transfer requirement using Transaction LB01, the system will display an error message, and the creation of the transfer requirement cannot proceed if the movement type doesn't allow the manual entry of a transfer requirement.

Figure 4.14 shows a manual transfer requirement that has been created for movement type 968. In this case the movement type is not triggered by an inventory management movement, and you can create a transfer requirement manually.

After you've created and processed a transfer requirement, either automatically or manually, your next step for the movement of the material is the transfer order.

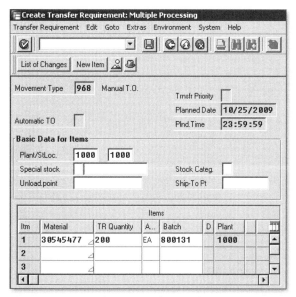

Figure 4.14 Manual Creation of a Transfer Requirement

4.2.2 Transfer Order

You use a transfer order move materials and confirm that move once it is completed. You can create the transfer order with reference to a source document from either warehouse management or inventory management. The information that you need to move materials into the warehouse, out of the warehouse, or from one storage bin to another within the warehouse is found in the transfer order.

A transfer order is required for performing the movement of materials

The transfer order is comprised of a header and a number of lines items. The header contains the transfer order number and the dates of creation and confirmation. If the transfer order has been created with reference to a transfer requirement, then the transfer requirement number appears in the header.

A transfer order can have a single or multiple line items that give you information about where the material is coming from and going. Each line item is an individual movement of a certain quantity of material from a source storage bin to a destination storage bin. To maximize the functionality of the transfer order in warehouse management, the processing should aim to have as little intervention as possible. To do this, create the automatic transfer order in the relevant movement types.

A transfer order can have one or many line items

Automatic Transfer Order

You can automatically create a transfer order for a movement when the respective movement type is configured to allow it. You can find this configuration by going to IMG • Logistics Execution • Warehouse Management • Activities • Transfers • Set Up Automatic TO Creation for TR's.

You have several options for this configuration step. You can find the definition for the automatic transfer order creation in the Control Data option. In this area, you can create one or more options for the automatic transfer for each warehouse. In Figure 4.15 the transaction shows that two options are configured for warehouse 100. However, you only need to configure one option to create automatic transfer orders.

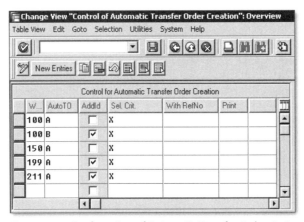

Figure 4.15 Configuration of Automatic Transfer Order Options

The second part of the configuration is found in the Assign Control option. Figure 4.16 shows the configuration for warehouse 100 and movement type 261. Option A has been selected in the Automatic TO field to create automatic transfer orders when the movement type is used.

A background job is needed to automate transfer orders

The final part to the configuration of automatic transfer orders is to create a background job that runs the report RLAUTA10. For each of the automatic transfer order indicators, you need to use a separate variant. This allows different starting times and repetition cycles to be defined for the different indicators. Once the background is running and automatic transfer orders are being generated, this is will help you maximize the efficiency of operations in the warehouse.

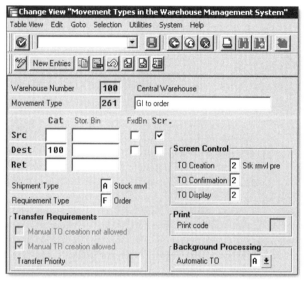

Figure 4.16 Configuration for Automatic Transfer Order

Manual Transfer Orders

There may be occasions when you have to create manual transfer orders. Although this requires warehouse resources, sometimes it's necessary. The most common occurrence of a manual transfer order is when materials need to be moved internally within the warehouse. However, the movement type, which determines the materials movement in the warehouse, must be configured to allow the creation of manual transfer orders.

Manual transfer orders may be required

Figure 4.17 shows the configuration for a user-defined movement type 969. The movement type allows manual creation of transfer orders because the Manual TO creation not allowed checkbox has not been selected. You can create the manual transfer order using Transaction LT01 or access it by going to SAP • LOGISTICS • LOGISTICS EXECUTION • INTERNAL WAREHOUSE PROCESSES • STOCK TRANSFER • CREATE TRANSFER ORDER • NO SOURCE OBJECT.

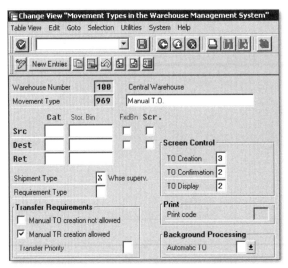

Figure 4.17 Configuration for Manual Transfer Order

Figure 4.18 shows the initial screen and input fields for manually creating a transfer order. The key to creating a manual transfer order is the movement type, which you must configure in order to allow the process (shown in Figure 4.17). You can select the control for the creation of the transfer order to be in the background, which allows the system to control the storage bin selection, or in the foreground, where you can change the destination storage bin proposed by the system.

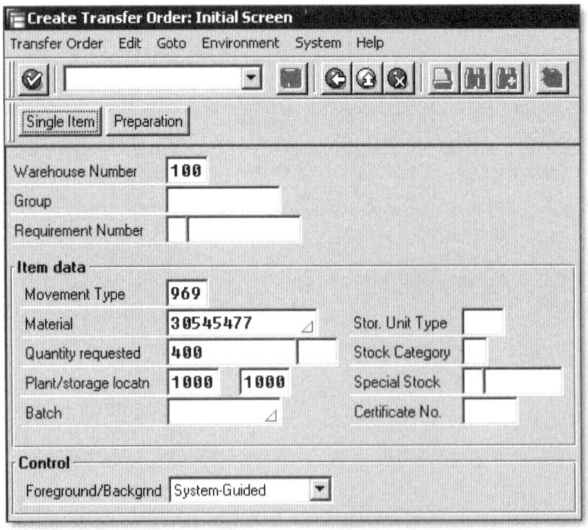

Figure 4.18 Initial Screen for Manual Transfer Order Creation

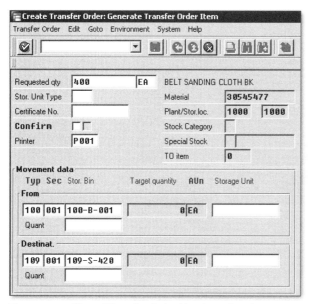

Figure 4.19 Manual Transfer Order Line Item Creation

Figure 4.19 illustrates the line item information for the manual transfer order. The system has selected the destination storage bin, but you can override this if you require a specific storage bin. The amount of manual entry for this type of transfer requires warehouse resources to be moved from primary warehousing tasks and makes the warehouse operation less efficient. Although you can't always avoid manual transfer orders, they should not be considered part of an efficiently run warehouse.

Confirming Transfer Orders

The transfer order can be confirmed to verify that the materials movement has been completed. The confirmation process is not required but may be necessary for certain storage types in your warehouse. For example, in a storage type that contains high-volume and high-value items, it may be a company policy to confirm transfer orders to reduce liability. The confirmation of a transfer order can depend on the configuration of the relevant storage type and the movement type.

Confirmation of transfer order verifies that movement is complete

Each storage type has a configuration option to require the confirmation of transfer orders for stock placement and stock removal. You can find the configuration for the storage type by going to IMG • LOGISTICS EXECUTION • WAREHOUSE MANAGEMENT • MASTER DATA • DEFINE STORAGE TYPE.

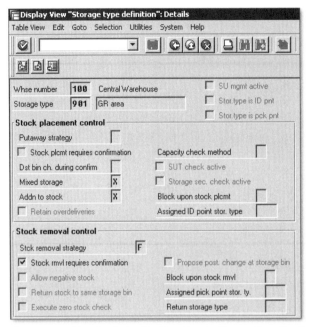

Figure 4.20 Transfer Order Confirmation in Storage Type Configuration

Figure 4.20 shows the transfer order confirmation setting for both stock removal and stock placement control in the storage type configuration. You can also control the confirmation of a transfer order with the configuration of the movement type. This allows warehouse staff to confirm that materials have been moved for specific movement types, such as goods issue to scrap.

You can configure the movement type by using the menu path IMG • LOGISTICS EXECUTION • WAREHOUSE MANAGEMENT • ACTIVITIES • TRANSFERS • DEFINE MOVEMENT TYPES.

Figure 4.21 shows the transfer order confirmation options that are available in the movement type configuration. You have two configuration options: an option to allow the confirmation to be performed when a transfer order is created and an option to allow a confirmation to be proposed, which can be processed later. The most efficient method is to ensure that the, TO item can be confrmd immed. checkbox is selected so that there is no requirement for a manual confirmation.

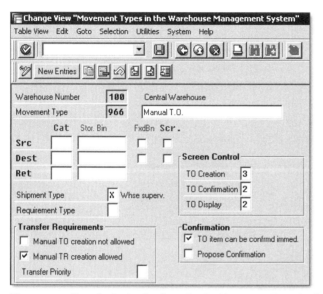

Figure 4.21 Transfer Order Confirmation in Movement Type Configuration

Transfer requirements and transfer orders are the mainstay of moving materials within the warehouse. There is one other type of movement that is part of the warehouse operation, the posting change, which we'll discuss in the next section.

4.3 Posting Changes in the Warehouse

A posting change can be processed in the warehouse and will change the information about or status of a quantity of material, for example, when materials have been inspected and can be moved from quality inspection to unrestricted stock. For most posting changes, the materials remain in the same physical location, and no changes are made to the overall quantity of the materials.

Posting change will change the status of materials

You can initiate a posting change in either inventory management or warehouse management functionalities in SAP ERP, depending on the posting change. If the posting change is triggered in inventory management, a posting change notice is created in the warehouse management functionality in SAP ERP with two equal quants of material in a posting change interim storage type. When processing the posting change notice, the system creates a transfer order with two lines: one for each item on the posting change notice. One line item is used to move the material quant into the interim posting change type, and the other is used to move it back out again with the status change. The posting change is complete when the transfer order is confirmed.

4.3.1   Reviewing Posting Changes

Posting changes can be triggered in inventory management or warehouse management functionalities

As we mentioned earlier, posting changes are produced by either the inventory management or warehouse management functionality in SAP ERP. You can review a list of posting changes in the system by using Transaction LU04 or by going to SAP • LOGISTICS • LOGISTICS EXECUTION • INTERNAL WHSE PROCESSES • POSTING CHANGE • DISPLAY • IN LIST.

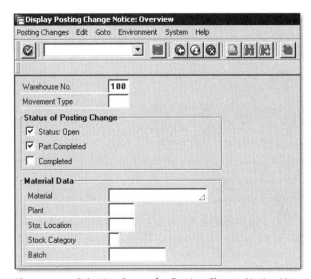

Figure 4.22 Selection Screen for Posting Change Notice List

The initial selection screen, as shown in Figure 4.22, allows you to select posting changes for a warehouse or, more specifically, for a certain movement type. The report also shows open, partially complete, or completed posting notices, depending on the option selected.

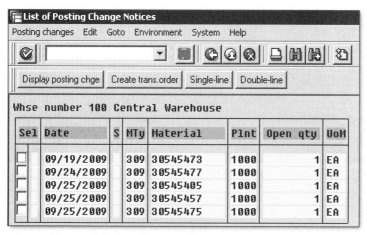

Figure 4.23 List of Posting Change Notices

Figure 4.23 shows the list of posting change notices for warehouse 100. The five posting changes are all for movement type 309, which is the movement type for a posting change in the warehouse. From this list you can select a posting change, reviewed it, and create a transfer order if necessary.

4.3.2 Automatic Processing of Posting Change Notices

The most efficient method of processing posting change notices is to have the transfer orders created automatically for each posting notice. The configuration is the same for the automatic transfer order processing that we discussed in Section 4.2.2 of this chapter. The transfer order can be automatically processed for each posting notice that is created.

Posting changes should automatically create transfer orders

To automate the creation of transfer orders for posting change notices, create a background job that runs the report RLAUTA11. For each of the automatic transfer order indicators, a separate variant must be used. This allows different starting times and repetition cycles to be defined for the different indicators. Once the background is running and automatic transfer orders are being generated for each posting change, this is will help you to maximize the efficiency of operations in the warehouse.

There are a number of scenarios in which posting changes are made in the warehouse, including the following.

- ▶ Releasing materials from quality inspection to unrestricted
- ▶ Converting blocked stock to quality inspection
- ▶ Converting unrestricted materials to inspection stock
- ▶ Changing the material number for a quantity of material
- ▶ Splitting available materials into two or more batches
- ▶ Converting special stock, such as consignment stock or returned stock, into own stock

Each of these posting changes can require manual intervention to create and confirm the transfer order that logically changes the status. However, if the process is automated, you'll reduce the level of warehouse resources required.

4.4   Business Examples – Efficient Internal Movements

Businesses that use the warehouse management functionality in SAP ERP have the ability to implement efficient internal movements of materials in the warehouse. The functionality within SAP ERP provides the ability to automate the processes that move materials, both logically and physically, in the warehouse with the minimum of resources expended.

4.4.1   Materials Movement Concepts

Companies that implement warehouse management functionalities in SAP ERP should understand that movements in inventory management trigger warehouse management movements. However, companies can expend significant warehouse resources if they don't take advantages of the efficiencies that are available in their SAP system.

Example

A U.S. distributor of electrical components purchases the majority of its stock from manufacturers in a number of Asian countries. The company has several vendors for each of the parts it buys. The items are shipped to the U.S. via containers and arrive in bulk at the warehouse. Unloading the containers results in hundreds of movements into the warehouse. To make the process more efficient, but still keep a high degree of visibility, the company decided to change the way they receive materials. When they implemented SAP ERP warehouse management functionalities, the company used predefined interim storage bins, but couldn't easily identify which document triggered the transfer requirement. The company changed to dynamic coordinates for interim storage bins so that it could identify the purchase order and vendor for a transfer requirement if it became necessary. Although the change did not make the process of moving materials into the warehouse more efficient, it did give the company additional visibility of its incoming purchase orders.

When we talk about movement of stock into the warehouse, it's important to remember that a company's inventory is reflected in two SAP ERP functionalities: inventory management and warehouse management. Without an efficient process in place, the situation may arise where totals in the two systems aren't identical.

Example

An English chemical company had implemented an SAP system with an interface to a legacy warehouse management system (WMS). When the company upgraded their SAP system, they decided to replace their aging WMS with warehouse management in SAP ERP. After implementation, the company found that despite implementing a series of warehouse efficiency programs, their putaway and picking processes often failed because storage bins were full when the system indicated that they were empty. The company was running the stock comparison reports, but because they didn't understand the implications of the report, very little was done. The stock mismatch between inventory management and warehouse management became greater each day. The company found that because many confirmations were not completed, the stock in the warehouse did not correspond to the stock indicated in inventory management in SAP ERP. They changed the process so that the stock comparison report was run once every shift, and any issues were dealt with during that shift.

4.4.2 Goods Movements

You can create an automatic transfer requirement when you execute a transaction for a goods movement. The configuration of the movement type determines if a transfer requirement is automatically created.

A Canadian manufacturer of vitamin and herbal supplements implemented an SAP system without any process improvements and considered it to be a straight replacement for a number of disparate computer systems. As a result, the warehouse staff manually processed items when they were received into the plant. They manually created transfer requirements, manually created transfer orders for those transfer requirements, and in turn manually confirmed each of the transfer orders.

An external audit of the company's operations found that the warehouse had increased its hourly staff by over 50% since the implementation of the SAP system. The audit found that most of the new resources were employed in dealing with data entry. A number of recommendations came out of the study focusing on improving efficiency in the warehouse and reducing warehouse staff to pre-SAP system levels. The company decided that it wanted to keep the manual confirmation of transfer orders, but chose to start the process changes with the automatic creation of transfer requirements based on the movement types they used. After configuring the necessary movement types, the warehouse shift supervisors found that they could assign more resources to working on the warehouse floor rather than on the SAP system creating documents.

After two weeks of the new processes, a review committee found that the headcount for each shift could be reduced. Based on that initial reduction, the review committee believed that the headcount for the warehouse would fall to below pre-SAP system levels once all of the automated processes were adopted.

The transfer order takes the planned movement of the transfer requirements and performs the physical movement of the materials. A transfer order can be automatically created for a movement when the respective movement type is configured to allow it.

A U.S. manufacturer of industrial tools implemented an SAP system and was fully utilizing the warehouse management functionality. The company had configured the system to allow automatic transfer requirements for each inbound delivery, but the transfer orders were manually created when the warehouse staff had time to put away material. The warehouse operators would wait for the shift manager to create the necessary transfer orders, which resulted in a bottleneck when the goods receiving area needed to be cleared. The company decided to try to alleviate this problem by adopting a process to automate transfer orders for the most used movement types. This removed the bottleneck because warehouse operators no longer waited for transfer orders to be created.

4.4.3 Posting Changes

Posting changes are processed in the warehouse and change the information about or status of a quantity of material. The materials remain in the same physical location and there aren't any changes to the overall quantity.

A French chemical company implemented the warehouse management functionality in SAP ERP as part of their company-wide SAP project. Every day the company received deliveries of raw materials that required quality inspection to ensure that the materials were within a range of tolerances. The quality department would perform its complex analysis in a separate system and decided to reject or accept the materials. The results would be sent to the warehouse each morning during the first shift, and the warehouse staff would then manually perform the change in material status. The process would result in warehouse staff being overloaded with having to perform posting changes while new deliveries were arriving. Warehouse operators on the first shift often had to wait for transfer orders to be created. The delay in dealing with incoming deliveries often continued late into the second shift. In an attempt to reduce the workload on the first shift, the company decided to automate the posting change process, which meant the warehouse staff no longer spent time creating transfer orders for posting changes.

4.5 Summary

This chapter has examined how a company can achieve efficiency in the way they move materials around the warehouse.

When items are moved in the warehouse efficiently, the system creates an automatic transfer requirement when a goods movement is executed. Automatically created transfer requirements remove the need for manual intervention, resulting in a reduction in the resources needed. Although this requires configuration, the automatic creation of transfer requirements is an excellent example of where warehouse management functionality can make materials movements extremely efficient

To maximize the functionality of the transfer order in warehouse management, the process should have as little intervention as possible. To do this, automatic transfer order creation should be configured in the relevant movement types.

The most efficient method of processing posting change notices is to have the transfer orders created automatically for each posting notice. The transfer order can be automatically processed for each posting notice that is created.

The movements of goods in the warehouse should require as little intervention by warehouse staff as possible, and this will effectively speed up the materials movement process. This chapter has examined the internal warehouse operations and described a number of processes you can implement to maximize efficiency.

The next chapter will review the processes of effective picking operations and review the use of storage unit management.

Picking operations are vital to the successful outbound process. The correct picking strategy will improve efficiency of the warehouse. In addition, storage unit management is important when you use containers to move items around the warehouse.

5   Effective Picking Operations and Storage Unit Management

Efficiently run warehouses maximize the components of the warehouse management functionality in SAP ERP. The strategy a company uses to pick materials for the outbound process can make a significant difference in the overall efficiency of that process. Although it isn't necessary to introduce picking strategies into the outbound process, you should discuss the way in which materials are removed from the warehouse and choose or adopt the most suitable strategies.

Picking strategies can make a significant difference in overall efficiency

After you've made decisions on the picking strategies, the SAP system uses that strategy to assign the appropriate picking location. Accepting the system-generated picking location removes the manual intervention by warehouse staff and reduces the overall picking time. Any changes that do require manual intervention should be kept to an absolute minimum and reviewed periodically so you can ensure that the picking strategies still contain the most effective configuration.

In the second part of this chapter, we'll examine the efficiencies of storage unit management. In a warehouse that doesn't use storage unit management, materials are managed as separate quants at the storage bin level. When storage unit management material is active for a storage type, materials are managed at the storage unit level in that storage type, which may mean materials are stored on pallets or in a container. By using storage unit management, your company will be able to optimize warehouse capacity and control materials flow by using storage units within the warehouse.

Storage unit management can optimize warehouse capacity

When materials are controlled in a storage unit–managed storage type, you can move them in a container or on a pallet. The storage unit is a logical grouping of the container and the materials in or on the container.

Storage units are identified by a storage unit number

All storage units are identified by a storage unit number, which you can use to locate the storage unit in the warehouse, so warehouse staff can identify the quantity of materials contained in a storage unit, and the operations have been processed or planned for it.

In the first section, we'll discuss the different picking strategies available for a company's outbound process.

5.1   Defining Picking Operations

In Chapter 3 we examined the strategies for the placement of stock into the warehouse. In this chapter we'll look at the different strategies you can use to move materials out of the warehouse and deliver them to customers with the minimum of delay.

For outbound movements, you can configure the warehouse management functionality in SAP ERP to use the optimum picking strategy so that the best picking location is assigned. The first picking strategy we need to examine is the first in, first out (FIFO) picking strategy.

5.1.1   First In, First Out (FIFO)

FIFO picking proposes the storage bin with the oldest quant of materials

The first in, first out (FIFO) picking strategy is designed so that when it is assigned to a storage type, a transfer order for an outbound movement will propose a storage bin that contains the oldest quant for specified materials.

Many companies use the FIFO picking strategy because it ensures that the oldest materials are removed from the warehouse. This strategy gives companies a basic picking strategy that ensures that the correct quant of material is selected without manual intervention by warehouse staff.

Sometimes companies use this strategy when it's not suitable. In a warehouse with racking that is two pallets or more deep, the materials identified on the transfer order may be in a storage bin at the back of a rack. The removal of the correct quant identified by the FIFO strategy would then require several movements of materials by the warehouse operator to get the correct quant. The warehouse operator then has to spend time storing the correct quant and replacing the unwanted materials back on the rack.

The picking strategy should accommodate the warehouse operations

It's important to review picking strategies to ensure that they're suitable for a company's warehouse operations rather than just fitting the requirements of the finance or sales department.

Configuring a Storage Type for FIFO

If you decide to pick materials from a storage type via the FIFO method, you need to complete the configuration to reflect this by following the menu path IMG • Logistics Execution • Warehouse Management • Strategies • Stock Removal Strategies • Define FIFO Strategy.

Figure 5.1 shows the storage type control configuration where you configure the picking and the putaway strategies. In this example storage type 105 has been configured with the FIFO stock removal strategy, indicated by the letter F.

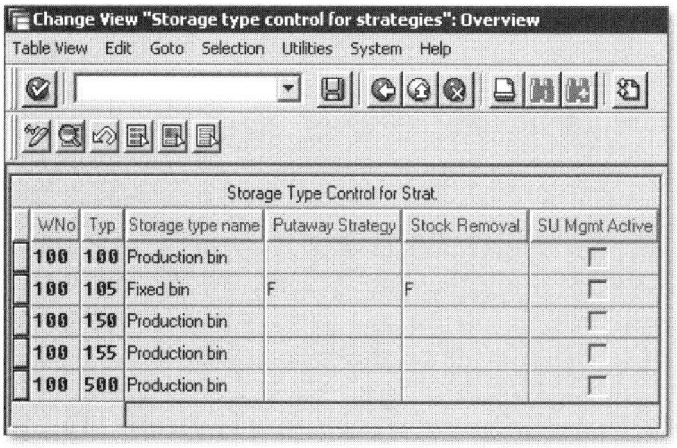

	WNo	Typ	Storage type name	Putaway Strategy	Stock Removal.	SU Mgmt Active
	100	100	Production bin			☐
	100	105	Fixed bin	F	F	☐
	100	150	Production bin			☐
	100	155	Production bin			☐
	100	500	Production bin			☐

Figure 5.1 FIFO Picking Strategy for Storage Types

To see the details behind the configuration, you can highlight the relevant line and select Goto • Details from the main menu.

Figure 5.2 shows the details that can be configured for the storage type. Apart from the picking strategy, you can select several configuration options, including allowing for negative stock, returning stock to the same storage bin, rounding off the quantity, and much more.

5.1.2 Picking Using Stringent FIFO

The normal FIFO picking strategy is applied to a single storage type. The picking process reviews the storage types based on the storage type search and selects the first suitable quant. Although this is an efficient picking strategy, some companies need a more complete, or *stringent,* search.

Stringent FIFO looks across the plant for materials

The stringent FIFO picking strategy is different from other picking strategies because it reviews not just a single storage type, but all relevant storage types to find the oldest quant. However, there may be some storage types that should not be included in the stringent FIFO picking strategy, and these can be configured, as shown in Figure 5.3.

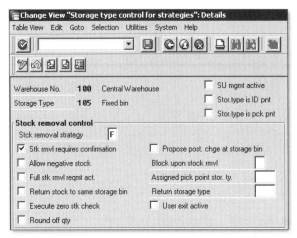

Figure 5.2   Details of Storage Type Control

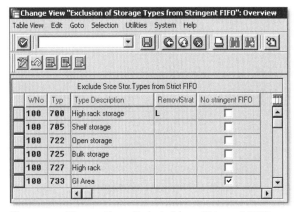

Figure 5.3   Storage Types Excluded from Stringent FIFO

You should use the stringent FIFO picking strategy when a company needs to ensure that the oldest quant in the warehouse is picked.

Configuring the Stringent FIFO Strategy

When a company decides that it requires stringent FIFO picking, they need to complete several configuration steps. You can define the stringent FIFO picking strategy using Transaction OMM8 or by going to IMG • LOGISTICS EXECUTION • WAREHOUSE MANAGEMENT • STRATEGIES • STOCK REMOVAL STRATEGIES • DEFINE STRATEGY FOR "STRINGENT FIFO".

Figure 5.3 shows the configuration that allows certain storage types to be excluded from the stringent FIFO picking strategy. Including storage types such as goods issue interim storage types and posting change interim storage types, may result in the picking strategy producing invalid results.

You should confirm the storage type search with a storage type indicator designated for stringent FIFO. Configure the search for all storage types, except those that are excluded, as shown in Figure 5.3.

Figure 5.4 shows the storage type search for stringent FIFO. A storage type indicator is defined for the picking strategy, in this case, SFI. The *** in the first storage type column indicates that all storage types will be checked for stringent FIFO.

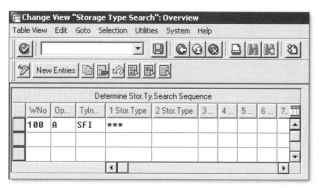

Figure 5.4 Storage Type Search for Stringent FIFO

5.1.3 Last In, First Out (LIFO)

For some companies the FIFO picking strategy may not be suitable for their warehouse operations. An alternative may be the last in, first out (LIFO) picking strategy, which is based on the principle that the last quant of material to be placed in the warehouse should be the first to be picked. The financial aspects of this strategy mean that the existing materials in the warehouse do not change in value when new materials are received. Because of the LIFO method, the older materials aren't affected by the potentially higher prices of the new deliveries of materials. If the older materials aren't affected, they aren't valuated at the new material price. If the older material value isn't increased, this stops any false valuation of current inventory.

LIFO proposes that the last quant is the first to be selected

The LIFO method may be suitable for the company's financial goals, but for the warehouse it may not be the most efficient picking method. There has to be some compromise between company departments so that the financial benefits are not outweighed by the cost of moving materials around the warehouse.

Configuring a Storage Type for LIFO

When you decide that materials should be picked from a storage type via the LIFO method, you need to configure the system to reflect this. You can define the LIFO picking strategy for a storage type by following the menu path IMG • LOGISTICS EXECUTION • WAREHOUSE MANAGEMENT • STRATE-GIES • STOCK REMOVAL STRATEGIES • DEFINE LIFO STRATEGY.

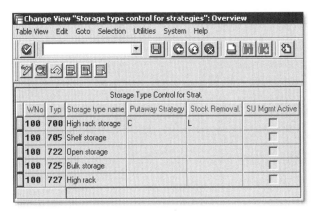

Figure 5.5 LIFO Picking Strategy for Storage Types

Figure 5.5 shows the storage type control configuration where the picking strategy is defined. In this example storage type 700 has been configured with the LIFO stock removal strategy, indicated by the letter L.

5.1.4 Partial Quantity Picking

When companies have implemented FIFO or stringent FIFO picking, they adhere to using whatever quant is the oldest, no matter what condition that quant is in. The partial picking strategy allows warehouse staff to pick partial pallets of material first before picking full pallets. The benefit of this strategy isn't important for all businesses, but for companies that store items in pallet loads, reducing the number of partial pallets in the warehouse can be beneficial.

The partial quantity picking strategy does require that a company has adopted the storage unit management functionality, which is described later in this chapter.

> **Example**
>
> A beverage company stores their 330-ml cans in trays of 24, with 96 trays to a pallet. The pallet is then covered with stretch wrap plastic before being placed in the warehouse. If warehouse staff notices damage on a pallet, they remove the stretch wrap and dispose of the damaged items. They amend the quantity on the pallet in the warehouse management functionality and return the pallets to the warehouse. Because the majority of sales are for full pallets, the company found that partial pallets stay in the warehouse too long because they were not picked. Eventually, the beverage on the partial pallet would near its sell-by date, and the company couldn't sell it. They should adopt partial quantity picking to reduce the chances of partial pallets being unpicked before the product expires.

The partial quantity picking strategy looks at a number of specific scenarios in deciding which storage bin to select for a transfer order. If you chose this strategy, it will select partial storage unit quantities if no standard storage units are available. If the required quantity in the outbound transfer order is less than the quantity of a standard storage unit, the system will first attempt to remove partial storage unit quantities from the stock. Unfortunately, if a transfer order is for a quantity less than a standard storage unit and no partial quantities are available, a full storage unit selected using FIFO and will be broken down.

Partial pallet picking means there will be fewer partial pallets

Configuring a Storage Type for Partial Quantity Picking

When you decide to use the partial quantity picking method, you need to configure the system by going to IMG • Logistics Execution • Warehouse Management • Strategies • Stock Removal Strategies • Define Strategy for Partial Pallet Quantity.

Figure 5.6 shows the storage type control configuration where the picking strategy is defined. In this example, the storage types A20 through A24 have been configured with the partial quantity picking stock removal strategy, indicated by the letter A. In this instance the storage unit management (SU Mgmt Active) checkbox must be selected.

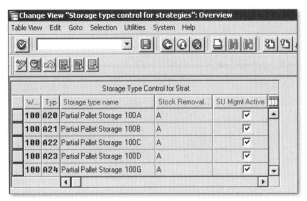

Figure 5.6 Partial Quantity Picking Strategy for Storage Types

5.1.5 Picking According to Quantity

Picking by quantity decides on the pick location based on quantity

This picking method can improve the operation of the warehouse because it allows the system to pick quants based on the quantity required by the transfer order comparing the quantity in the storage bins. This strategy is particularly useful for companies that store small quantities of material in a fixed bin in the fast picking area or in a storage carousel while larger quantities of the material are stored in a reverse area.

By implementing a picking strategy based on quantity, the operation of the warehouse can be dramatically improved. Without this type of picking strategy the storage bins in a fast-moving picking area may need to be replenished several times a shift, if large quantities of materials need to be picked.

Configuring Picking According to Quantity

To implement this picking strategy, you need to take a number of steps. First, you configure the storage type control to indicate that a storage type has been assigned to the quantity picking strategy.

You can define the picking according to quantity strategy for a storage type by going to IMG • LOGISTICS EXECUTION • WAREHOUSE MANAGEMENT • STRATEGIES • STOCK REMOVAL STRATEGIES • DEFINE STRATEGY FOR LARGE/SMALL QUANTITIES • ACTIVATE.

Figure 5.7 shows the storage type control configuration where the picking strategy is defined. In this example storage types 512 through 515 have been configured with the picking by quantity picking stock removal strategy, indicated by the letter M.

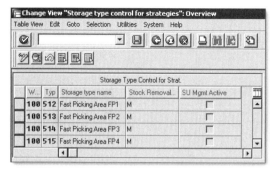

Figure 5.7 Picking by Quantity Strategy for Storage Types

Make the next setting in each material master record that is appropriate for the picking by quantity strategy. You can set the control quantity field in the warehouse management section of the material master so that the system knows the value at which the picking strategy should change.

> **Example**
>
> In Figure 5.8 material 100-002704 is stored in quantities of up to 100 pieces in storage type 512, one of the fast picking areas. In quantities greater than 100 pieces in storage type 728, this is the high-racking area. With picking according to quantity, the configuration needs to be set where strategy M is used for storage type 512 and strategy F for FIFO, for the high-racking storage type 728. When configuring the storage type search for picking, the storage type where quantities below the control quantity 100 can be picked need to be first priority, and the storage types for quantities greater than 100 are the second priority. In this case storage type 512 should be first in the search, followed by storage type 728.

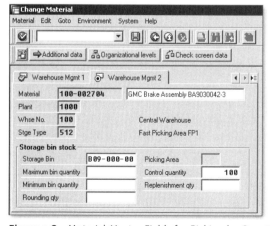

Figure 5.8 Material Master Fields for Picking by Quantity

In Figure 5.8 the control quantity is 100, and the unit of measure is taken as the base unit of measure for the materials. The value is the threshold below which the system decides whether to use the picking according to quantity strategy.

After configuring the storage type control for picking strategy and the relevant material master records, you need to configure the storage type search to allow the system to search efficiently. You can define the storage type search for the picking according to quantity strategy by going to IMG • LOGISTICS EXECUTION • WAREHOUSE MANAGEMENT • STRATEGIES • STOCK REMOVAL STRATEGIES • DEFINE STRATEGY FOR LARGE/SMALL QUANTITIES • DETERMINE SEARCH SEQUENCE.

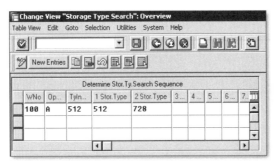

Figure 5.9 Storage Type Search for Picking by Quantity

Figure 5.9 shows the storage type search required for the picking by quantity strategy. The first storage type to be searched is the location where the smaller quantities, below the control quantity on the material master, can be picked. The second storage type in the search is the area from which the larger quantities above the control quantity can be picked.

5.1.6   Picking by Shelf Life Expiration Date

Picking by expiration date uses oldest materials first

For companies that sell materials that have a shelf life expiration date, the picking of materials must reflect the need to move the oldest materials out of the warehouse in the most efficient manner. Because items in the warehouse have a shorter shelf life, the possibility of selling them to customers is smaller. Some customers require the shelf life of items to be not less than a certain number of days. For example, in the food and beverage industry the shelf life for food items may be as much as two years for canned goods, but customers may only want to purchase items with more than 18 months of shelf life remaining, so it's important for these manufacturers to pick the oldest quants first.

You can assign the picking strategy for shelf life expiration in the storage type control configuration by going to the navigation path IMG • LOGISTICS EXECUTION • WAREHOUSE MANAGEMENT • STRATEGIES • STOCK REMOVAL STRATEGIES • DEFINE STRATEGY FOR EXPIRATION DATE.

The first part of this configuration step is to ensure that the warehouse is active for shelf-life expiration date, as shown in Figure 5.10.

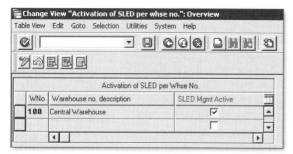

Figure 5.10 Activating Shelf Life Expiration for the Warehouse

The second part to the configuration step is to ensure that the picking by expiration date strategy is activated for the necessary storage types.

Figure 5.11 shows that storage types 1B1, 1B3, 1B4, and 1B5 have all been assigned to picking strategy H, which indicates the picking by shelf life expiration date.

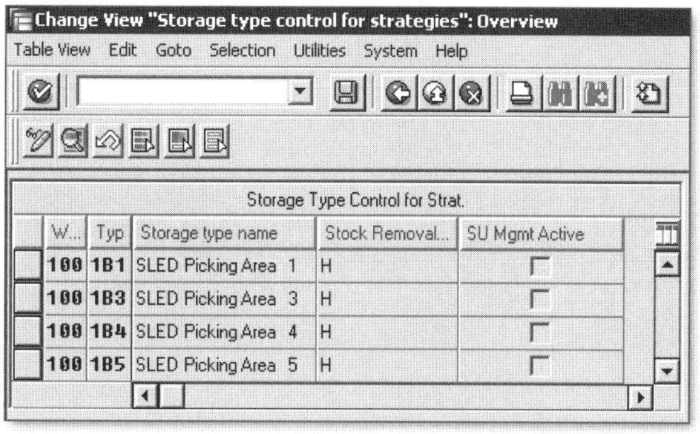

Figure 5.11 Storage Type Search for Picking By Expiration Date

Figure 5.12 shows the shelf life data in the material master record that is used in the picking by expiration date strategy. In this case, the material has a total shelf life of 480 days with a 45 day minimum shelf life. This implies that the system will no longer identify a quant as being valid with less than 45 days of shelf life remaining.

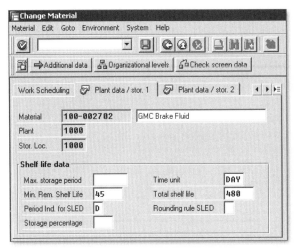

Figure 5.12 Shelf Life Data in the Material Master Record

5.1.7 Fixed Bin Picking Strategy

Fixed bin picking uses the same storage bin all the time

For some companies the location where materials are to be picked from never varies. If materials are always picked from the same storage bin for certain storage types, then it is possible to enter this fixed storage bin in the material master record. Although this isn't the most efficient method of picking, for some companies this is the optimum way for the warehouse operations to work.

The fixed storage bin for picking strategy is in the material master record in the warehouse management screens. The fixed storage bin is the same for picking and putaway for a particular storage type.

Figure 5.13 shows the fixed storage bin, 095-01-420, that material 700000066 is stored in for storage type 005. The fixed bin picking strategy will select this storage bin when a transfer order requests materials for this storage type.

At the storage type control level, the configuration has to indicate that a storage type is operating fixed bin picking. You can define the fixed bin picking strategy using the menu path IMG • LOGISTICS EXECUTION • WAREHOUSE MANAGEMENT • STRATEGIES • STOCK REMOVAL STRATEGIES • DEFINE FIXED BIN STRATEGY.

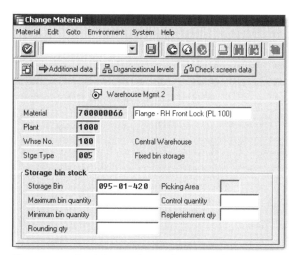

Figure 5.13   Fixed Storage Bin in the Material Master Record

Figure 5.14 shows that storage types 1P0, 1P3, 1P4, and 1P5 have been configured for the fixed bin picking strategy.

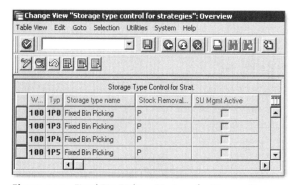

Figure 5.14   Fixed Bin Picking Strategy for Storage Types

In this section, we've looked at the different picking strategies you can use in the warehouse. Any of the strategies examined here can be used in any warehouse and may by the optimum strategy for a company.

5.2   Business Example – Effective Picking Strategies

The picking strategies available to companies in the warehouse management functionality in SAP ERP cover every picking scenario that could occur. Choosing the most appropriate picking strategy can significantly increase the efficiency of warehouse operations.

The picking strategies can improve warehouse operations

5.2.1 FIFO

One method used by companies that require FIFO picking and want to ensure that the oldest materials are picked on the rack is to use gravity flow racks for materials. With this type of racking, items are placed at the back, and the flow racks are filled so that when a pick is made at the front of the rack this moves materials toward the front from the back.

Example

A small British brewing company became successful by brewing small batches of beer and selling the product in bottles. To expand their business, the company started to produce beer in kegs for the local pubs close the brewery. One downside was that the product had a relatively short shelf life, so it was imperative that the oldest beer was sold first. However, the warehouse layout was such that the kegs were stored four to a pallet, and the pallets were stored in open storage types. When sales of the product were strong, the inventory in the warehouse was low, and no problems occurred. However, with slower sales the inventory in the warehouse built up, and finding the oldest shelf life became increasingly difficult. The company decided to use FIFO picking and forego open storage. The kegs were no longer stored on pallets, and instead the company used gravity racks to ensure that the oldest keg was always available.

5.2.2 Partial Quantity Picking

Companies that store materials on full pallets don't necessarily sell materials in pallets, so picking the materials usually involves breaking down full pallets. To make picking more effective, companies can adopt the partial quantity picking strategy.

Example

A Canadian manufacturer of refrigeration compressors stored parts on pallets in the warehouse. The compressors were stored 12 to a pallet and shipped to distribution centers on the pallets. To increase sales revenues the company began selling the parts via the Internet and through telephone sales. The sales were usually for one or two items rather than a pallet. Initially, the warehouse did not implement any picking strategy, and the complete pallets were routinely broken down leaving many partial pallets. Not only was this an issue when the picking for the distribution centers required full pallets, but it also meant picking took significantly longer because operators had to break full pallets. In an attempt to reduce the number of partial pallets, the company introduced the partial quantity picking strategy. The picks for Internet sales began selecting storage bins that contained partial pallets. After five weeks, 90% of the existing partial pallets had been consumed, and the warehouse operations had significantly improved.

5.2.3   Picking According to Quantity

This picking method is particularly useful for companies that store small quantities of material in a fixed bin in the fast picking area and larger quantities in a reserve area. Without this picking strategy the storage bins in a fast-moving picking area may need to be replenished several times a shift if large quantities of material need to be picked.

Example

A British automotive parts company has a regional warehouse that supplies approximately 100 retail stores. Each evening the transfer orders are created for picking the orders for the retail stores. The storage bins closest to the shipping dock contain the 500 most popular items ordered by the stores, and each bin contains a limited number of items. The slower-moving items and the reserve quantity for the fast-moving items are stored in high-racking. On occasion, the retail stores order a quantity of a certain item far in excess of the normal order quantity because of a customer's requirement. In this case the pick should not remove the quantity from the closest storage bin, but should select the materials from the high-racking area where the reverse stock is held.

5.2.4   Picking by Shelf Life Expiration Date

Many companies produce items that have an expiration date. In most of these companies it's important to pick the oldest quant of material first so that no materials in the warehouse expire. Because items in the warehouse have shorter shelf lives, the possibility of selling them to customers is smaller. Some customers require the shelf life of items to be not less than a certain number of days.

Example

A Canadian manufacturer of vacuum parts had been producing replacement bags, belts, and brushes for 40 years. During that time the items had never been given expiration dates. In 2004 several manufacturers informed the company that they needed to include an expiration date for items that contained rubber, which included some replacement vacuum bags and rubber belts. Initially, the company didn't track the expiration date of its products in the warehouse, and the picking of items was based on a fixed bin strategy. When an annual physical inventory found a large amount of inventory that had either expired or was close to expiring, the company decided to implement a new picking strategy. The warehouse began monitoring shelf life data and implemented shelf life date picking so that the correct date was picked for each order. At the next physical inventory, the amount of expired product was almost zero.

The picking strategies available in the warehouse management functionality of SAP ERP allow companies to increase the efficiency of their warehouses. In the next section we'll examine storage unit management and how you can use it in the warehouse to increase productivity.

5.3 Using Storage Unit Management

Storage unit management moves items on a pallet or container

Storage unit management was developed exclusively for the warehouse management functionality in SAP ERP. The primary component is the storage unit, which is used to contain a quantity of material while it is moved around the warehouse. The storage unit consists of one or more materials and a container, such as a pallet or a packing box. The items combined together make up the uniquely identifiable storage unit that can be moved and stored within the warehouse.

Some warehouses receive materials on pallets or in containers but then unpack the items prior to storing them in the warehouse. For other materials that arrive on a pallet or container, it's more efficient to move and store them along with the pallet or container. In other instances materials may arrive without any packaging, and the company may decide to place the materials in a container or on a pallet to be stored in the warehouse. The use of containers or pallets as a storage medium in the warehouse may require the use of storage unit management for several storage types in the warehouse.

Storage unit management can improve efficiency in the warehouse, but you need to perform some configuration to ensure that storage unit management operates successfully.

5.3.1 Activate Storage Unit Management

For each warehouse where storage unit management is to be used, you need to activate the functionality by going to IMG • LOGISTICS EXECUTION • WAREHOUSE MANAGEMENT • STORAGE UNITS • MASTER DATA • ACTIVATE STORAGE UNIT MANAGEMENT PER WAREHOUSE.

Figure 5.15 shows the control data configuration for a warehouse, where you can activate the storage unit management. No storage unit management can take place until the SU Management Active checkbox is selected for the relevant warehouse.

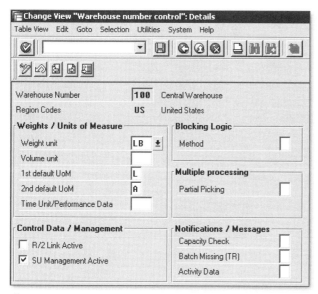

Figure 5.15 Activate Storage Unit Management for a Warehouse

5.3.2 Activate Storage Unit Management for a Storage Type

When you decide to use storage unit management in a warehouse, the next decision concerns what storage units you'll use. Once we've examined the picking strategies, you'll see that some require storage unit management, such as partial quantity picking. So, an understanding of what is required from storage unit management and how this relates to the stock placement and removal strategies is important. Once you've decided, you can configure storage types to activate storage unit management by going to IMG • Logistics Execution • Warehouse Management • Storage Units • Master Data • Define Storage Type Control.

Figure 5.16 shows the configuration for the storage type, in which the SU mgmt active checkbox has been selected. The next step after configuring the warehouse and storage type is to define what storage unit types you'll use in the warehouse. These can be as simple as pallets or wire baskets that are used to move materials around the warehouse.

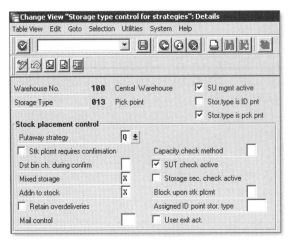

Figure 5.16 Storage Unit Management for a Storage Type

5.3.3 Storage Unit Type

Storage unit types identify different container types

You use the storage unit type to distinguish the containers that are used with materials to comprise the storage unit. The storage unit type can be a pallet or a wire basket. Companies often want to keep track of the containers, so it's important to create the correct storage unit types.

You can find the configuration steps by going to IMG • LOGISTICS EXECU-TION • WAREHOUSE MANAGEMENT • MASTER DATA • MATERIAL • DEFINE STORAGE UNIT TYPES.

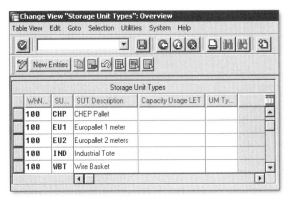

Figure 5.17 Creating the Storage Unit Types

Figure 5.17 shows the different storage unit types that are used in warehouse 100. When materials arrive in the warehouse, they can be placed in a container or on a pallet. This configuration defines the types of storage units that are available in the warehouse.

5.3.4 Storage Unit Record

A storage unit record consists of a header and at least one quant of material. The header contains the number of the storage unit record, the storage unit type, the status, and the storage bin where the storage unit is located. Storage units don't appear in functionality outside of warehouse management and can only exist when materials have to be moved within the warehouse. So, you create a storage unit when the quant of material that requires a storage unit is moved in the warehouse or is planned to be moved into the warehouse. You can create a storage unit record by a transfer order for materials arriving or in advance of that materials arriving.

Storage unit records show the information about the items

Creating a Storage Unit Record by Transfer Order

The transfer order is the mechanism used to create a storage unit. You can do this using Transaction LT07 or by going to SAP • LOGISTICS • LOGISTICS EXECUTION • INTERNAL WAREHOUSE PROCESSES • STOCK TRANSFER • CREATE TRANSFER ORDER • CREATE STORAGE UNIT.

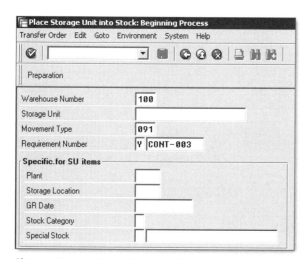

Figure 5.18 Creating a Storage Unit Record using a Transfer Order

Figure 5.18 shows the initial screen for Transaction LT07. The actual movement of the quant of material, with the appropriate container, requires that the transfer order create the storage unit as part of the process.

You can see the detail that is added to Transaction LT07 in Figure 5.19. Once you correctly enter the appropriate data into the screen, you can click on the Create Trans. Order button to create the transfer order and the storage unit. You can also plan the storage unit in advance of the materials arriving at the warehouse.

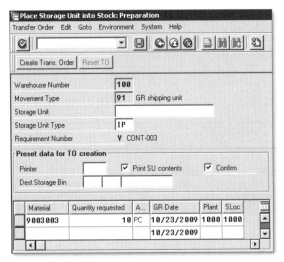

Figure 5.19 Detailed Entry for the Storage Unit

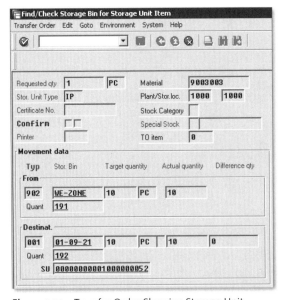

Figure 5.20 Transfer Order Showing Storage Unit

Figure 5.20 shows the created transfer order with the source and destination storage types. The destination storage type shows that there is a new storage unit, which has been created from the data entered into Figure 5.19.

Planning Storage Unit by Transfer Order

The planning of storage units is the process of creating the transfer orders but not confirming them. The creation of the transfer order creates the storage unit, so it exists when the materials arrive at the receiving dock.

Storage units can be planned and used when the materials arrive

You should use Transaction LT0A to plan storage units for incoming materials. To do so, follow the menu path SAP • LOGISTICS • LOGISTICS EXECUTION • INBOUND PROCESSES • GOODS RECEIPT FOR PURCHASE ORDER, ORDER, OTHER TRANSACTIONS • PUTAWAY • CREATE TRANSFER ORDER • PREPLAN STORAGE UNITS.

Figure 5.21 shows the initial screen for Transaction LT0A, which allows you to create storage units for planning purposes. The quantity of the material entered on the transfer order is the amount expected to arrive on the inbound delivery.

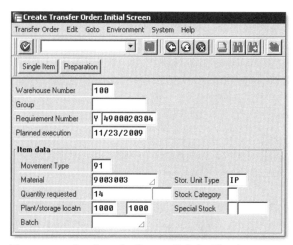

Figure 5.21 Creation of a Storage Unit for Planning

Figure 5.22 shows the transfer order that has been created for the inbound materials. The materials will be moved from the goods receipt area using the container, and this will be storage unit 1000080837. The storage unit will be moved to storage type 105, bin location 89-6060605.

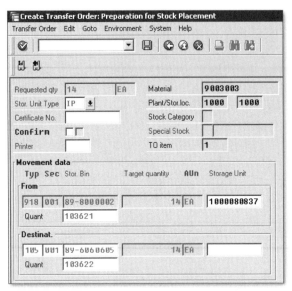

Figure 5.22 Transfer Order Showing Storage Unit

The transfer order is not confirmed, because this process only plans the movement. Storage unit documents are printed that and stored until the materials arrive. The confirmation takes place when the materials arrive at the receiving dock and are moved to the storage bin.

The storage unit functionality is extremely useful in warehouses that move and store materials in containers or on pallets. For companies that use rented pallets and want to monitor those pallets movements in the warehouse, the creation of a storage unit is an efficient way of achieving that goal.

5.4 Business Examples – Benefits of Storage Unit Management

You don't have to use storage unit management in the warehouse, but it may improve warehouse efficiency for some companies that need containers or pallets to move items around the warehouse. Items often arrive at a warehouse and stay on the pallet as it's moved and eventually shipped. Some companies don't need to track the container, but some that use rental pallets may need to know where each pallet is. The other benefit of using storage unit management is that it's possible to pack items in a packaging material and track that packaging material along with its contents in the warehouse.

A German automotive parts manufacturer sold some parts individually and then combined a number of parts to create a unique kit. The company sold parts and kits to automotive stores. The parts of the kit were not kept together, but were picked and combined as a kit, with the kit packaging, when the order was shipped. To increase productivity in the warehouse, the company decided to combine the parts and the packaging materials for the kit before the item was stored in the warehouse. The company used the storage unit management functionality to combine the parts with the packaging materials to create a storage unit.

Some companies receive different materials into the warehouse on the same pallet or in the same container. It's possible to break down the pallet and move the individual materials to separate bins, or the whole pallet can be stored as a storage unit.

An Indian computer parts distribution company supplied parts for retailers. Each retailer sent orders that required a pallet or partial pallet of items to be packed before shipping. The company received parts from manufacturers in China and Taiwan that were delivered in separate containers. The items were stored in the warehouse and pulled to the packing area when orders that contained multiple items were combined. The company found this to be very labor intensive, and the process added an extra day to the delivery time to the customer. In an attempt to reduce the delivery time to the customer and improve customer service, the company asked vendors to combine items on a pallet or in a container, based on customer orders, which could then be stored in the warehouse as a storage unit. The storage unit might not contain all of the items on the customer order, but it significantly reduced the amount of additional work needed at the warehouse.

In a further attempt to reduce warehouse resources, the company encouraged its freight companies to combine incoming materials to create storage units, which resembled customer orders.

5.5 Summary

This chapter has discussed the different picking strategies that are used in the warehouse and that can improve warehouse operations. All of the strategies we've discussed can be used at a variety of companies; the company decides which is the most appropriate strategy to maximize operations. Although FIFO and fixed bin picking strategies are very common, other picking strategies that may improve warehouse efficiency.

The functionality for storage unit management was designed for warehouses and is a useful tool for materials that need to be moved around the warehouse in a container. Storage units can contain one material or several different materials. You can use the storage unit management functionality to improve warehouse operations where the company needs to move and store materials in a container or on a pallet in the warehouse.

The next chapter will discuss the functionality that contributes to efficient shipment completion.

The shipping completion process can be complex and labor intensive. You need to clearly understand the outbound delivery function to use more complex strategies, ultimately maximizing efficiencies in the warehouse.

6 Efficient Shipment Completion

In warehouse management, the shipping process is a vital part of the supply chain. By ensuring that the process is as efficient as possible, you'll also maximize customer satisfaction and minimize operating costs. The outbound delivery is an integral part of the process and describes the movement of material from the warehouse to an external source, which can be another company location or a customer. The outbound process is an extremely important for a company because the shipping performance can affect customer satisfaction, increase revenue, and reduce operating costs. However, the process can be complex and can require significant resources to maintain efficiency.

6.1 Defining Your Shipment Completion Process

The shipping completion process involves shipping activities including packing, transportation, and goods issue. As part of the process, the company records shipping information, monitors the status of shipping activities, and documents data.

Shipment includes packing, transportation, and goods issue

When the outbound delivery is created, you schedule the shipping activities, initiate the delivery, and process documentation. The outbound delivery can be created from a sales order, a stock transport order, or a project, or it can be created without reference to a document.

6.1.1 Creating an Outbound Delivery

When you receive a sales order from a customer or produce a stock transport, you can create an outbound delivery. This allows your system to process several activities that move the material from the warehouse to

An outbound delivery can be created from a sales order

the customer with maximum efficiency. The outbound delivery also allows warehouse staff to monitor the activities and make changes if necessary.

You can create the outbound delivery for a sales order by using Transaction VL01N or by going to SAP • Logistics • Sales and Distribution • Sales • Order • Subsequent Functions • Outbound Delivery.

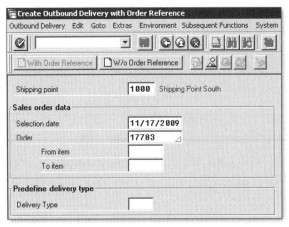

Figure 6.1 Creation of an Outbound Delivery

Figure 6.1 shows the initial screen for the creation of an inbound delivery. To create the document, you need the shipping point and the order number.

The shipping point is a location from which items are shipped

The shipping point is a location from which items are shipped. There is normally one shipping plant, but depending on your company's structure, there may be one shipping point for several plants. In large distribution or retail operations, the loading area for vehicles may be a separate location and facilitate a number of locations at the site. A shipping point can be further divided into individual loading points.

Figure 6.2 shows the detail screen for the outbound delivery. The information from the sales order or stock transport order is transposed, including the material number, the quantity to be delivered, and the planned goods issue date.

If this information doesn't require any modification, then you can create the outbound delivery by selecting Outbound Delivery • Save from the header menu or by pressing [Ctrl] + [S]. Once the processing is complete, the system will return you to the initial screen for outbound delivery creation and display the outbound delivery number on the screen.

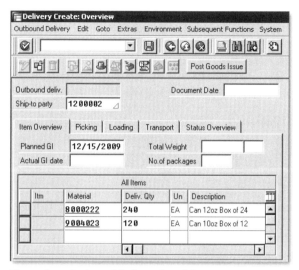

Figure 6.2 Outbound Delivery Detail Screen

Once the outbound delivery has been created, the system processes several activities, which include the following:

- ▶ Check the order and materials to ensure an outbound delivery is possible
- ▶ Determine the delivery quantity of an item and check the availability of the material
- ▶ Calculate the weight and volume of the delivery
- ▶ Pack the outbound delivery
- ▶ Redetermine the route
- ▶ Add information relevant for export
- ▶ Check delivery scheduling and change deadlines, if required
- ▶ Assign a picking location
- ▶ Carry out batch determination if material is batch managed
- ▶ Create an inspection lot if the material must pass a quality check
- ▶ Update sales order data and change order status

If any of the information changes after the outbound delivery is created, you can use Transaction VL02N.

The system processes several activities for outbound delivery creation

6.1.2   Review an Outbound Delivery

After the outbound delivery has been created, you update information when certain activities are processed. To review the status of the outbound delivery, you can use Transaction VL03N or go to SAP • Logistics • Sales and Distribution • Shipping and Transportation • Outbound Delivery • Display.

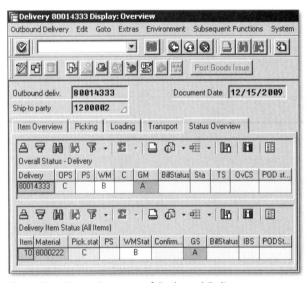

Figure 6.3   Status Overview of Outbound Delivery

Figure 6.3 shows the status of the outbound delivery. There are two elements that you can see: the overall status of the delivery and the line item status. Each element has several items for which a status is given.

Outbound delivery shows several statuses

You can review several statuses to identify the stage at which delivery should be set. First are the statuses that refer to the overall delivery.

Overall Status

▶ **OPS**

This is the overall status for picking the delivery:

　▸ A – Not processed

　▸ B – Pick is in process

　▸ C – Delivery has been completely picked

▶ **PS**

This field shows the packing status that indicates whether there are items that are relevant for packing.

- ▶ A – Packing has not been processed
- ▶ B – Delivery is partially packed
- ▶ C – Delivery is completely packed

▶ **WM**

This field shows the overall status of the warehouse management functionality in SAP ERP activities. The status shown is either a transfer order specifying if SAP ERP is required or not, and if required, whether it's confirmed or still open for processing.

▶ **C**

This field shows the status of pick confirmation. This confirmation status indicates whether picking must be explicitly confirmed for the delivery or whether picking has already been confirmed. The confirmation status is only relevant if transfer orders are not for picking.

▶ **GM**

This field shows the total goods movement status. It tells whether the delivery has already left the warehouse or is still being processed or whether processing has not yet begun.

▶ **Bill Status**

This field shows the billing status of the sales or delivery document. The status describes if the document is completely billed, partly billed, or not relevant for billing.

▶ **Sta**

This field shows the status for intercompany billing.

▶ **TS**

This field indicates the transportation planning status. The status is entered on the basis of the leg indicator (preliminary, subsequent, direct, and return) in the headers of the shipment documents to which the delivery has been assigned.

- ▶ A – Not yet planned
- ▶ B – Partially planned
- ▶ C – Completely planned

▸ **OvCS**

This field is relevant for the overall status of credit checks.

▸ **POD Status**

This field is the proof of delivery status (POD status) for the entire delivery. The status tells whether the customer reported a POD for this delivery. The values can be:

- ▸ A – Relevant for the POD process
- ▸ B – Differences were reported
- ▸ C – Quantities were verified and confirmed

Delivery Item Status

▸ **Pick.stat**

The status message indicates whether the item is relevant for delivery. Some items are not relevant for picking and show a blank field. These can include text or service materials.

- ▸ A – Not processed
- ▸ B – Pick is in process
- ▸ C – Line item has been completely picked

▸ **PS**

This field refers to the packing status of the line item.

▸ **WM Stat**

This field shows the warehouse management status of the delivery item. If the delivery processing uses the warehouse management functionality in SAP ERP, then the system updates the status for each item in a delivery.

▸ **Confirm**

This field specifies the pick confirmation status for each delivery item. When a delivery item is subject to pick confirmation, the item is assigned the status A to indicate that the line is subject to confirmation but not yet confirmed. Once the pick is confirmed, the system assigns either status B for partially confirmed or status C if the line item is fully pick confirmed.

► **GS**

This field is for goods movement status. For outbound deliveries, the status tells whether the item has already left the warehouse or company premises, or whether it's still being processed.

► **Bill Status**

This is the billing status of delivery-related billing documents. The status line displays whether the item is not yet billed, partly billed, completely billed, or not relevant for billing.

► **IBS**

This field shows the status for intercompany billing.

► **POD Status**

This field is for the proof of delivery status of each item. The status message tells whether the customer reported a proof of delivery for this item. This status can have the following values:

  ▸ Blank – Not relevant for the POD process

  ▸ A – Relevant for the POD process

  ▸ B – Differences were reported

  ▸ C – Quantities were verified and confirmed

6.1.3 Outbound Delivery Monitor

The outbound delivery monitor is a useful tool for warehouse staff because it allows you to view deliveries for a variety of options.

The delivery monitor displays and processes completed and open deliveries

You can access the outbound delivery monitor using Transaction VL06O or by going to SAP • Logistics • Logistics Execution • Outbound Process • Goods Issue for Outbound Delivery • Outbound Delivery • List and Logs • Outbound Delivery Monitor.

The outbound delivery monitor offers seven options and a selection for listing all outbound deliveries, as shown in Figure 6.4.

Warehouse staff can use the outbound delivery monitor to monitor and process completed and open deliveries. It allows you to create lists of deliveries for collective processing using selection criteria. The use of the outbound delivery monitor is key to making the warehouse as efficient as possible. By monitoring the status of deliveries, the warehouse manager can orchestrate how resources are used as efficiently as possible to ensure that deliveries are processed in a timely fashion.

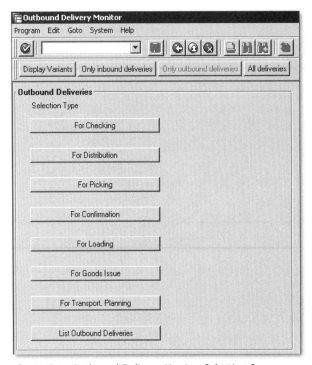

Figure 6.4 Outbound Delivery Monitor Selection Screen

For Picking

The delivery
monitor allows a
review of picking

The outbound delivery monitor is useful for warehouse staff that needs to review the picking that has to be processed on a specific workday. You can select the picking option from the delivery monitor, as shown in Figure 6.4. The picking selection screen allows the warehouse staff to enter a range of options so that the particular scenario can be monitored.

Figure 6.5 shows the selection screen for the picking data, where you enter the shipping point and the picking date range. In this case the selection is for a single work day at shipping point 1000. The selection can be for warehouse management in SAP ERP or non-SAP picking. In this case both have been selected.

Figure 6.6 shows the picking data that has been identified for the selection entered in Figure 6.5. The screen shows that six deliveries have been found for shipping point 1000 for the date selected.

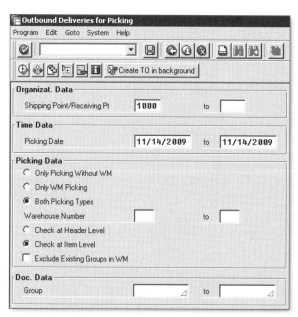

Figure 6.5 Outbound Delivery Monitor – Picking Selection Screen

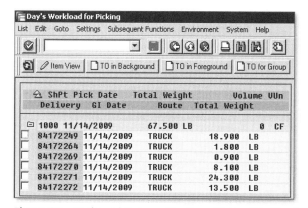

Figure 6.6 Outbound Delivery Monitor – Picking Workload

You can review each of the deliveries or select several other processes. The Subsequent Functions menu in the header menu allows the user to perform various tasks directly from the delivery monitor.

You can select a delivery and perform the following:

▶ Create a transfer order

▶ Create a billing document

The delivery monitor allows you to perform several processes

- ▸ Post a goods issue
- ▸ Display picking output
- ▸ Process delivery documents
- ▸ Create a group of deliveries

6.1.4 Grouping Outbound Deliveries

You can maintain a group of outbound deliveries for several reasons. In the warehouse it may be appropriate to group deliveries based on the shift they need to process in, the type of equipment needed to process the picking, the type of packing required for the delivery, or to group deliveries for a wave pick and so on. There are many reasons to create a group. Depending on the complexity of your warehouse operations, it can make operations more efficient to group deliveries together.

Deliveries can be grouped together
You can create a group from the list created by the outbound delivery monitor, as shown in Figure 6.6. For deliveries that need to be grouped, you can select SUBSEQUENT FUNCTIONS • GROUP • CREATE from the header menu.

Figure 6.7 Description for Creating a Group

The screen shown in Figure 6.7 will be displayed, and you can enter a description for the group you want to create. The group type defaults to K in this case, which represents a group for picking. Other group types include W for wave picks and M for freight lists. Once you enter the group you've created, its number will be displayed.

You can use the group in the selection criteria so that you can use the delivery monitor to show just the deliveries for the chosen groups.

Figure 6.8 shows the selection screen for the outbound delivery monitor that has an entry for groups that have been created. The resulting information only shows the details for the two selected groups.

Figure 6.8 Outbound Delivery Monitor – Picking Selection Screen

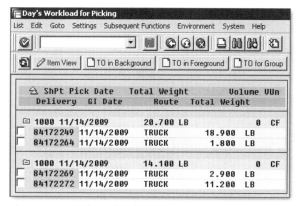

Figure 6.9 Outbound Delivery Monitor – Picking Workload for Groups

Figure 6.9 shows the deliveries that relate to the two groups entered in the selection criteria. The use of groups can ensure that in warehouses with large numbers of outbound deliveries during a shift, the warehouse staff can group deliveries with similar criteria so that they're easier to monitor. In this example two groups are selected, each with two deliveries. The appropriate number of deliveries to assign to a group depends on the number of outbound deliveries and the complexity of the warehouse

The use of groups can create efficiencies in the warehouse

operations. To achieve the most efficient use of grouping deliveries, you need to analyze the warehouse's outbound deliveries.

6.2   Adding Value to Shipment Completion

Outbound delivery
process can be
made more
efficient
The outbound delivery is the major process in shipping completion, and you can use several applications to add value to the overall process. The outbound delivery requires transfer orders to be created and items to be picked and packed, and these elements need to be sequenced so that warehouse resources can be most efficiently used.

6.2.1   Creation of Transfer Orders for Outbound Deliveries

One aspect of the outbound delivery is the creation of the transfer order in the warehouse management functionality in SAP ERP. The warehouse staff can do this in the outbound delivery monitor. When they create the list for the work to be processed in a shift or for groups, it's possible to then create the transfer orders for all of those deliveries at one time.

You can use the
delivery monitor
to create transfer
orders
On the delivery monitor screen you can create transfer orders in the foreground, background, or for groups. To reduce manual intervention, the transfer orders can be created in the background.

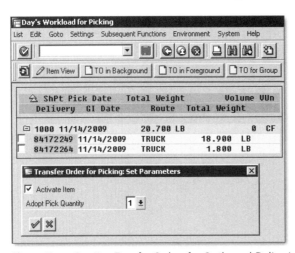

Figure 6.10   Creating Transfer Orders for Outbound Deliveries

Figure 6.10 shows the processing for creating transfer orders for the outbound deliveries in the background. The processing requires that the user select an option for the adoption of the pick quantity. There are five options.

- ▶ Blank – Control through the movement type
- ▶ 1 – Include picking quantities in delivery
- ▶ 2 – Include picking quantities in delivery and post goods issue
- ▶ 3 – Do not include picking quantities in delivery
- ▶ 4 – Do not take pick quantity as delivery quantity

In Figure 6.10 option 1 has been selected so that the quantities are picked and a goods issue processed. This option requires the minimum amount of intervention by warehouse staff.

6.2.2 Wave Picking

Wave picking can significantly increase the efficiency of the outbound delivery process for companies that process large numbers of deliveries each day. A wave pick can consist of a group of deliveries that are due to be processed at the same time, for example, at the beginning of a shift. You can create wave picks either manually or automatically according to time criteria.

Wave picking can consist of picks processed at the same time

You can create wave picks from the outbound delivery monitor's picking screen by selecting the appropriate deliveries and then selecting SUBSE-QUENT FUNCTIONS • GROUP • WAVE PICK from the header menu.

However, before you begin wave picking, you need to complete several configuration steps. The wave picking process is based on picking items for outbound deliveries that need to be processed at a similar time. For example, if the delivery trucks leave the warehouse at 8 AM, they'll need to be completely loaded by that time. Therefore, there will be a wave pick at 6 AM or 7 AM that picks the material that has to be on the delivery trucks leaving at 8 AM. You need to configure the picking times for the wave picks so that there are multiple timeslots that relate to when picking takes place.

Wave picking requires some configuration

Wave Picking Profile

The first configuration step is to create a wave picking profile for the warehouse. In this configuration step you define any capacity limitations. For example, if the first shift has 5 forklift operators that can perform 10 picks per hour each, then the capacity for an hour on the first shift is 50 picks per hour. The profile must then reflect this capacity limitation so that wave picking groups don't contain more than the capacity defined in the profile.

Capacity is a limitation to wave picking

You can configure the wave picking profile via the menu path IMG • LOGIS-
TICS EXECUTION • SHIPPING • PICKING • WAVE PICKS • MAINTAIN WAVE
PICKS PROFILE.

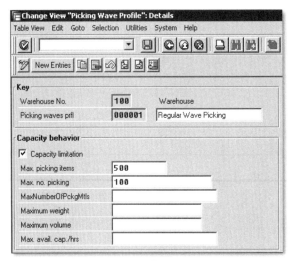

Figure 6.11 Wave Picking Profile

Figure 6.11 shows the configuration that has been entered for warehouse
100. The Capacity limitation checkbox is selected, and the profile limits the
number of picks to 100 and the number of items to 500. These capacity
limits are used when the wave picks are assigned to a time slot. When the
capacity is reached, no further picks are assigned.

Time Slots

Wave picks occur
at predefined
time slots

The next part of the configuration is to create the time slots when the wave
picks are generated. These can be at suitable time intervals for the individual warehouse. Regional distribution centers that replenish hundreds
of retail stores may have thousands of deliveries a day, and the time slots
may be configured for one per hour, whereas less busy warehouses may
get by with one wave pick per shift.

To configure the time slots for the wave picks, follow the menu path IMG •
LOGISTICS EXECUTION • SHIPPING • PICKING • WAVE PICKS • MAINTAIN TIME
SLOTS.

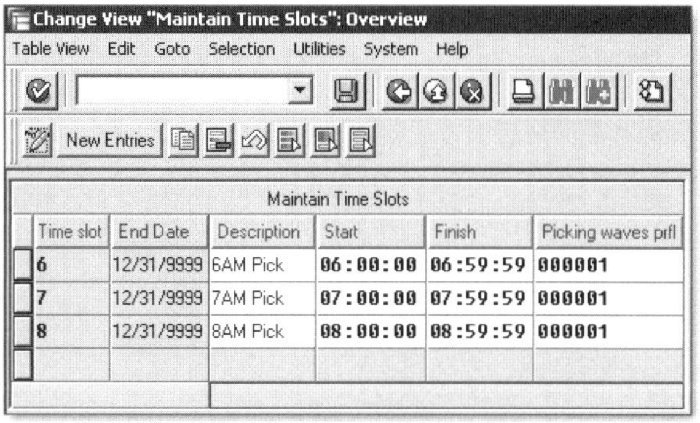

Figure 6.12 Configuration for Wave Time Slots

Figure 6.12 shows the time slots that are configured for the warehouse. The time slot is associated with a wave picking profile, which contains the capacity limitations. If the time slots have different capacity limitations, then they should be linked to a different profile.

Timeslot Group

You need to configure the timeslot group needs to be configured because the group combines a number of time slots. For example, a timeslot group could include a 6 AM timeslot, which may be the first timeslot of a shift, and then the 6 AM time slot the next day. A timeslot group should contain at least one timeslot, but timeslots should not overlap. You can configure the timeslot group by going to IMG • LOGISTICS EXECUTION • SHIPPING • PICKING • WAVE PICKS • MAINTAIN TIMESLOT GROUP FOR WAVE PICK.

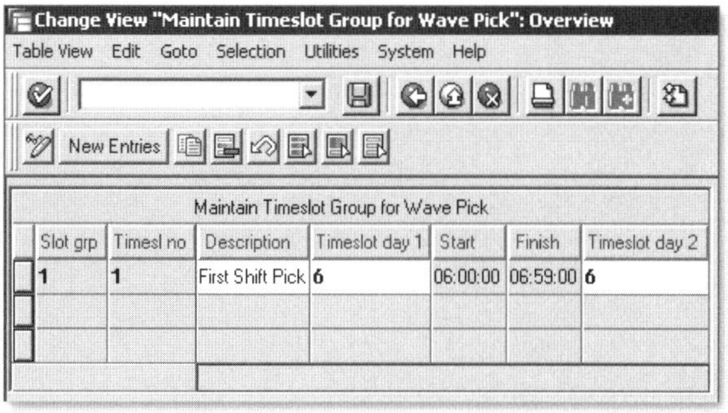

Figure 6.13 Configuration for a Timeslot Group

Figure 6.13 shows the configuration for a timeslot group. The group is created from a number of timeslots that can be on one or two days. In this example the timeslot group is for the 6 AM time slot for two consecutive days.

Create a Wave Pick According to Delivery Time

You can create a wave pick manually by adding deliveries or by using the outbound delivery monitor. To achieve the manual entry of deliveries to a wave pick, use Transaction VL35 or follow the menu path SAP • LOGISTICS • LOGISTICS EXECUTION • OUTBOUND PROCESS • GOODS ISSUE FOR OUTBOUND DELIVERY • PICKING • WAVE PICKS • CREATE • ACCORDING TO DELIVERY TIME.

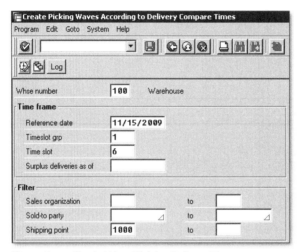

Figure 6.14 Create Wave Pick by Delivery Time

Figure 6.14 shows the initial selection screen to create a wave pick by delivery time. The warehouse operator can create a wave pick for a specific timeslot at the warehouse. In this example the wave pick is being created for timeslot 6, which is 6 AM.

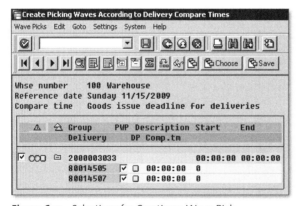

Figure 6.15 Selections for Creating a Wave Pick

Figure 6.15 shows the wave pick that has been created for the selection criteria entered in Figure 6.14. The wave pick shows the relevant selected deliveries.

Create a Wave Pick Using the Outbound Delivery Monitor

You can also create a wave pick using the outbound delivery monitor, which you can access using Transaction VL06P or by going to SAP • Logistics • Logistics Execution • Outbound Process • Goods Issue for Outbound Delivery • Picking • Wave Picks • Create • Via Outbound Delivery Monitor.

You can use the delivery monitor to create a wave pick

Here, you can enter the appropriate selection criteria, and the resulting picking workload will be displayed. You can also create wave picks by selecting the appropriate deliveries and then selecting Subsequent Functions • Group • Wave Pick from the header menu.

Release a Wave Pick

You can release the wave pick and print the documents with the shipping Transaction LT44 or by following the menu path SAP • Logistics • Sales and Distribution • Shipping and Transportation • Communication/ Printing • Release and Print Wave Pick.

Wave Pick Monitor

After they've created the wave picks, the warehouse staff can monitor the picks to ensure that they're being processed and print any necessary output documents. You can use Transaction VL37 to access the wave pick monitor or go to SAP • Logistics • Logistics Execution • Outbound Process • Goods Issue for Outbound Delivery • Picking • Wave Picks • Monitor.

Use the wave pick monitor to review the picks

The selection screen shown in Figure 6.16 requires warehouse number and a range of other selection criteria, including the document date, timeslot group, and timeslot. The warehouse staff can then monitor the wave picks for the timeslot.

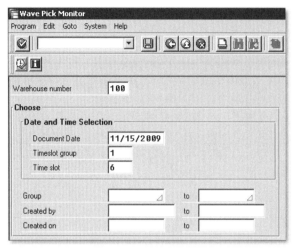

Figure 6.16 Selection Screen for the Wave Pick Monitor

Print Pick Lists

If you need to print the pick lists for the deliveries in a wave pick, you can process this from the wave pick monitor.

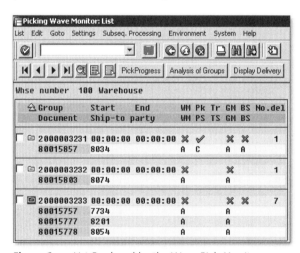

Figure 6.17 List Produced by the Wave Pick Monitor

Figure 6.17 shows the wave picks for the timeslot specified. In the wave pick monitor you can initiate several activities. To print the pick list for a wave, select SUBSEQUENT FUNCTIONS • PICK LIST.

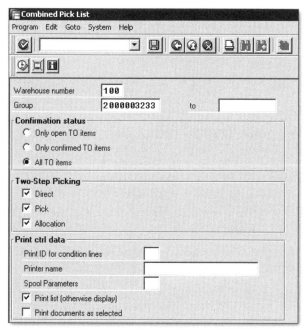

Figure 6.18   Pick List Printing for Wave Pick

Figure 6.18 shows the selection screen for the transaction that prints the pick lists for the deliveries associated with the wave pick. In this example the program will print the pick lists for deliveries that are in wave pick 2000003233.

Print Delivery Notes and Freight Papers

From the wave pick monitor, you can print the delivery notes and freight papers for the deliveries in the wave pick. To initiate the delivery notes for a pick list, select SUBSEQUENT FUNCTIONS • OUTPUT/PAPERS • OUTPUT DELIVERY NOTE from the header menu. You can process the freight papers by selecting SUBSEQUENT FUNCTIONS • OUTPUT/PAPERS • OUTPUT FREIGHT PAPERS, also from the header menu.

Delivery documents can be vital to the shipping process

Figure 6.19 shows the selection screen for printing freight papers. The output type, LL00, is specifically for freight papers, whereas the transmission medium 1 is to print the documents.

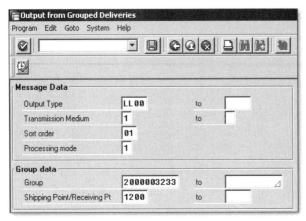

Figure 6.19 Print Procedure for Freight Papers

Other Processing from the Wave Pick Monitor

You can initiate several other processes from the wave pick monitor that allow the warehouse staff to use this one transaction to control warehouse picking.

▸ Plan replenishment for fixed storage bins

▸ Create transfer orders for wave picks

▸ Release transfer orders for printing

▸ Reprint of transfer orders

▸ Confirm transfer orders for wave picks

▸ Create shipments using collective processing

▸ Post goods issues for wave picks

▸ Create billing documents

The wave pick monitor is a useful transaction for the warehouse staff to ensure that picks are efficiently processed.

6.3   Auditing, Reporting, and Clean-Up Activities

The complexity of the outbound delivery process requires that the warehouse staff manage any issues that may arise. To maintain an efficient warehouse the staff has to monitor for incomplete deliveries and move materials when deliveries are modified or cancelled.

6.3.1 Incompletion Log

It's important to check that the outbound deliveries are complete so the picking and shipment can take place when required. An outbound delivery is incomplete if any of the fields required for the delivery have not been filled. The incompletion log checks for omissions in the header data, item data, partner information, and delivery texts.

Incomplete deliveries can result in missed deliveries

You can access the incompletion log using Transaction V_UC or by going to SAP • LOGISTICS • LOGISTICS EXECUTION • OUTBOUND PROCESS • GOODS ISSUE FOR OUTBOUND DELIVERY • OUTBOUND DELIVERY • LIST AND LOGS • INCOMPLETE OUTBOUND DELIVERIES.

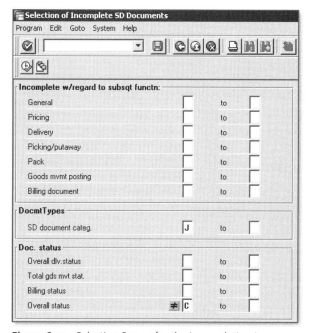

Figure 6.20 Selection Screen for the Incompletion Log

Figure 6.20 shows the selection screen that you use to create the incompletion log. For the incompletion log the document type is set to J for deliveries, and deliveries should be excluded where the overall status is C, for complete. Leaving the other selections blank results in all incomplete deliveries being displayed, but if staff wants to just see certain lists of incomplete deliveries, they can select the appropriate selection criteria.

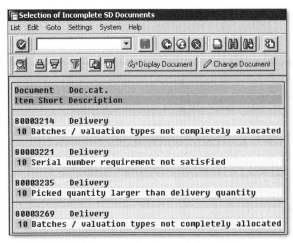

Figure 6.21 Deliveries on the Incompletion Log

Figure 6.21 shows the incomplete deliveries and the description of the missing element. To select a delivery can and change it to complete the delivery, click on the Change Document button. The delivery can be processed once the changes are made.

6.3.2 Shipping Output

You can print shipping documents separately from the wave pick monitor

You can print documents from the wave pick monitor, but it can be more efficient to print the shipping output for a group of outbound deliveries. The shipping output can be several standard or customized forms, including the delivery note, packing list, freight list, and shipping notification. You process the shipping output using Transaction VL71 or by following the menu path SAP • LOGISTICS • SALES AND DISTRIBUTION • SHIPPING AND TRANSPORTATION • COMMUNICATION/PRINTING • OUTBOUND DELIVERY OUTPUT.

Figure 6.22 shows the selection screen for the outbound delivery output, where you can print all of the necessary output. In this example the delivery notes, output type LD00, will be printed for shipping point 1200. You can print several standard and customized output types, for example, packing list PL00, shipping notification LAVA, and freight list LD00.

To print the output documents for a wave pick or multiple wave picks, you can use Transaction VL72 or follow the menu path SAP • LOGISTICS • SALES AND DISTRIBUTION • SHIPPING AND TRANSPORTATION • COMMUNICATION/ PRINTING • GROUP OUTPUT.

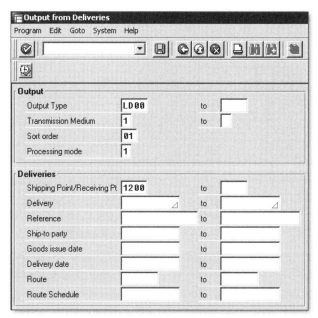

Figure 6.22 Outbound Delivery Output Selection Screen

6.3.3 Creating a Transfer Order for a Cancelled Delivery

When outbound deliveries are cancelled, for example, by the customer or if the material was incorrectly picked, then the material needs to be removed from the shipping area and returned to the warehouse.

Material needs to be moved back to the warehouse if not used for deliveries

The transfer order to clean up errors or cancellations in outbound deliveries can only be initiated when the transfer order to initially pick the material for the delivery has been confirmed.

To transfer material back to the warehouse, use Transaction LT0G or follow the menu path SAP • Logistics • Logistics Execution • Outbound Process • Picking • Cancel Transfer Order • Return Transfer for Outbound Delivery.

Figure 6.23 shows the initial screen to clean up materials that are not required for an outbound delivery. If multiple deliveries are cancelled, you can enter a range to process them as a group. In this example only one delivery has been entered.

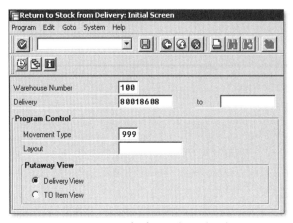

Figure 6.23 Return Transfer for Outbound Delivery

Figure 6.24 shows the transfer proposed for the movement of material 6630085 back to the warehouse, storage type 005, from the shipping area, storage type 916. There is an option to perform this in the foreground if any manual changes need to be made.

Figure 6.24 Details for Transfer from Delivery

6.4   Business Example – Efficient Shipment Procedures

Efficiencies in shipping can be obtained by using the SAP functionality

The shipping of materials to customers is a vitally important part of the supply chain because an efficient shipping process can reduce overall resources while helping to improve customer satisfaction. As companies become leaner, competition becomes less focused on margins and more focused on service. When businesses have maximized the utilization of the resources they have, a customer's perceived level of service can make the difference in maintaining and increasing business.

The outbound delivery process in the warehouse management functionality in SAP ERP offers companies a range of functionality that when utilized, can increase the productivity of the warehouse.

6.4.1 Outbound Delivery Monitor

The outbound delivery can be created from a sales order, stock transport order, or project, or it can be created without reference to a document. The outbound delivery allows the warehouse staff to monitor the aspects that make up the delivery process in the warehouse.

Warehouse staff can use the outbound delivery monitor to monitor and process completed deliveries and deliveries that are still open. It allows you to create lists of deliveries for collective processing using selection criteria and is a key component in making the warehouse as efficient as possible.

> **Example**
>
> A U.S. candy manufacturer had recently implemented the warehouse management functionality in SAP ERP after decommissioning some aging legacy systems. The implementation of warehouse management in SAP ERP had been successful, and the shipment of goods had not suffered from the change. However, the logistics management had hoped to see an improvement in resource utilization in the warehouse and a decrease in time it took to ship materials to the customer.
>
> Although the implementation had addressed and adopted the use of outbound deliveries, the warehouse staff hadn't understood the importance of the outbound delivery monitor. The warehouse staff was not monitoring the overall status of the deliveries, so items were remaining on the shipping dock until the transport staff requested shipping documents.
>
> After some retraining of warehouse staff, the use of the outbound delivery monitor was adopted, and warehouse shift leaders were proactive in selecting deliveries for picking and grouping together deliveries for specific warehouse operators to usher through the process. After three months of using the outbound delivery monitor, the shipping process in the warehouse had improved and delivery times to customers had been reduced.

6.4.2 Wave Picking

Wave picking can significantly increase the efficiency of the outbound delivery process for companies that process large numbers of deliveries each day. A wave pick can consist of a group of deliveries that are due to be processed at the same time, for example, at the beginning of a shift. It's possible to create wave picks either manually or automatically according to time criteria.

A U.S. automaker opened a central distribution center in Mexico that received parts from vehicle plants in Canada, the U.S., China, and Mexico. The distribution center in Mexico supplied parts to retail outlets, repair shops, and car dealerships throughout Latin America that had previously been supplied by five small regional distribution centers. Initially, the plan was for the distribution center to process approximately 200 sales orders per day, with on average, four lines per order. The design of the SAP system was to pick the deliveries during the first shift and spend the second shift dealing with inbound deliveries. However, at the time of go-live, the number of orders transferred from the decommissioned regional distribution centers numbered just below 1000 per day. At the opening of the center, the inventory was not complete, and many orders couldn't be fulfilled until parts arrived from overseas. In addition to the open orders, the trucks containing the outbound deliveries had to be filled quickly because the incoming parts couldn't be received. In the first week, ten trucks arrived daily with parts, and only a maximum of five trailers could be emptied during the second shift. At the end of the first week 20 trailers were still waiting to be unloaded, and 3000 orders couldn't be picked owing to the materials being on the parked trailers and not in the warehouse.

At the beginning of the second week the plant decided to implement wave picking and increase the staff on the first shift. This gave the warehouse more picking capacity, which would complete the loading of the outbound trucks faster and allow the parked trailers to be unloaded starting on the first shift. The benefits of the wave picking were that the warehouse staff could determine the capacity for each timeslot and ensure that the maximum amount of successful picking could be attained. The warehouse had four timeslots for the first shift, where the pick tickets were printed each hour and given to the forklift drivers. At the end of the last timeslot, the remaining unpicked deliveries required manual intervention, but the majority of the loading was complete, halving the time required the previous week.

The wave picking process allowed the warehouse to achieve a higher percentage of successful picks, while dealing with the problem of parked trailers waiting to be unloaded. It took only 11 more days to clear the parked trailers, and the wave picking remained in place as the sale orders rose to over 2500 per day.

6.4.3 Wave Pick Monitor

After you create the wave picks, the warehouse staff can monitor the picks to ensure that they're being processed and to print any necessary output documents.

> **Example**
>
> A British electrical component company picked over 4000 items each day for orders to retail stores and Internet sales. The company had implemented full warehouse management in SAP ERP and was using wave picking for each hour of their first shift, which corresponded to approximately 500 items per hour. The electrical items were stored in a series of horizontal carousels, which consisted of an oval track with rotating bins containing shelves that delivered items to the carousel operator.
>
> The picking lists were printed at the beginning of each hour and passed to the carousel operators. The items were picked with accuracy and efficiency, and often the operators had completed their picks after 20 or 30 minutes. Because the wave picks were printed each hour, the operators were not being utilized for half of their shift.
>
> To increase the utilization of their carousel operators the warehouse managers began a more stringent use of the wave pick monitor. In particular, the warehouse manager was able to monitor the picking and ascertain when the operators were close to completing the wave pick. When the wave pick was almost complete, the warehouse manager triggered the printing of the next wave pick from the wave pick monitor. With the use of this transaction, the carousel operators' productivity increased, and the deliveries to customers were able to leave the warehouse earlier than before the use of the wave pick monitor.

6.5 Summary

This chapter has discussed the shipment completion processes used in the warehouse that can improve the overall outbound delivery process. Not every company wants to expend the effort of developing a comprehensive shipping process, but to maximize the functionality available in a standard SAP ERP system, the topics covered in this chapter can easily be adopted.

The functionality of the outbound delivery and the outbound delivery monitor gives the warehouse manager a clear understanding of the current warehouse situation and has the tools to maximize efficiency. The functionality of wave picking along with the delivery monitor can significantly increase utilization of resources and decrease the amount of time it takes to ship product to a customer. With customer satisfaction playing a more important role in maintaining and winning work, any improvement can be as significant as a reduction in overall cost.

The next chapter will discuss the functionality to create an efficient returns process.

Processing returns is an important aspect of a company's business. By maximizing the process a company can provide repair services to customers and refurbish return items, both of which can increases profitability for your company.

7 Maximizing Returns Processing

When a customer returns materials, often the materials are received into the warehouse and stored until they quality department examines or scraps them. Not only does this scenario use precious warehouse space, but it fails to address the potential benefits of repairing items for customers or refurbishing returns for potential resale. Both of these options can turn the loss due to the cost of disposal into a profit for your company.

Returns processing is also called reverse logistics

The term *reverse logistics* describes the value added processes that are performed on customer returns, as well as the whole returns process. This process covers the customer returning items and servicing processing the returns and either returning them to the customer, putting them back into stock, or refurbishing them for resale. The returns process has become an important part of the processing that takes place in the warehouse.

7.1 Introduction to Returns Processing

Customers return materials for many reasons; the items your customer received are damaged, the product failed after a period of time, or the product was not on their purchase order and therefore was sent in error. Whatever the reason, your customers will send materials back to your warehouse, and your company must have procedures in place to quickly and efficiently receive the items, inspect them, and make a decision on returning the items to stock, scrapping them, or refurbishing them for resale.

Customers return materials for a variety of reasons

Many parts of your organization are involved in the returns process. When a customer buys an item, there are often instructions on how to return it, if necessary. The method depends on the characteristics of the materials.

Different parts of your organization are involved in returns processing

Many items cannot be returned because of their status when they sold, that is, the product was a refurbished item and not returnable.

7.1.1   Notification of a Return

Customers call your sales rep to return materials

When your company sells products to customers, the documentation you supply with those products should clearly explain the process by which you'll accept their return. Some companies allow customers to return materials without a return order being processed or a return material authorization (RMA) number being issued. In this case the product is sent directly from the customer and arrives at your warehouse, where it will need to be processed. This method is particularly inefficient because you cannot plan for materials arriving, and warehouse resources are expended in matching the materials to a sales order and then assessing if the materials can be restocked, refurbished, or scrapped.

An efficient returns method should be employed that allows you to manage the process from the moment the customer calls to the time the items are processed in the warehouse.

Sales representatives should obtain as much information as possible

When your returns process requires that a customer call your sales department and talk to a customer service representative to initiate a return of material, your representative should not only enter the basic information into a return order, such as sales order number and customer number, but should try to collect as much information as possible about why the customer is returning the materials. This information can be used to decide whether the returned materials can be refurbished, placed back into stock, or will have to be scrapped. In addition, the sales representative should ascertain whether the materials can be brought back into the plant. In some industries, especially pharmaceutical and chemical, some materials become unstable or dangerous after a period of time and therefore cannot be returned to the warehouse. In those cases the items should be sent to a designated facility that can process hazardous returns.

Packaging and Documentation

Special packaging may be needed to return materials

Some returns require that you send the customer special packaging so the materials can safely be returned. You may charge the customer for the packaging or send it free of charge, but no matter what the cost, a sales order and delivery need to be created for the packaging.

Specialty computer company manufacturers found that if they sent custom packaging to customers who needed to return their system units, the items would arrive at the warehouse without further damage. Before packaging was sent to customers, the majority of return items were poorly packed by customers and were not repairable when they arrived.

If your company issues customers a return material authorization (RMA) number when they call the sales department, then you may require that documentation such as a returns label or a repair questionnaire be sent to the customer prior to them sending in the item. The RMA label is useful for the receiving dock because it clearly displays all of the information they need to receive the item, without having to open the packaging. A repair questionnaire is important if the customer is requesting an item to be repaired. Not only will the information help the service department complete the repair, but it will also help them decide whether the item should be repaired.

Some companies insist on return material authorization (RMA)

Warranties

Some customers request that an item they have purchased be fixed or replaced under a warranty agreement. This is be different from a return because the item is subject to a service notification, service order, or repair order, where the item will be repaired at the customer site or sent back to the service department at your company.

A warranty claim may be different from a straightforward return

7.1.2   Receipt of Return at the Warehouse

When the return order is created, a return delivery can be created so that the warehouse can plan for the arrival of the item. Planning is a crucial activity in an efficient warehouse, and a return order should be treated as another inbound delivery. When a return delivery arrives, it requires resources to receive and process the item. Usually, warehouse staff visually checks the returned item for damage and to ensure that it's what was expected from the customer. Many companies have found that returned items are either completely different from the item the customer said they were returning or the returned item was never sold to the customer, based on model number or serial number.

The planning of a return order is important for efficiency

Inspection

A visual inspection can quickly determine if an item is damaged

After warehouse staff visually checks the item, they can prepare it either for placement in the warehouse or for quality inspection. The inspection of the item determines if it's faulty and whether the customer should receive a replacement or refund.

Shelf Life

An item's shelf life can deem it unsellable even if there is no damage

You may not be able to return items that have a shelf life to the warehouse even if they're not damaged. Items that are close to their expiry date or have already expired may be reworked or more likely scrapped. It is important for the warehouse staff receiving the return order to know if the item is shelf life managed because they may give the return a higher priority if it means the item can be restocked rather than being scrapped.

7.1.3 Placing Returns in the Warehouse

You need a transfer posting to assign the correct item status

If the return items have been inspected and classified for restock, refurbishment, or scrap, they should be moved from the goods receiving interim storage area back into the warehouse. Warehouse staff can create transfer orders to move the items to the appropriate storage types. However, the materials still have a status of returns, and a transfer posting needs to take place to either move the material to *unrestricted* stock, *blocked* stock, or *quality inspection* stock based on the quality review.

7.2 Successful Returns Processing

Customers have many reasons for returning items

The returns process starts with your customer deciding that they don't need the items that have been sent to them. This may be because the item is damaged, fails after a period of time, or was sent to them in error. The customer can has several options: send back the item and request a replacement, send back the item and request a refund, or not send the item back, because it isn't physically possible to return it, and request a replacement or refund.

7.2.1 Return Order

When your customer calls to return an item, your customer service representative creates a return order, which is a type of sales order. You can create the return order with reference to a sales order, if your customer has the appropriate sales order number, or without reference to a sales order.

A return order in SAP is similar to a sales order

You can create a return order using transaction VA01, or you can follow the menu path SAP • Logistics • Sales and Distribution • Sales • Order • Create.

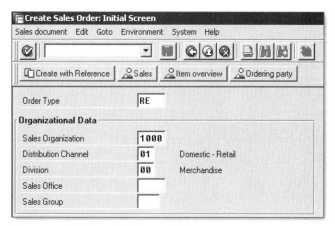

Figure 7.1 Creation of a Returns Order

Figure 7.1 shows the initial screen that your customer service representative uses to create a return order. The order type that is used for a return order is denoted by the letters RE. You can enter the sales organization, distribution channel, and division on this initial screen.

Figure 7.2 shows the detail screen for entering the items the customer is returning. Certain details need to be entered for the return order such as the sold-to party number, customer's purchase order number, order reason, and payment terms. In addition, you must include the details on the items to be returned, such as the material number and quantity.

A return order requires information on the original sales document

You can save the return order on this screen, and the system will display a return order number.

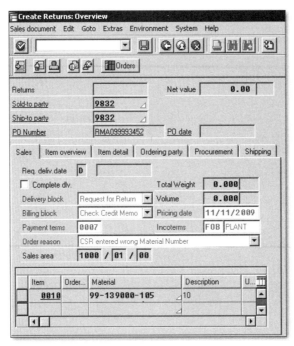

Figure 7.2 Details on a Return Order

7.2.2 Return Delivery

After your customer service representative creates the return order, the customer either returns the goods directly or asks for the items to be picked up.

The next step is to create a return delivery in the system. You can create the delivery by using Transaction VL01N or by following the menu path SAP • LOGISTICS • LOGISTICS EXECUTION • INBOUND PROCESS • GOODS RECEIPT FOR INBOUND DELIVERY • INBOUND DELIVERY • CREATE • CUSTOMER RETURNS.

Figure 7.3 shows the initial screen to create an outbound delivery based on the return order. You need to enter the shipping point that will receive the customer return along with the return order number.

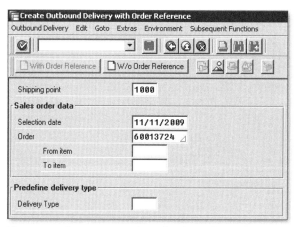

Figure 7.3 Creating an Outbound Delivery for the Return Order

Figure 7.4 shows the information in the outbound delivery that has been copied from the return order. After you enter and check all of the relevant items, you can save the delivery, and the system will display a return delivery number for the customer return.

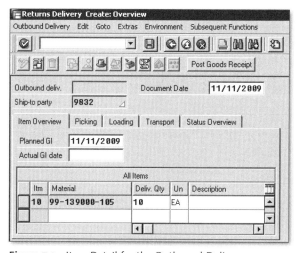

Figure 7.4 Item Detail for the Outbound Delivery

7.2.3 Outbound Delivery Monitor

You can find the return delivery from the customer using the outbound delivery monitor. The Transaction to use for the outbound delivery monitor is VL06O, or you can access it through the menu path SAP • Logistics •

The outbound delivery monitor displays the incoming return orders

Logistics Execution • Outbound Processes • Goods Issue for Outbound Delivery • Lists and Logs • Outbound Delivery Monitor.

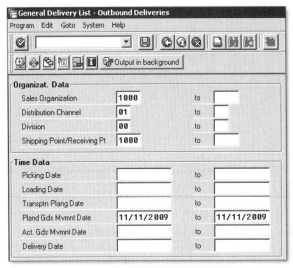

Figure 7.5 Selection Screen for the Outbound Delivery Monitor

Figure 7.5 shows the selection screen for the outbound delivery monitor. To find the return delivery, the sales organization, shipping point, distribution channel, and division are entered along with the date for the return.

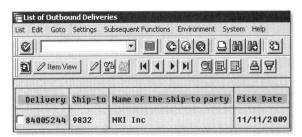

Figure 7.6 List Showing Return Delivery

Figure 7.6 is a display of the output from the outbound delivery monitor. The screen shows the single line item that is for the return delivery.

You can view the full return delivery by selecting Subsequent Functions • Display Outbound Deliveries from the header menu.

7.2.4 Post Goods Issue

When the material has arrived at the warehouse, you can process the return delivery. To process the goods issue for the return, use Transaction VL02N or access it through the menu path SAP • LOGISTICS • LOGISTICS EXECUTION • OUTBOUND PROCESSES • GOODS ISSUE FOR OUTBOUND DELIVERY • POST GOODS ISSUE • OUTBOUND DELIVERY SINGLE DOCUMENT.

Posting the goods issue moves the return into the warehouse

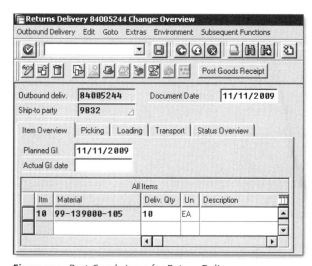

Figure 7.7 Post Goods Issue for Return Delivery

Figure 7.7 shows the return delivery. Click on the Post Goods Receipt button to process the incoming return. Once it's complete, the system returns with a message indicating that the return delivery has been processed.

7.2.5 Return Materials in the Warehouse

When you process the return delivery, the materials are placed in an interim storage type. You can see the returned materials via Transaction LS24, or you can follow the menu path SAP • LOGISTICS • LOGISTICS EXECUTION • INTERNAL WHSE PROCESSES • BINS AND STOCK • DISPLAY • BIN STOCK PER MATERIAL.

Returned materials are received into an interim storage type

Figure 7.8 shows the returned materials in the interim storage for returns, 904, in warehouse 100. The line item shows that the stock category is R, for return stock.

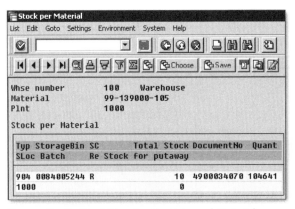

Figure 7.8 Bin Stock Showing the Returned Materials

7.2.6 Transfer Requirement for Returned Materials

The delivery automatically produces the transfer requirement

The returned materials arrive at the warehouse and are automatically placed in the interim storage area for returns. You create a transfer requirement to plan the movement of the material back into the warehouse. To access the transfer requirement, use Transaction LB11 or follow the menu path SAP • LOGISTICS • LOGISTICS EXECUTION • INTERNAL WHSE PROCESSES • TRANSFER REQUIREMENT • DISPLAY • FOR MATERIAL.

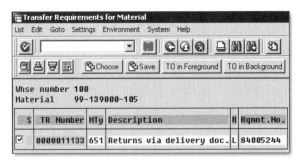

Figure 7.9 Transfer Requirement for Returned Material

The transfer order can be created in the background or foreground

Figure 7.9 shows the transfer requirement for the returned materials. The transfer requirement contains the return delivery number. It is possible to create the transfer order in the background or foreground to move the material to the warehouse. You can also create the transfer order manually by using Transaction LT04.

If the system is configured to automatically create and process a transfer order for a return, it will bypass this step. However, this step may be required when you want to perform a quality check on the returned material before it reaches the warehouse.

7.2.7 Transfer Order for Returned Material

If the quality department checks the returned materials and believes they can be placed back into stock, you can create a transfer order to perform that movement.

You can create the transfer order to move the returned materials back to the warehouse in the actual transfer requirement or create it manually. When you view the transfer requirement in Transaction LB11, as shown in Figure 7.9, you can create the transfer order by clicking on the TO in Foreground or TO in Background button.

When the transfer order is created, the system displays the document number on the screen. You can display the newly created transfer order using Transaction LT21, or you can follow the menu path SAP • Logistics • Logistics Execution • Internal Whse Processes • Stock Transfer • Display Transfer Order • Single Document.

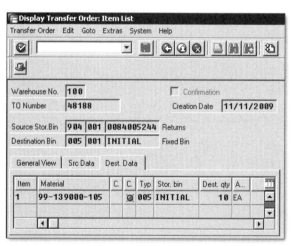

Figure 7.10 Transfer Order to Place Returns Back in the Warehouse

Figure 7.10 shows the transfer order for the returned materials. The transfer order moves the materials from the returns interim storage area to fixed bin storage type 005. In the figure the transfer order isn't confirmed. You can confirm the transfer order by selecting Transfer Order • Confirm Transfer Order from the header menu. This will take you to Transaction LT12, where you can start the confirmation process.

The transfer order needs to be confirmed for the material to move in the system

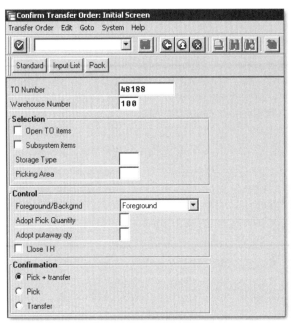

Figure 7.11 Confirming the Transfer Order for the Return Material

Figure 7.11 shows the initial screen for confirming the transfer order for the return material. In the selection screen you can enter the transfer order number and warehouse and decide whether you want to confirm in the foreground or background.

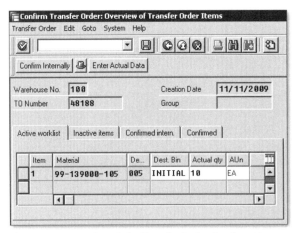

Figure 7.12 Item Details for Transfer Order Confirmation

Figure 7.12 shows the line item details from the transfer order, which include the storage type, the destination storage bin, and the quantity of the returned materials. To confirm the transfer order without changes, you can click on the Confirm Internally button. This will confirm the move of the returned materials to storage type 005 and the storage bin called INITIAL.

7.2.8 Review of Warehouse Inventory

After the transfer order is processed, the materials are placed in the destination storage type. You can review the returned materials in the warehouse via Transaction LS24 or the menu path SAP • LOGISTICS • LOGISTICS EXECUTION • INTERNAL WHSE PROCESSES • BINS AND STOCK • DISPLAY • BIN STOCK PER MATERIAL.

The returned material shows it has a return status in the bin stock report

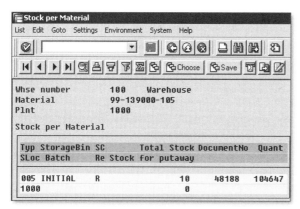

Figure 7.13 Review of Returned Materials in the Warehouse

When the transfer order is confirmed, the materials are moved into storage type 005 and storage bin INITIAL. Figure 7.13 shows the materials in the warehouse, referencing transfer order number 48188. However, the materials aren't in unrestricted stock; they have the returns status. If the quality department gives the approval to move the material back to unrestricted stock, then you can change the status of the stock in the inventory management functionality in SAP ERP.

7.2.9 Transfer Materials from Returns to Own Stock

If the returned materials are suitable for resale, you need to change their status from returns to unrestricted stock. You achieve this using a transfer

Inventory management transfer posting is required to move materials out of the returns status

posting in the inventory management functionality in SAP ERP. You can perform a transfer posting using one of two transactions. Transaction MB1B is in current and older versions of SAP, whereas Transaction MIGO is only in the more recent versions of SAP. You can access these transactions via the menu path SAP • Logistics • Materials Management • Inventory Management • Goods Movement • Transfer Posting.

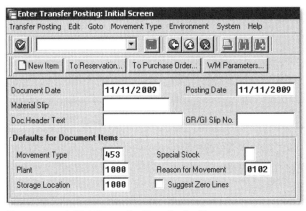

Figure 7.14 Initial Screen for Transfer Posting

You can move materials from returns to QI and from unrestricted or blocked status

To transfer the status of the material from returns to unrestricted, use movement type 453. In Figure 7.14 Transaction MB1B has been used. Also, reason code 0102 has been entered, which refers to an incorrect quantity sent to the customer. You can configure the reason codes can be configured for each movement type, as appropriate for your company.

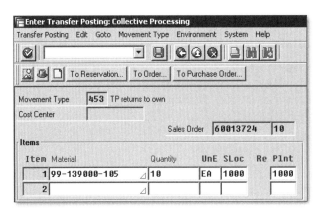

Figure 7.15 Details of Transfer Posting

Figure 7.15 shows the details of the transfer posting. The quantity of material is the same as is in the warehouse because all of the material is deemed to be suitable for resale. If only some of the material was suitable, then the quantity in the transfer posting would be less. Executing this transaction changes the status of the material from returns to unrestricted.

The status of materials suitable for resale is changed from returns to unrestricted

When you have executed the transaction, the system will display the material document number, which shows the details of the movement in the inventory management functionality in SAP ERP.

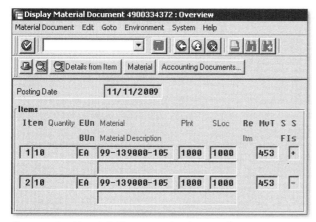

Figure 7.16 Materials Document for the Transfer Posting

Figure 7.16 shows the transfer posting to change the returned materials to unrestricted. The materials don't physically move; only the logical status changes. The materials are then part of the unrestricted inventory and are available for sale.

7.3   Business Example – Benefits of Returns Processing

Many companies have seen customer returns as a painful reminder of inadequate quality control, customer dissatisfaction, and an inaccurate shipping process. But for companies that have improved their business practices, returns processing, or reverse logistics as it's sometimes called, can be developed to become a revenue stream rather than a loss. The functionality in SAP can be used to create an efficient returns process that can provide a new revenue stream over time.

Processing returned product can be a new source of revenue

Example

A toy distributor based in Southern California imported toys from China, Taiwan, and the Philippines. It supplied independent toy stores and department stores in Canada and the U.S. Just before the height of the holiday season, one of their major customers informed the company that an item that they exclusively supplied to them would have to be returned owing to safety issues reported by the U.S. Consumer Product Safety Commission. The returns from the customer were less than 50% of the original sales order because the customer had shipped the rest of the products to their stores overseas.

The toy distributor received almost 20 pallets of toy scooters that couldn't be sold owing to the safety issue. The company couldn't send the items back to the vendor in China, so the items were stored in the warehouse awaiting a decision to scrap them.

The toy scooters sat in the warehouse for over a year, and during that time the company improved their quality control processes for overseas vendors so the issue would not occur again. In addition, the company reengineered several processes in the finance, purchasing, and warehousing departments as part of an SAP system upgrade. The company also started a pilot project to investigate the possibility of improving the returns process and implementing some of the aspects of reverse logistics. The company found that many of the returns they received from customers were due to damaged packaging rather than a damaged product. In response, the company required their vendors to supply all new items with additional packaging so that in the event of returns due to packaging, the product could be repackaged and placed back into stock.

With the relative success of the pilot reverse logistics project, the company reviewed the returned toy scooters prior to scrapping them. After some analysis they found that the safety issue with the scooter related to an attachment that could come loose and be a potential choking hazard. Based on collaboration with the original vendor, the company realized that they could remove the loose part and replace it with a larger part that would not be a choking hazard. To show good faith, the original vendor produced the parts and sold them to the company at cost. The scooters were sent to a subcontractor for retrofitting with the new part, and the modified scooters were sold to the customer who returned the items but at a higher cost that covered the retrofitting.

Many companies have expended significant resources on the implementation of an SAP system only to continue to use outdated and inadequate processes. The warehouse management functionality in SAP ERP offers companies the opportunity to improve their business procedures, and the returns process is an excellent example of how this can be done.

Example

A chemical company headquartered in Alabama specialized in coatings for commercial applications such as sheet metal and mirrors. The company's processes had been established when the plant opened in the early 1970s. The company had replaced their aging BPCS system with an SAP system in 2004. The implementation was a straightforward system replacement, with no new functionality being used over and above that required to ensure that the system worked. Along with the failure to use additional functionality, the company also didn't change any of their warehouse procedures unless forced to do by the change in computer processing.

The returns process at the company assumed that the customer was always right. A customer would call their local sales representative to say they were returning an item. The sales representative would call the sales department, which would process a credit memo for the amount the customer said they would return. The warehouse was rarely informed of any returns, and often they would receive several drums that were usually unidentifiable and did not indicate which customer had sent them. This process continued until one drum arrived at the receiving dock with a leak that caused a number of warehouse staff to be taken to the hospital complaining of stinging eyes.

After that incident the local Occupational Safety and Health Administration (OSHA) office cited the company and imposed a fine. To ensure that the company complied with OSHA regulations, some changes were made to the returns process. The initial changes required that if the customer wanted to return product, they had to call the sales department, and a representative would issue an RMA. The sales representative would create a return delivery and email the warehouse that a return would arrive. The company trained the warehouse staff on inbound and outbound deliveries and the delivery monitors. The return deliveries began to arrive when they were expected, and the warehouse staff received the drums into a hazardous materials area until they were checked by the quality department. The inspection checked that the returned material wasn't hazardous, and then the warehouse staff moved the drums to the appropriate areas. Only after the quality department had checked the drum was a credit memo issued to the customer.

After several weeks of the new process the warehouse staff began to notice that the majority of returned drums lacked labeling information about the contents. The company's assumption was that the customers were sending the product they had communicated about with the sales representative. The warehouse manager asked the quality department to test a sample of the returned drums and compare the results against the return order.

The quality department found that the vast majority of returned drums contained a combination of chemicals that sometimes did include the chemical on the return delivery.

Based on the results from the sample of returned drums, the company changed the returns process again. This change was to ensure that no credit memo was processed before the quality department had tested the returns and confirmed that the contents matched those on the return delivery.

7.4   Summary

The return process is something that every company has to deal with. Making the process as efficient as possible can not only save warehouse resources, but create a new revenue stream if returned items can be refurbished or resold rather than being scrapped. Many different parts of your organization are involved in the returns process, and for the process to be successful those departments need to work together and approach the process with the same level of commitment. If any one of the departments doesn't participate fully in the process, any efficiency achieved will be squandered.

In the next chapter we'll discuss the efficiencies that can be achieved in the physical inventory functionality of warehouse management in SAP ERP.

The often overlooked physical inventory process is an important process. Accurate inventory figures ensure warehouse efficiency and customer deliveries.

8 Efficient Physical Inventory

Inventory accuracy is an important feature of an efficiently operated warehouse. Most companies only talk about inventory accuracy when there are problems. If the accuracy of the items in the warehouse is in doubt, companies can no longer guarantee that they know the state of the inventory. This lack of knowledge can be reflected in several costs to the business. Once the inventory accuracy is below an optimum level, there are costs involved in carrying larger safety stocks to offset potential stock-outs, which can cause production disruptions or delays in shipments to customers. In addition, companies pay dearly for rapidly replenishing stock, as well as the costs of inefficiencies that naturally creep into the production schedules.

Inventory accuracy is important in any warehouse

The warehouse management functionality in SAP ERP has counting procedures such as continuous and cycle counting that reduces the need for companies to perform a traditional annual count. In this chapter we'll discuss the inventory procedures that businesses use to maximize the efficiency of their inventory accuracy and how they perform these within the system.

8.1 Cycle Counting

Cycle counting is basically the process of continually validating the accuracy of the inventory in the warehouse by regularly counting a portion of the inventory, on a daily or weekly basis, so that every item in the warehouse is counted at least several times a year.

Cycle counting counts some materials several times a year

Cycle counting is a sampling method where a certain sample is selected and measured. It's then inferred that the measurement, or count accuracy, is characteristic of the overall count accuracy of the warehouse. For many companies with tens of thousands of items in the warehouse, this is the

Cycle counting is a sampling method

only method they can employ because it's not physically possible to perform an annual inventory, counting all materials, without severely affecting normal operations.

8.1.1 Benefits of Cycle Counting

Cycle counting is a cost-effective method

Many companies choose the cycle counting method, because they can't afford the cost or inconvenience involved in performing annual inventories. Frequent cycle counting can shorten the period of time between physical counts of any material, and as a result, shorten the time required to discover the causes of any discrepancies discovered during a recent cycle count. This gives you with the opportunity to understand the cause of the discrepancy and perform any remedial action. Inventory write-offs can be much lower with regular cycle counting.

8.1.2 ABC Method of Cycle Counting

The ABC method is based on the Pareto principle, sometimes called the 80/20 principle

The ABC method is based on the Pareto principle, named after the Italian economist Vilfredo Pareto, who created a mathematical formula to describe the unequal distribution of wealth in Italy, observing that 20% of the population owned 80% of the wealth. The ABC method when related to cycle counting introduces a bias on the inventory that has a higher value. The A materials only represent 20% of the materials in the warehouse but make up 80% of the value. Therefore, these valuable materials are counted more often than other materials, which are termed B and C materials. The percentage values of the B materials are usually 30% of the materials carrying 15% of the value, and the C materials make up 50% of the materials in the warehouse but only make up 5% of the value.

With ABC analysis, 190% of the inventory is counted each year

The ABC method is designed to count approximately 190% of the materials each year, with the obvious bias toward the highly valued materials, which are counted more frequently.

8.1.3 Configuration for ABC Cycle Counting

Some configuration is needed to use cycle counting

You need to complete several configuration steps before implementing cycle counting in your warehouse. These include the ABC analysis and the configuration of the storage types in the warehouse.

Define ABC Percentages

The first step in implementing the ABC method for cycle counting is to decide on the percentages your company needs to assign to the ABC indicators. In some companies counting 20% of materials may not be necessary if only 5% of their materials have any significant value. Depending on the types of materials your company has in the warehouse, you want to configure the values for the ABC indicators accordingly. To set the parameters for each plant, use Transaction OMCO or access it via the menu path IMG • MATERIALS MANAGEMENT • INVENTORY MANAGEMENT AND PHYSICAL INVENTORY • PHYSICAL INVENTORY • CYCLE COUNTING.

You need to define the percentage of A, B, and C items

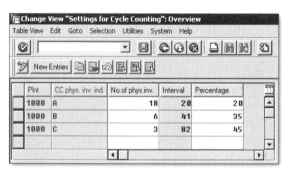

Figure 8.1 Setting Parameters for Cycle Counting

Figure 8.1 shows the cycle counting parameters for the A, B, and C indicators. In this example the A indicator is set for 20% of the items in the warehouse, the B indicator is set for 35% of items, and C items are set to 45%. The configuration also denotes how many times per year each item assigned to the respective indicator will be counted. In this case the A items will be counted 18 times a year at 20-day intervals.

ABC Indictor and the Material Master

The next configuration step is to assign an indicator, A, B, or C, to each material in the warehouse. There is functionality in SAP ERP to automatically perform this operation. You can run the ABC analysis for cycle counting by using Transaction MIBC, or you can follow the menu path SAP • LOGISTICS • MATERIALS MANAGEMENT • PHYSICAL INVENTORY • SPECIAL PROCEDURES • CYCLE COUNTING • SET CYCLE COUNTING INDICATOR.

The ABC indicator is located in the material master

Figure 8.2 shows Transaction MIBC, which allows you to enter the plant and a material type. In this example the ABC analysis will be performed on material type FERT, finished goods, in plant 1000.

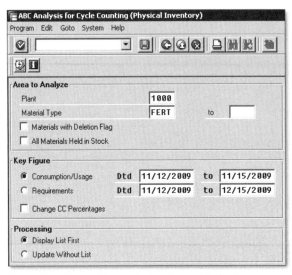

Figure 8.2 Transaction to Assign the ABC Indicators

SAP ERP can automatically assign the ABC indicator

The selection screen shows that you can propose a range of dates for either consumption or requirements. You then decide to use either the material consumption data or material requirement data as the basis to define the ABC indicator. You also have the option to alter the percentages that were already configured for the plant, as shown in Figure 8.1. You can set the transaction to just update the materials or display them in a list before any updates are made. It's always best to review the assignment of the ABC indicator before any updates are made. In case there are some anomalies that require modification.

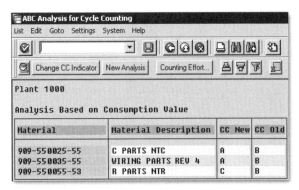

Figure 8.3 Analysis of ABC Indicators

Figure 8.3 shows the three materials that can have their ABC indicator changed based on the consumption dates entered in the selection screen of Transaction MIBC.

When you execute this transaction and you agree with the changes the program proposes, you can save the changes, and the ABC indicator is updated on the material master record. It's important that this analysis is performed on a regular basis to ensure that the correct materials are being counted (i.e., the most valuable).

To reduce the level of manual input into this process, it's possible to automate the ABC analysis by creating a batch job to run program RMCBIN00 at regular intervals, such as weekly or monthly.

Create a batch job to automate the ABC analysis

To check that the ABC indicator for cycle counting has been updated, you can go to the plant data screen of the material master record. Use Transaction MM03 to view the material master record or go to SAP • LOGISTICS • MATERIALS MANAGEMENT • MATERIAL MASTER • MATERIAL • DISPLAY • DISPLAY CURRENT.

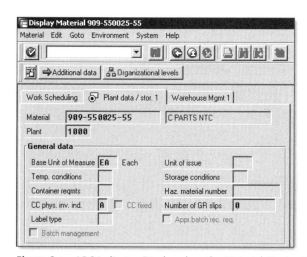

Figure 8.4 ABC Indicator Displayed on the Material Master Record

Figure 8.4 shows the updated ABC indicator for material 909-550025-55. The ABC indicator is listed in the CC phys. inv. ind. field. Note that the CC fixed checkbox isn't selected. If this checkbox was selected, the ABC indicator for this material at plant 1000 couldn't be updated despite the changes proposed in ABC analysis program. Use this checkbox wisely because it remains the same until it's unselected. There are several reasons warehouse

You can set the indicator so it cannot be changed

management wouldn't want an ABC indicator to not change. For example, if an A material was temporarily taken off the market and there was subsequently no consumption, running the ABC analysis program would propose a change to the indicator. However, if the business was reintroducing that item at a later date, they might still want the item to be counted as an A item. The materials that have the CC fixed checkbox selected should be reviewed regularly to ensure that the business decision is still valid.

Defining Storage Types for Cycle Counting

Some storage types aren't suitable for cycle counting

Each storage type has the ability to be defined for cycle counting. If this isn't relevant, then the material that is stored there won't be counted. Some storage types don't lend themselves to regular counting; for example, deep racks require the material to be removed, identified, counted, and then put back. This isn't a good use of resources, so these storage types may need to be excluded from cycle counts.

You can find the configuration to define cycle counting for the storage types by following the menu path IMG • LOGISTICS EXECUTION • WAREHOUSE MANAGEMENT • ACTIVITIES • PHYSICAL INVENTORY • DEFINE TYPES PER STORAGE TYPE.

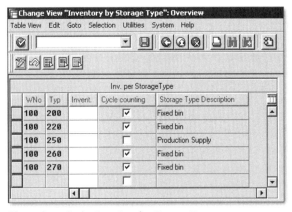

Figure 8.5 Cycle Counting for Storage Types

Figure 8.5 shows the cycle counting configuration for several storage types. The Cycle counting checkbox is selected when cycle counting can be performed at a storage type. In this example the fixed bin storage types are all relevant for cycle counting, whereas the production supply storage type isn't. It's important to understand your warehouse and what storage types should or shouldn't be cycle counted.

8.1.4 Cycle Counting Documents

The documents for cycle counting can be produced manually or automatically. It's more efficient for warehouse staff to allow the SAP system to calculate and generate the cycle count documents.

You can use the program RM07ICN1 to create the physical inventory documents for cycle counting, and a batch job can be created to run this on a daily or weekly basis depending on warehouse activity.

Use a batch job to calculate and print cycle count documents

The program RM07ICN1 calculates the planned count date by using the date of the last count and then adding the number of days between counts, which is defined in configuration. If a count is due, the documents can be printed.

You can manually create a cycle count document with Transaction LX26 or by going to SAP • Logistics • Logistics Execution • Internal Whse Processes • Physical Inventory • In Warehouse Management • Physical Inventory Document • Create • Cycle Counting.

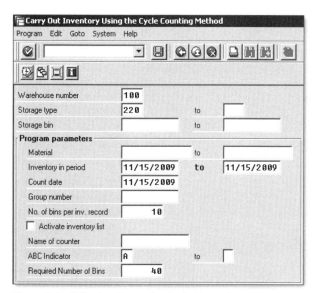

Figure 8.6 Selection Screen for Cycle Count Documents

Figure 8.6 shows the selection screen for Transaction LX26. You can specify a certain warehouse, storage type, and ABC indicator to obtain a list of cycle counts that need to be performed.

The transaction
shows items for
which the count is
overdue

When you execute this transaction, a list of materials that are available for cycle counting will be displayed. You can then select the items you want to count.

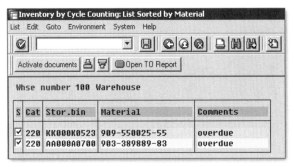

Figure 8.7 Storage Bins that Require Cycle Counting

Figure 8.7 shows an overview of the count documents that can be created for the warehouse number and storage type entered in the initial selection screen. In this example two storage bins have been selected, KK000K0523 and AA000A0700, where the cycle count is overdue.

If you want to activate a count document, highlight the line item click on the Activate documents button. The transaction will return the inventory count document number for the cycle count selected.

8.1.5   Printing the Count Document

After you create the cycle count document, you can print it via Transaction LI04 or the menu path SAP • LOGISTICS • LOGISTICS EXECUTION • INTERNAL WHSE PROCESSES • PHYSICAL INVENTORY • IN WAREHOUSE MANAGEMENT • PHYSICAL INVENTORY DOCUMENT • PRINT WAREHOUSE INVENTORY LIST.

```
    WAREHOUSE INVENTORY LIST via CYCLE COUNTNG
    ============================================

Wareh.number: 100 Warehouse          Inventory no.: 11
Storage type: 220 Fixed bin          Page.........: 1/1
Date........: 11/16/2009             Main count
                                     _____

It.   Stor.bin   Plnt Material number....   Qty.   UoM
      Quant no.  SLoc Material short text

0001 KK000K0523 1000 909-550025-55          _____ EA
      51323      1000 Rear Lock
```

Figure 8.8 Print Output of the Cycle Count Document

You can give the cycle count document to a member of the warehouse staff to perform the count as part of their daily warehouse operation. Figure 8.8 shows the printout of the count document that the warehouse operator will use to record the count of the storage bin.

Print the count document for the person performing the count

8.1.6 Enter the Cycle Count

Once you have printed the cycle count document, the warehouse operator will count the items in the specified storage type. After the items have been counted, you can enter the count result into the system using Transaction LI11N, which you can find by following the menu path SAP • LOGISTICS • LOGISTICS EXECUTION • INTERNAL WHSE PROCESSES • PHYSICAL INVENTORY • IN WAREHOUSE MANAGEMENT • COUNT RESULTS • ENTER.

When the count document is complete, enter the count in your SAP system

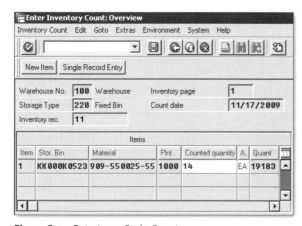

Figure 8.9 Entering a Cycle Count

Figure 8.9 shows the information for the storage bin that has been counted. Once you've entered all of the figures, you can save the count. If you've entered the count for this storage bin and determined that it's correct, the material doesn't need to be counted until the date determined by the configuration.

8.1.7 Recounts and Clearing Differences

If the count of the material is inaccurate, it can be repeated. You can use Transaction LI14 to process the recount document or follow the menu path SAP • LOGISTICS • LOGISTICS EXECUTION • INTERNAL WHSE PROCESSES • PHYSICAL INVENTORY • IN WAREHOUSE MANAGEMENT • COUNT RESULTS • RECOUNT.

Sometimes mistakes are made on the count and it needs to be repeated

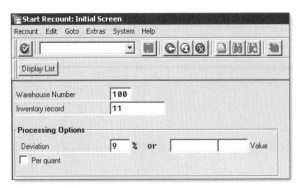

Figure 8.10 Cycle Count Document Recount

Allowing a variance makes the count more effective

Figure 8.10 shows the initial screen for recounting a cycle count document. The key point about using the recount document is that you can allow a deviation on the recount document rather than recounting and then clearing the differences. By using the deviation, either a percentage or a specific value, you can close the count at the recount stage rather than having to execute more transactions. However, the recount can only be processed if the deviation is less than the figure you enter.

Find out what the company's maximum allowed variance should be

If the deviation between the count and the system inventory is greater than the variation entered, then you have to clear the differences in the warehouse management functionality in SAP ERP by using Transaction LI20. You can access this transaction via the menu path SAP • LOGISTICS • LOGISTICS EXECUTION • INTERNAL WHSE PROCESSES • PHYSICAL INVENTORY • IN WAREHOUSE MANAGEMENT • CLEAR DIFFERENCES • WAREHOUSE MANAGEMENT.

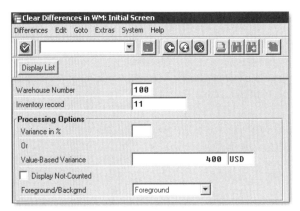

Figure 8.11 Clearing the Differences for a Cycle Count

Figure 8.11 shows the initial screen that you use to clear any differences in the cycle count performed in the warehouse. In this example if the difference is below a value of $400, then the count document will be processed and the differences will be cleared.

If the variance is greater than company policy allows, further investigation should be implemented to understand why the cycle count is so inaccurate. In an efficient warehouse the count shouldn't show wide variations between the system inventory and the physical cycle count.

Investigation may be needed if the discrepancy is greater than the variance

8.1.8 Understanding the Error

To maximize the warehouse management functionality in SAP ERP, the accuracy of the inventory is important, but the accuracy also affects sales, production, and finance. Clearing differences that occur in cycle counting is a valid process, but correcting errors without understanding why the error occurred won't help produce an effective warehouse. Investigating why an error has occurred or why errors continue to occur may be time consuming, but if they continue to occur over a period of time, it's less efficient and more costly to just clear differences rather than find the root cause.

8.2 Continuous Inventory

The principle of continuous inventory is basically to divide the annual physical inventory count into a number of smaller inventory counts performed over the year, ensuring that all material is counted. Many companies are required to count items in inventory at least once per year but prefer the continuous inventory method over a once a year process, because it reduces the effort required and the stress involved in a single count.

Continuous inventory divides the annual physical inventory count into smaller numbers

The key to performing a successful continuous inventory is to ensuring that all storage bins are counted in a systematic manner and to ensure that the counts are successfully documented.

8.2.1 Configuration for Continuous Inventory

Configuration needs to be completed before your company uses the continuous inventory process. Each storage type that is part of the continuous inventory process needs to be configured. You can configure the storage types using Transaction OMNK, or you can follow the menu path IMG • LOGISTICS EXECUTION • WAREHOUSE MANAGEMENT • ACTIVITIES • PHYSICAL INVENTORY • DEFINE TYPES PER STORAGE TYPE.

Configuration of the storage types is needed for continuous inventory

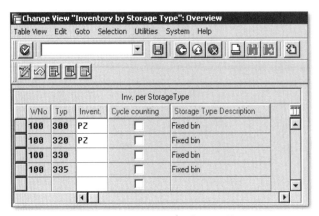

Figure 8.12 Continuous Inventory for Storage Types

Figure 8.12 shows that for storage types 300 and 320, the indicator for continuous inventory, PZ, has been assigned. This means continuous inventory will be relevant for those materials in those storage types.

8.2.2 Creating a Continuous Inventory Count Document

Continuous inventory counts can be performed when there is downtime

The continuous inventory process allows the warehouse manager to count items in the warehouse when there is downtime in the warehouse, on weekends, or during a scheduled plant shutdown.

The transaction you can use to produce the count documents for continuous inventory is LX16, which you can also find by following the menu path SAP • Logistics • Logistics Execution • Internal Whse Processes • Physical Inventory • In Warehouse Management • Physical Inventory Document • Create • Continuous Inventory.

Figure 8.13 shows the selection screen for the transaction to create a continuous inventory count document. You enter the warehouse number and storage type and if necessary select a range of storage bins.

Figure 8.14 shows that there are four storage bins with material that can be counted in warehouse 100, storage type 300. You can highlight these and activated them for counting by pressing `Shift` + `F4` or selecting Physical Inventory Document • Activate from the header menu.

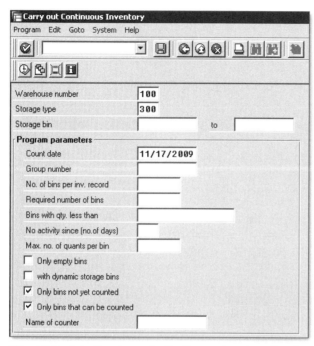

Figure 8.13 Selection Screen for Continuous Inventory Count

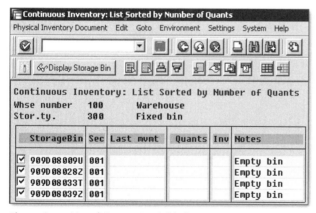

Figure 8.14 List of Quants Available for Continuous Inventory

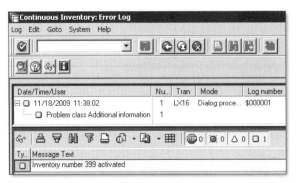

Figure 8.15 Continuous Inventory Count Document Is Created

Figure 8.15 shows that after the four storage bins are activated, continuous count document 399 is created via Transaction LX16. You can print this document by using Transaction LI04.

8.2.3 Entering a Count for Continuous Inventory

It's important to record if a bin is empty

After you print the continuous inventory count document, it goes to the warehouse staff, who perform a count on the relevant storage bins. You can then enter the count into the SAP system via Transaction LI11N, which you can find by following the menu path SAP • LOGISTICS • LOGISTICS EXECUTION • INTERNAL WHSE PROCESSES • PHYSICAL INVENTORY • IN WAREHOUSE MANAGEMENT • COUNT RESULTS • ENTER.

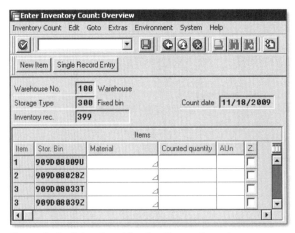

Figure 8.16 Enter Count for Continuous Inventory

Figure 8.16 shows the count document that the warehouse operators can complete if they find any material in the storage bins listed on the document. Once all of the figures are entered, you can save the count.

When the four storage bins have been counted, they don't need to be counted again until the next fiscal year. If the bins were mistakenly included in another count document, they wouldn't be displayed.

Once a bin is counted, it won't be counted again until next year

After the fiscal year is complete and all of the bins have been counted, the storage bins should then become available to count again. To ensure that the storage bin table is clear of the count date and time of the previous fiscal year, you need to run an end of year report called RLREOLPQ using Transaction SE38 or included as part of an end of year batch job. Ensure that the BASIS team knows this needs to be performed.

8.3 Business Example – Benefits of Physical Inventory

A company needs accurate inventory records for many reasons. Financially, the company requires an accurate record of its inventory so it can accurately state its financial position. The manufacturing department needs to know if items are in stock to ensure that MRP runs successfully. Without accurate inventory there is the potential for production disruptions. The efficient warehouse operates with the minimum of resources performing the maximum number of processes. By implementing efficient counting procedures such as cycle counting or continuous inventory, the warehouse can continue to operate at maximum efficiency using the warehouse management functionality in SAP ERP.

Companies are more efficient when inventory records are accurate

8.3.1 Cycle Counting

Companies choose the cycle counting method because it can be more cost effective and is less of an inconvenience than performing traditional annual inventories. Frequent cycle counting of high-value materials shortens the time between physical counts, and as a result the root cause of any discrepancies can be investigated. This gives the warehouse management the opportunity to understand the causes of any discrepancy and to perform any remedial action.

Cycle counting is cost effective and is less of an inconvenience

A U.S. manufacturing company found that over a three-month period they had seen several disruptions to their production schedule. This was due to some components not being available in the warehouse when they were required for a production order, despite the system indicating that the items were in stock.

The company implemented a continuous inventory process to count all materials over the fiscal year. Warehouse and production managers were concerned that this was not adequate for items that were important to the production process. As a result, the company decided to implement a cycle counting process that would count certain materials on a more regular basis. The A materials were configured to be counted at least once a month.

After the first cycle count of the A materials, several items were found have discrepancies, and the missing items couldn't be found in the warehouse, so the variance was cleared. On the second count of A materials, the same materials had a variance similar to the first month. Unwilling to clear the differences a second time, the management started an investigation of the root cause of the discrepancy. After a week of analysis and interviewing warehouse staff, they found that the missing materials were being removed from the warehouse by temporary staff working for the quality department. The items were taken during the third shift, when there were very few warehouse staff, and the movements were never entered in the SAP system. The quality department performed checks on the items and stored the results in their stand-alone laboratory information management system (LIMS). At the end of the testing procedure, the items were returned to the warehouse and placed in the returns storage location, which was not part of the count process.

8.3.2 Continuous Inventory

Continuous inventory is more convenient than an annual inventory

Continuous inventory allows companies to divide the annual physical inventory count into several smaller inventory counts performed over the year, ensuring that all material is counted. This is more efficient for warehouses because it allows counts to be performed when the warehouse resources are available.

Example

A UK beverage company had been using a stand-alone warehouse management system prior to their implementation of an SAP system, which included the warehouse management functionality in SAP ERP. For many years the company had been performing an annual inventory during the yearly two-week plant shutdown, which occurred in the summer. As part of the introduction of the SAP system, the company implemented several other process reengineering projects that reduced the yearly two-week shutdown to only three days, which could occur over a holiday weekend.

As part of the SAP implementation, they performed an inventory count of all items to ensure that the inventory was accurate at start-up of the SAP system. During the first shutdown after the implementation of the SAP system, the annual inventory was planned and started on the first day of the shutdown. By the final day of the shutdown, the inventory count was only 60% complete and no recounts had been performed. Because the inventory in the warehouse was blocked for movement, shipping couldn't begin unless the count was completed or abandoned. For customer orders to be shipped, they decided to stop the count and perform recounts on those count documents that were found to be incorrect.

As a result of the count issues, the company decided that the annual count should be changed to be a continuous inventory count process so that the inventory count could take place over the fiscal year.

8.4   Summary

This chapter has discussed the ways a company can accurately keep track of its physical inventory and ensure that it's reflected in the warehouse management system. In efficient warehouses, the traditional annual inventory is being superseded by frequent cycle counting or changed to continuous inventory, which takes advantage of downtime in the warehouse. More counting produces a more accurate picture of the stock in the warehouse and eliminates the stress on the warehouse that is caused by the annual inventory.

In the next chapter, we'll discuss the processes involved in cross-docking and how its efficient use can benefit warehouse operations.

Cross-docking matches inbound and outbound deliveries so that the material avoids storage in the warehouse. The cross-docking process can reduce labor costs, delivery time to the customer, and the amount of warehouse space needed.

9 Successful Cross-Docking

The term *cross-docking* refers to moving available finished products from the production plant and delivering them directly to the customer with limited materials handling. In efficient warehouse operations the materials sent from the production plant to the loading dock are allocated for outbound deliveries prior to the materials' arrival. There are several benefits to the company:

Cross-docking can reduce labor, increase customer satisfaction, and reduce warehousing needs

- Reduction in labor costs, because the materials no longer require put-away and picking in the warehouse
- Reduced time from production to the customer, which can maintain or improve overall customer satisfaction
- Reduced need for warehouse space, because materials aren't stored.

At the warehouse, the internally produced finished goods are delivered from the production area directly to a location near the loading dock and from there is packed and shipped to the customer. When materials that are being shipped to a customer arrive at the warehouse from an external production facility, external warehouse, or vendor, they arrive at the loading dock and are moved directly to the shipping area.

Cross-docking means incoming items can be moved directly to outbound deliveries

You can use the cross-docking functionality in SAP ERP to perform this process at your warehouse, but is only applicable to unrestricted materials, not items that are blocked or in quality inspection. Cross-docking is an efficient process that can help your company improve deliveries to customers while reducing use of warehouse resources.

9.1 Defining the Cross-Docking Process

Cross-docking is used in warehouses in many industries, but with the drive to reduce costs and increase customer satisfaction, companies are using cross-docking as a component in their overall drives for improving warehouse efficiency.

9.1.1 Types of Cross Docking

There are many types of cross-docking

Several cross-docking scenarios are available to warehouse management.

Manufacturing Cross Docking

This type of cross-docking involves the receipt of purchased and inbound materials required by manufacturing. The warehouse receives the materials and prepares subassemblies for production orders.

Distributor Cross-Docking

This process includes the consolidation of inbound materials from different vendors into a mixed material pallet, which is delivered to the customer when the final material is received. For example, computer parts distributors often source their components from various vendors and manufacturers and combine them into one shipment for the customer. The consolidation occurs in the shipping area.

Transportation Cross-Docking

This operation combines shipments from different shippers in the less-than-truckload (LTL) and small package industries to gain economies of scale.

Retail Cross-Docking

This process involves the receipt of materials from multiple vendors and sorting onto outbound trucks for several retail stores. This method was a key to cost saving for Wal-Mart in the 1980s. Wal-Mart procured two types of products, materials they sell each day of the year, called staple stock, and large quantities of materials that are purchased once and sold by the stores and not usually stocked again. This second type of procurement is called direct freight, and Wal-Mart minimizes any warehouse costs with direct freight by using cross-docking and keeping the goods in the warehouse for as little time as possible.

Opportunistic Cross-Docking

This can be used in any warehouse, transferring materials directly from the goods receiving dock to the outbound shipping dock to meet a known demand, such as a customer sales order.

9.1.2   Materials Suitable for Successful Cross-Docking

Many companies haven't introduced cross-docking because the materials stored in their warehouses may not be suitable or their customers don't require immediate delivery. However, for companies that do want to use cross-docking, some materials are better suited to cross-docking than others. The types of material that are more suited to cross-docking include the following:

> Not all materials are suitable for cross-docking

- ▶ Perishable materials that require immediate shipment
- ▶ High-quality items that don't require quality inspections during goods receipt
- ▶ Materials that are pretagged (bar coded, RFID), preticketed, and ready for sale at the customer's location (i.e., retail items)
- ▶ Promotional items and materials that are being launched
- ▶ Retail materials with a constant demand or low demand variance
- ▶ Prepicked, prepackaged customer orders from an external production plant, distribution center, or warehouse

9.1.3   Planned Cross Docking

The warehouse management functionality in SAP ERP offers companies the ability to plan the cross-docking process or allow opportunistic cross-docking. The main difference between the two is that the planned cross-docking allows you to make decisions before materials arrive at the warehouse, whereas opportunistic cross-docking decisions occur after materials arrive.

> You can plan cross-docking before items arrive at the warehouse

You may want to use both types of cross-docking in the same warehouse, but planned cross-docking reduces the need to deal with materials once they arrive at the warehouse. For planned cross-docking several prerequisites and configuration need to be in place prior to making decisions.

9.1.4 Cross-Docking Configuration

Configuration is needed to implement cross-docking

The configuration for cross docking initially is to define the type of cross-docking for the warehouse and the storage type, that is, whether it's planned or opportunistic cross-docking. You can access the transaction to do this by following the menu path IMG • LOGISTICS EXECUTION • WAREHOUSE MANAGEMENT • CROSS DOCKING • GENERAL SETTINGS • MAINTAIN WAREHOUSE LEVEL SETTINGS.

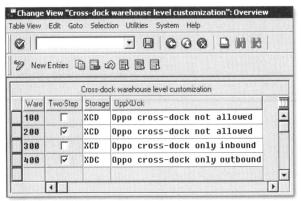

Figure 9.1 Warehouse Configuration for Planned Cross-Docking

Figure 9.1 shows the configuration you can enter for the warehouse when you're considering cross docking. The storage type entered is the location where the two-step cross-docked material will be located. In this example the storage type is called XCD, shorthand for cross docking. You should select the Two-Step checkbox when planned cross docking is required.

This transaction allows the configuration for opportunistic cross-docking in the warehouse and cross-docking for inbound, outbound, both, or not at all.

You need to configure movement types for cross-docking

The next configuration step is to confirm that a movement type to be used for cross-docking is set to allow cross-docking. To find the transaction to use, follow the menu path IMG • LOGISTICS EXECUTION • WAREHOUSE MANAGEMENT • CROSS DOCKING • GENERAL SETTINGS • DEFINE CROSS-DOCKING RELEVANCY FOR MOVEMENT TYPES.

Figure 9.2 shows the configuration for the movement type applicable in each warehouse. Select the CD Relevant checkbox for movement types that are to be used for cross-docking.

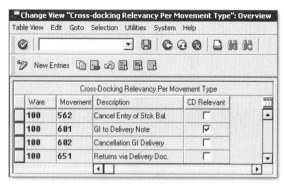

Figure 9.2 Configuration of Movement Types for Cross-Docking

9.1.5 Cross-Docking Decisions

A cross-docking decision is defined as a link that can be made between a planning document, which can be an inbound or outbound delivery, and a candidate document, which is another inbound or outbound delivery. For example, if you're expecting an inbound delivery for 20 units of material XYZ, and there's a planned outbound delivery of 20 units of XYZ to a customer, then these two documents, the planning and the candidate, can be linked by a cross-docking decision.

An inbound delivery and an outbound delivery are linked by a cross-docking decision

You can use two methods to make the cross-docking decision.

▶ **Manual creation**
The warehouse staff can make the decision to link a planning and a candidate document.

▶ **Automatic creation**
The system can make the decision automatically. When a transfer order is created for an inbound or outbound delivery, the system reviews all potential candidate documents to determine whether a link can be made and a cross-docking decision created.

9.1.6 Cross-Docking Monitor

When you need to make decisions to get the most efficient use of resources in the warehouse, you should use the cross-docking monitor. It allows you to review the cross-docking situation in the warehouse, and then you can make any necessary changes. The monitor displays all inbound and outbound deliveries and transfer requirements, shipments, groups, and cross-docking decisions.

The cross-docking monitor displays all relevant deliveries

You can access the cross-docking monitor by using Transaction LXDCK, or you can follow the menu path SAP • LOGISTICS • LOGISTICS EXECUTION • CROSS DOCKING • CROSS DOCKING MONITOR.

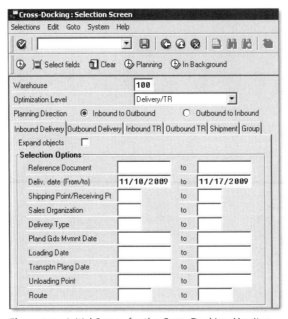

Figure 9.3 Initial Screen for the Cross-Docking Monitor

The date range is important in deciding to match inbound and outbound deliveries

Figure 9.3 shows the initial screen for the cross-docking monitor. The transaction allows you to enter the warehouse and a relevant date range. You can also select the planning direction: inbound to outbound or outbound to inbound. The date range is an important selection. If cross-docking in the warehouse is operated with small delays between inbound and outbound delivery, maybe owing to a lack of floor space or material requirements, the dates entered should be narrow in range. In this example the date range is a week, so the materials can sit on the dock for a period of time if they're matched up with a delivery that is due to leave the warehouse a few days later.

Figure 9.4 shows the inbound and outbound transfer requirements for the date entered into the selection screen. The warehouse manager has the option to go to the planning tool, by clicking on the Plan button, or to select documents for creating manual decisions for cross-docking.

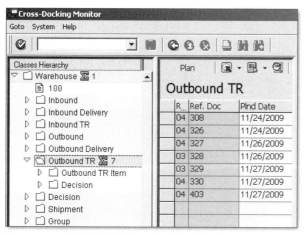

Figure 9.4 Detail of the Cross-Docking Monitor

Planning Tool

Next, you use the cross-dock planning tool with the selected documents from the planning monitor. The left side of the screen shows the inbound documents, and the right shows the outbound documents. The planning tool shows which documents are planning or candidate documents. From this screen you can make a cross-docking decision.

Use the planning tool to perform cross-docking decisions

Alert Monitor

Another important part of the cross-docking monitor is the alert monitor, which informs warehouse staff of any issues occurring with the cross-docking process. You can access the alert monitor from the cross-docking monitor by clicking on the alert button, via Transaction LXDCA, or through the menu path SAP • LOGISTICS • LOGISTICS EXECUTION • CROSS DOCKING • ALERT MONITOR.

The alert monitor informs staff when any cross-docking issues occur

Figure 9.5 shows one of the three alert screens that are available in the cross-docking alert monitor. It shows the deliveries for warehouse 100 that have been released and that are now outside of the tolerance. The other two alert screens are for transfer requirements that are outside of their tolerances and cancelled transfer orders that are without a replacement.

The alert monitor shows missed or cancelled deliveries

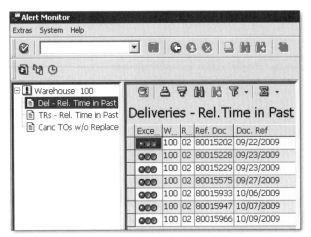

Figure 9.5 Cross-Docking Alert Monitor

▶ **Deliveries with release time in the past**
This alert shows cross-docking-relevant outbound deliveries whose release times and latest release times have passed. The yellow alert means the release time is passed. The red alert means the latest release time has passed.

▶ **Transfer requirements with release time in the past**
This alert shows cross-docking-relevant transfer requirements whose release times and latest release times have passed. The yellow alert means the release time is passed. The red alert means the latest release time has passed.

▶ **Cancelled transfer orders without replacement transfer orders**
This alert shows transfer orders that have been cancelled but for which no replacement transfer orders have been created as substitutes.

9.2 Cross-Docking Movements

Cross-docking can be one- or two-step movements

When you make a cross-docking decision before materials arrive at the warehouse, you can process the movement as a one-step or two-step cross-docking process. The actual movement is made using a transfer order, which should be processed as efficiently as possible, for example, with radio frequency handheld devices.

9.2.1   One-Step Cross-Docking

One-step cross-docking is the movement that processes the direct cross-docking of materials in one step. Materials are received into the inbound goods receiving area and moved to the outbound delivery area. This is the default method, although you can configure two-step cross-docking for a warehouse if required.

One-step cross-docking means inbound items are moved directly to outbound deliveries

In planned cross-docking the inbound delivery is linked to the outbound delivery, and a transfer order is created to move the materials from the goods receiving area to the outbound delivery area. The transfer order moves the materials from the goods receipt area, storage type 902, to the goods issue area, storage type 916.

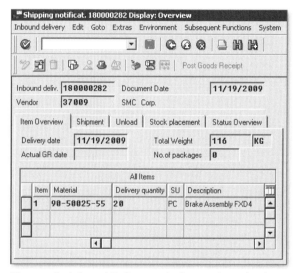

Figure 9.6   Inbound Delivery Linked to Outbound Delivery

Figure 9.6 shows the shipping notification for an inbound delivery, 180000282. The material, 90-50025-55, to be received from this inbound delivery is linked to outbound delivery to a customer for the same material. By linking these two documents, the material is cross-docked and doesn't enter the warehouse.

When the material arrives in the goods receipt area, it's unloaded, and a goods receipt is posted in the inventory management functionality in SAP ERP.

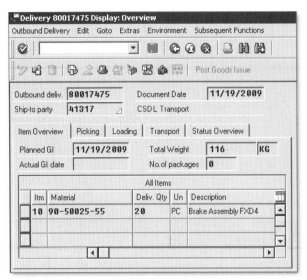

Figure 9.7 Outbound Delivery Linked to the Inbound Delivery

Figure 9.7 shows the outbound delivery with a planned goods issue of a quantity of 20 for material 90-50025-55. This is the same quantity of material that is expected from the inbound delivery.

A transfer order is created to move materials from storage type 902 to 916

When the goods receipted material is put away, a transfer order is created for the material. If this cross-docking is planned, the transfer order processing retrieves that cross-docking decision. It then creates a transfer order that moves the materials from the goods receipt storage type 902 and proposes the goods issue area, storage type 916, as the destination storage type on the transfer order.

Figure 9.8 shows the transfer order for the cross-docking decision that links the inbound goods receipt with the outbound delivery. The transfer order shows the quantity of 20 being moved from the goods receipt area, 902, to the goods issue area, 916.

After the transfer order is confirmed, the delivery documents are processed

Once the material has been moved and confirmed, the inbound delivery and outbound delivery documents are updated with the actual pick and putaway quantities that were recorded. The material is then available for outbound delivery to the customer.

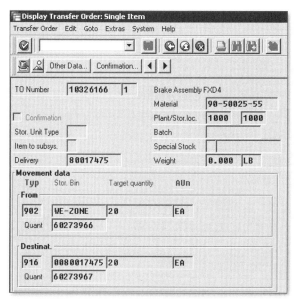

Figure 9.8 Transfer Order Produced by One-Step Cross-Docking

9.2.2 Two-Step Cross-Docking

Sometimes cross-docking cannot be processed in a single move. This may because of a small outbound delivery area or cross-docking decisions being made where there is a delay between inbound and outbound deliveries. Therefore, an area is set aside where the cross-docking materials from the inbound delivery are placed before being required for the outbound delivery.

Two-step cross-docking means items aren't moved directly

Several issues can arise with the two-step cross-docking process. Because materials are stored in an area close to either the goods receiving or outbound delivery area, they must be clearly identified for cross-docking so they're not confused with materials for other deliveries. In addition, the cross-docking decisions should take into account that the cross-docking area is not general storage and too much material will cause issues with identification of items and create a bottleneck. Warehouse managers should have a clear picture of what materials are in this area and understand the limitations of the physical space.

Two-step cross-docking requires a storage type to store items

Because the default for cross-docking is one-step, warehouses that want to perform two-step cross-docking should ensure that the configuration has been completed.

To set the two-step cross-docking indicator for a warehouse, you need to access the transaction found using the menu path IMG • LOGISTICS EXECUTION • WAREHOUSE MANAGEMENT • CROSS DOCKING • GENERAL SETTINGS • MAINTAIN WAREHOUSE LEVEL SETTINGS.

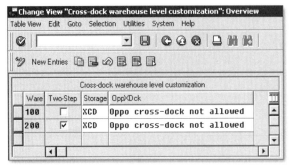

Figure 9.9 Configuration for Two-Step Cross-Docking

One-step cross-docking is the SAP system default

Figure 9.9 shows the configuration for two-step cross-docking for warehouse 200. The cross-docking storage type has been entered as XCD. When you make a cross-docking decision, the system decides whether the one-step or two-step process is applicable.

In a two-step process you'll see that the system has created two transfer orders.

▸ A transfer order for the inbound delivery materials is created to move materials from the goods receipt storage type to the cross-docking storage type.

▸ A transfer order from the cross-docking storage type is created to move materials from the cross-docking storage type to the goods issue storage type.

Delay between inbound and outbound deliveries necessitates two-step processing

Figure 9.10 shows a shipping notification for an inbound delivery that has been linked to an outbound delivery that will occur in two days. The two-step process is suitable for this type of cross-docking. The materials will be stored in the cross-docking storage type when it arrives. When the inbound delivery arrives at the goods receipt area, the materials are unloaded, and a goods receipt is posted in the inventory management functionality in SAP ERP.

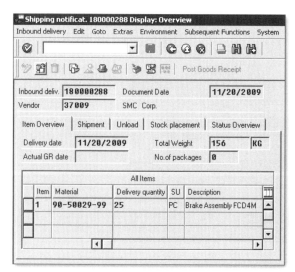

Figure 9.10 Shipping Notification for Inbound Delivery

Figure 9.11 shows the transfer order that is created for the first step of the two-step cross-docking. The materials are received, a goods receipt is posted, and a transfer order is created to move the materials from the goods issue storage type, 902, to the cross-docking storage type, XCD, where they remain until the outbound delivery is ready to be goods issued.

Items are stored in the cross-docking storage type after the inbound delivery

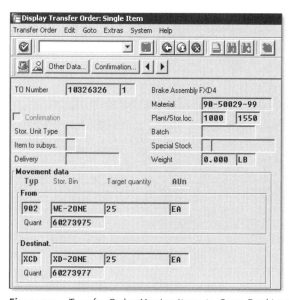

Figure 9.11 Transfer Order Moving Items to Cross-Docking Storage

Figure 9.12 shows the outbound delivery with a planned goods issue of a quantity of 25 for material 90-50029-99. This is the same quantity of material that is expected from the inbound delivery.

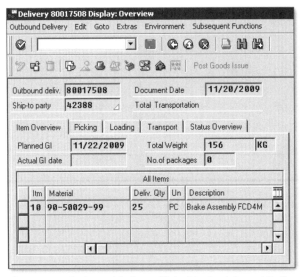

Figure 9.12 Outbound Delivery Linked to the Inbound Delivery

The transfer order moves the items from cross-docking storage type to the outbound delivery

When the outbound delivery is released, the system creates a transfer order that moves the cross-docked material from the cross-docking storage type, XCD, and proposes the goods issue area, storage type 916, as the destination storage type on the transfer order.

Figure 9.13 shows the second transfer order in the two-step cross-docking. The materials are removed from the cross-docking storage type, XCD, and placed in the goods issue storage type for the outbound delivery.

After both transfer orders are confirmed, the inbound delivery and outbound delivery documents are updated with the actual pick and putaway quantities that were recorded.

Figure 9.13   Transfer Order for the Second Part of the Two Step Cross-Docking

9.3   Business Example – Effective Cross-Docking

Several elements of the cross-docking process make it an important factor in creating efficiencies in the warehouse. Because materials aren't moved into the warehouse, there is a saving in resources used in putaway and picking and a monetary saving because the material doesn't require warehouse space. This is very important in a small warehouse or a warehouse approaching maximum capacity. Cross-docking can also help maintain or improve customer satisfaction because the outbound delivery is processed as soon as materials arrive at the warehouse.

Efficient warehouses use cross-docking

9.3.1   One-Step Cross-Docking

One-step cross-docking is the default in the SAP system and allows for materials to be processed in the outbound delivery as soon as they arrive at the plant. Materials aren't stored at the warehouse in a temporary location but are moved directly to the outbound delivery area. In the most efficient warehouses, materials are unloaded by forklift from a trailer on the receiving dock and immediately placed in the truck on the outbound delivery dock by the same forklift, without the pallet ever touching the warehouse floor.

Items aren't stored in the warehouse with one-step cross-docking

A Canadian food retailer used a single warehouse in Hamilton, Ontario, to receive all nonperishable food items, which it then supplied to its stores in eastern Canada. The company had implemented the warehouse management functionality in SAP ERP but hadn't maximized the functionality, and it was basically being used as the previous warehouse management system. Cross-docking had been discussed during implementation, but the company decided the warehouse configuration wasn't suitable for the process.

A year after the SAP implementation, a Dutch supermarket chain purchased the company and executed a rationalization of the warehouse operations. The results of the analysis were that the warehousing costs in the Canadian operation were far in excess of those in the U.S., Mexico, and Europe. The Canadian operation was tasked with reducing the size of the warehouse, reducing the number of items stored in the warehouse, and improving throughput.

The first result of the rationalization was that a new warehouse location was found less than a mile from the existing location. The new warehouse lease was 30% cheaper per square foot, but it was only 40% of the size of the existing warehouse. After bringing in a consulting company to optimize the warehouse layout, all of the current warehouse items would fit in the warehouse, but it would be close to capacity.

The company decided to review the original requirements that were part of the SAP ERP implementation to see if any of the SAP ERP functionality would help with increasing throughput and ensuring that the capacity of the warehouse was not critical.

They reviewed the benefits of cross-docking, and based on the new warehouse layout, the management believed it could be implemented, with one-step cross docking being most efficient.

Cross-docking began a month after the move to the new warehouse because the warehouse staff had to be trained on the new process. Within three months the capacity of the warehouse had been reduced from 93% to 78%, which management believed was due to a combination of product rationalization and the cross-docking process.

9.3.2   Two-Step Cross-Docking

Two-step cross-docking isn't as efficient as one-step cross docking, but in some instances the two-step process is a necessity. For the two-step process to work an area must be set aside where the cross-docking materials from the inbound delivery are placed before they're needed for the outbound delivery.

Several issues can arise with the two-step cross-docking process that have to be overcome for the process to be as efficient as possible, including the capacity limitations of the cross-docking storage type.

A Spanish electrical goods manufacturer sold its own products and items that were sold under their brand but were manufactured by companies in the UK and Germany. The re-badged goods were received at their warehouse in Zaragoza, which was attached to the main production facility. Before the implementation of the warehouse management functionality in SAP ERP the goods from the UK and German manufacturers were fully received into the warehouse. After the introduction of the warehouse management functionality in SAP ERP, this process continued.

In an attempt to reduce overall manufacturing costs, the company decided to move some production capacity to Mexico and China. Although the production facility in Zaragoza was not closed, production was cut by approximately 60%. The result of this reduction in production was that the warehouse was operating at less than 30% capacity, with items manufactured in China and Mexico not being sent to the warehouse in Zaragoza. The items were unloaded from ships to a third-party warehouse near the port of Algeciras before being shipped to customers.

The company evaluated the feasibility of the warehouse at Zaragoza and decided to hire a third-party logistics company (3PL) to operate the warehouse and allowed the 3PL to lease the unused capacity for its own warehousing needs.

The 3PL company used the existing SAP system but suggested that several warehouse efficiency measures that they used in their other operations be put in place. The 3PL suggested that a more efficient manner of dealing with the products arriving from the UK and German vendors was needed. They proposed that they should implement a cross-docking procedure so that warehouse space was not used on these items because they generally were shipped to customers shortly after being received. The delay between the inbound deliveries from the UK and Germany and the outbound deliveries to Spanish customers was always less than a week, and on average two days, so they implemented a two-step cross-docking process. The 3PL created a holding cage between the receiving and outbound delivery docks where the incoming items were stored and checked. The process was quickly implemented because the 3PL didn't want to expend unnecessary resources on the placement of the imported goods; they just wanted to pull them from the warehouse soon after their arrival. In addition, the 3PL managed to maximize the warehouse capacity for its own warehousing operation.

9.4   Summary

Companies are constantly investigating how to make warehousing more efficient, improve customer satisfaction, and cut costs. If possible, materials are shipped directly from the manufacturer to the customer to avoid any warehouse costs. An efficient method is to implement cross-docking. As discussed in this chapter, the process of cross-docking removes the need for inspection on goods receipt, good receipt staging, putaway, storage, picking, and goods issue staging. However, not all materials are suitable for cross-docking, but with the use of the cross-docking functionality in SAP ERP, it's possible to operate cross-docking for some items. Many large organizations use cross-docking, but it's most effective in the movement of items in the retail industry, where items are stored for as little time as possible, and the speed of delivery to the retail store is of the upmost importance.

In the next chapter, we'll review the most efficient ways to work with hazardous materials in your warehouse.

Hazardous materials are used in many production processes and need to be stored in the warehouse. The hazardous materials part of the warehouse management functionality of SAP ERP provides a structure for efficiently managing these materials.

10 Working with Hazardous Materials

Hazardous materials are often found in warehouses, and they are capable of producing many harmful physical effects such as a fire, sudden release of pressure and explosion, and acute health effects such as burns, convulsions, and chronic effects such as organ damage and cancer.

When you know that hazardous materials are in your warehouse, it's your responsibility as the warehouse operator or owner to operate within the boundaries set by federal, state, and local agencies, in the U.S., that regulate hazardous materials in order to protect human health and the environment.

These agencies have regulations that pertain to the handling, storage, and distributing of the hazardous material. In the U.S., these can include the Federal Clean Air Act, the Clean Water Act, the Safe Drinking Water Act (SDWA), the Hazardous Materials Transportation Act, the Toxic Substances Control Act (TSCA), and many others.

Apart from the federal laws, states each have a variety of strict regulations you must observe, for example, the California Safe Drinking Water & Toxic Enforcement Act.

In other countries organizations exist to work in the same manner as the Environmental Protection Agency (EPA) in the U.S. These include the Canadian Environmental Assessment Agency (CEAA), the Department of the Environment and Water Resources in Australia, and the Department for Environment, Food, and Rural Affairs (DEFRA) in the UK.

In addition to managing hazardous materials in warehouses, in the U.S. the Occupational Safety and Health Administration (OSHA) has been tasked to prevent work-related injuries, illnesses, and deaths. Since its inception in 1971, occupational deaths have been cut by 62%, and injuries have declined by 42%. OSHA helps companies with safety and health training and is a valuable resource for policies and procedures involving the handling of hazardous materials.

10.1   Introduction to Hazardous Materials

Many hazardous materials are present in warehouses

To safely and properly handle and store hazardous materials, it's important to know the hazards of those materials. You'll find several hazardous materials a warehouse including flammable and combustible liquids, corrosive and poisonous items, and radioactive and biomedical materials.

To ensure that your warehouse can effectively deal with hazardous materials and the issues that arise with the movement of those materials, your SAP system must be fully configured to allow for their efficient handling.

10.1.1   Configuration for Hazardous Materials

If the warehouse contains hazardous materials, you must take a number of configuration steps to define the sections, warnings, and hazardous material management strategy.

Fire Containment Sections

Fire containment may be required in your warehouse

Fire containment sections must be configured if there are areas in the warehouse that have different fire containment properties. For example, some areas in the warehouse that may contain hazardous materials may have a two-hour minimum fire resistance, whereas other areas may have a four-hour minimum. It's important to understand the construction of your warehouse and the safety features that have been built into it.

> **Example**
>
> A third-party warehouse in Fresno, California, advertises the safety features of its warehouse. It has a 200-horsepower fire pump that supplies the sprinkler system and can pump 2000 gallons per minute. The warehouse has seven self-contained 50,000-square-foot rooms with two-hour fire walls and automatic fire doors. It also has a clay-lined holding pond that has a capacity of 1 million gallons of water and is equipped with a safety valve. In case of fire, the safety value is closed to contain everything on the sealed surface to prevent ground or water contamination.

You can find the configuration for fire containment sections by following the menu path IMG • LOGISTICS EXECUTION • WAREHOUSE MANAGEMENT • HAZARDOUS MATERIALS • MASTER DATA • DEFINE FIRE-CONTAINMENT SECTIONS.

Figure 10.1 shows the configuration for the fire containment sections that can be set up for each warehouse. Some warehouses may have a series of fire containment storage cabinets or areas that can be identified as configurable sections.

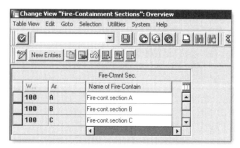

Figure 10.1 Fire-Containment Section Configuration

Hazardous Material Warnings

You can configure the warnings that can be used with hazardous materials in this section. The configuration allows for many material warnings to be created and assigned when dealing with hazardous materials.

Hazardous materials require warnings to be configured

To configure the material warnings, follow the menu path IMG • LOGISTICS EXECUTION • WAREHOUSE MANAGEMENT • HAZARDOUS MATERIALS • MASTER DATA • DEFINE HAZARDOUS MATERIAL WARNING.

Figure 10.2 shows the warnings you can use at the site to indicate a variety of hazardous environments. Don't just accept the SAP defaults. Find out the correct warnings for the materials in your warehouse. The local environmental agency for the country where each warehouse is located may be able to give advice on hazardous material warnings.

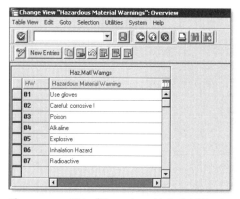

Figure 10.2 List of Hazardous Material Warnings

Hazardous Material Storage Warnings

Warnings are required when hazardous materials are transported or when they're placed in the warehouse. You can create storage warnings that are used when hazardous materials are stored in the warehouse. You should ensure that all hazardous materials that could be in the company warehouses have the appropriate warnings configured.

You can add the storage warnings by completing the configuration found via the menu path IMG • Logistics Execution • Warehouse Management • Hazardous Materials • Master Data • Define Hazardous Material Storage Warning.

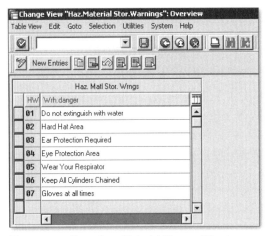

Figure 10.3 Hazardous Material Storage Warnings

Figure 10.3 shows the storage warnings that have been entered for the hazardous materials that could be stored at any warehouse in the company. Ensure that you have reviewed all of the potential hazardous materials at all warehouses in your company to cover all eventualities.

Storage Classes

The storage class is configured so that it can classify hazardous materials based on their features. The storage class can be used in stock putaway strategies. The definition of the storage classes in SAP ERP is based on the guidelines issued by the U.S. Department of Transportation. Several of the classes are preset in the standard SAP system, as shown in Figure 10.4, so you need to check to ensure that the classes used at your company are in the system; otherwise they'll need to be added.

You can configure storage classes by following the menu path IMG • LOGIS-
TICS EXECUTION • WAREHOUSE MANAGEMENT • HAZARDOUS MATERIALS •
MASTER DATA • DEFINE STORAGE CLASSES.

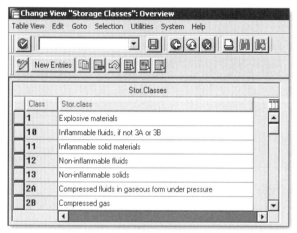

Figure 10.4 Storage Classes for Hazardous Materials

You can use the storage classes in the storage type search so that the correct
storage type is selected based on the appropriate storage class. For example, a material may be only allowed in a storage type that is applicable for
hazardous material storage class 2A. If the material is stored in the wrong
storage type, a potential safety issue can occur.

10.2   Hazardous Materials in the Warehouse

The importance of identifying and dealing with hazardous materials in
the warehouse cannot be stressed enough. Although the management of
hazardous materials does not increase the efficiency of the warehouse, it
should be noted that less than perfect management may lead to a serious
safety issue and cost your company money in lost production and possible
fines from safety organizations such as OSHA.

Hazardous
materials must be
identified when
stored in the
warehouse

10.2.1   Activating the Functionality for Hazardous Materials

The activation of the hazardous materials management in the warehouse
is important because it forces the system to look for hazardous materials and take their characteristics into account when placing them in the
warehouse.

You can begin to activate the hazardous material management by using Transaction OMM2 or by following the menu path IMG • Logistics Execution • Warehouse Management • Hazardous Materials • Strategies • Activate Hazardous Material Management.

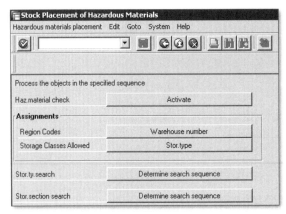

Figure 10.5 Activation of Hazardous Material Functionality

Figure 10.5 shows the configuration that is required for hazardous material management. The first configuration step is to activate the hazardous material check.

Activation of Hazardous Material Check

The steps shown in Figure 10.5 activate the section check, the hazardous material management, and the water pollution class for a designated storage type in a warehouse.

The water pollution class classifies a material in terms of its capability of polluting water

SAP recommends that you set the hazardous material check for all physical storage types but not for the interim storage types. In warehouses that contain minimal hazardous materials, there may be a tendency to configure only those storage types that are most likely to contain hazardous materials, but processes change, as do the materials stored in the different storage types, so to offer as much safety as possible, you should set the indicator for all storage types.

In Figure 10.6 the configuration has been entered for warehouse 260, and the storage types have been activated for the section check. The X in the field indicates that the storage section is determined and a check made. A Y would indicate that a storage section determination was made, but no check.

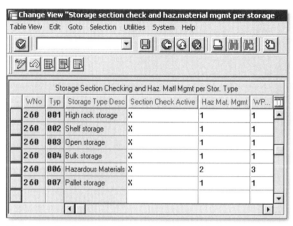

Figure 10.6 Activating Hazardous Material Management

The hazardous material management field has been configured with the value 1. This means the hazardous material check is made at the storage type level only. The entry of a 2 in this field would have required a check at the storage type and storage section levels.

The water pollution class (WPC) classifies a material in terms of its capability of polluting water. The values are defined as:

▶ 0 – Not a water pollutant

▶ 1 – Minimal water pollutant

▶ 2 – Water pollutant

▶ 3 – Extreme water pollutant

Entering a 1 in the WPC field allows materials with WPCs of 0 and 1 to be stored in the storage type.

Storage Classes per Storage Type

In this configuration step for hazardous materials, it's possible to assign all of the storage classes to a certain storage type in the warehouse. For example, some storage types are suitable for compressed gas but not flammable solids.

You can use the storage class in the storage type search

Figure 10.7 shows the assignment of storage classes to storage type 006 in warehouse 260. The example shows that storage type 006 allows the storage of materials of class 8 but not 6.1 or 6.2. Ensuring that the correct hazardous materials are allowed or blocked for each storage type is an important safety measure.

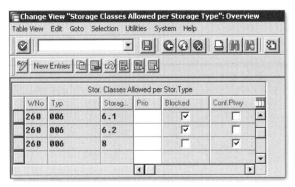

Figure 10.7 Assignment of Storage Classes to Storage Types

Materials can be blocked from being stored in specific storage types

You can use the Blocked checkbox to temporarily block the storage type for a particular storage class. This may occur if certain materials have been stored in the storage type, rendering it unavailable for hazardous materials of other storage classes.

The Conf.Ptwy checkbox requires that any stock placement for this storage class is performed in the foreground, overriding any other requirement for that storage type.

Storage Type Search

A storage type search can take into account the storage class and WPC

This allows additions to be made to the storage type search to allow for any storage class configuration that has been made. For example, if a storage type allows materials of class 6.1 and 6.2, then that can be used in the storage type search.

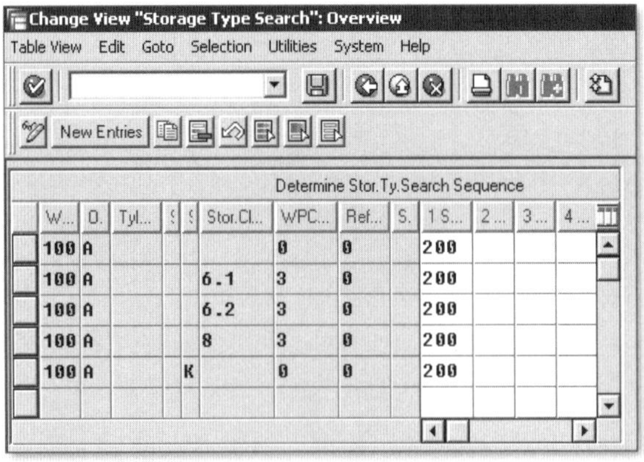

Figure 10.8 Storage Type Search Configuration

Figure 10.8 shows that there are storage types in the storage type search that include reference to a hazardous material storage class. The storage type search now includes a search in which the storage classes are 6.1, 6.2, and 8. In this example the search will try to find an empty storage bin in storage type 200 if the material has a storage class of 6.1 and a water pollution class of 3.

Storage Section Search

If your warehouse uses storage section search and storage type search, it's possible to configure the storage section search to include the storage class.

10.2.2 Hazardous Material Record

To ensure that all of the relevant safety documentation is assigned to a material, you create a hazardous material record. It should contain all of the necessary warnings, water pollution class, and composition.

The hazardous material record contains all relevant safety information

You can create a hazardous material record by using Transaction VM01, or you can follow the menu path SAP • LOGISTICS • LOGISTICS EXECUTION • MASTER DATA • MATERIAL • HAZARDOUS MATERIAL • CREATE.

Figure 10.9 shows the data for the hazardous material record. The hazardous material number is not internally assigned, so you'll have to get management to decide on an external number range.

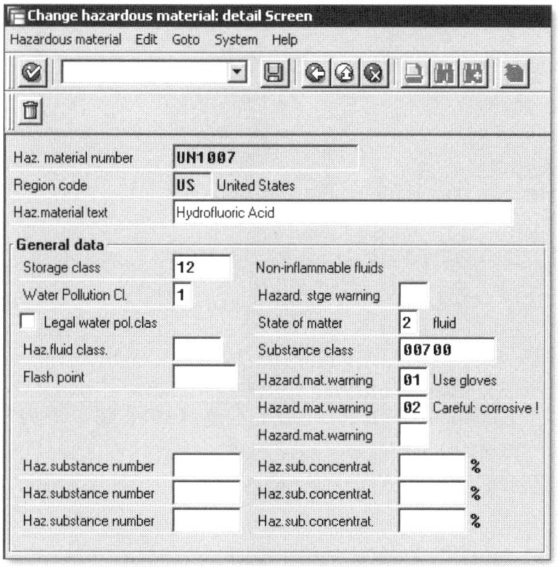

Figure 10.9 Hazardous Material Record

This transaction allows you to include more detailed information for the hazardous material, including the storage class, water pollution class, aggregate state and flash point. Once the hazardous material has been created, it can be assigned to a material master record.

10.2.3 Assigning the Hazardous Material to a Material Master Record

The hazardous material number is assigned to the material master record

Because the hazardous material information is stored in the warehouse management functionality of SAP ERP, the hazardous material number is assigned to the material master record in the warehouse management screen of the material master.

You can enter the hazardous material in the warehouse management screen using Transaction MM02, which is the Material Master Change transaction.

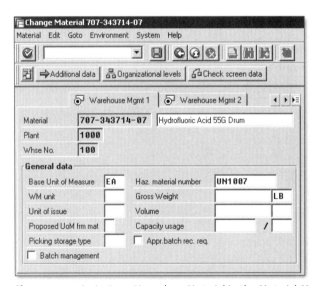

Figure 10.10 Assigning a Hazardous Material in the Material Master

Figure 10.10 shows the warehouse management screen for material 707-343714-07. The material is a 55-gallon drum of hydrofluoric acid that has hazardous material number UN1007. The hazardous material number is assigned to the material master record. Therefore, any warehouse movements of the material will show that it's a hazardous material, and special handling will occur.

10.2.4 List of Hazardous Materials

It's important that warehouse management ensure that all hazardous materials are tracked. The warehouse can use several reports and, in case of emergency, reports for the fire service of HAZMAT teams to work with, detailing where the hazardous materials are.

The first report shows the hazardous materials that are allowed in warehouses in a given region. The transaction for this is LX24, and you can find it via the menu path SAP • LOGISTICS • LOGISTICS EXECUTION • INFORMATION SYSTEM • WAREHOUSE • STOCK • HAZARDOUS MATERIAL • LIST.

The list of hazardous materials shows allowed materials within the region

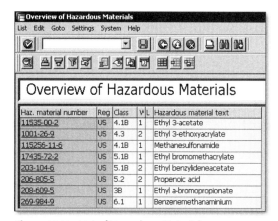

Figure 10.11 List of Hazardous Materials

Figure 10.11 shows a list of all of the hazardous materials that have been entered for the particular region. It's the company's responsibility to monitor the storage of those materials in the warehouse.

10.2.5 Fire Department Inventory List

Periodically, regulatory authorities or the local fire department may inspect the warehouse. You can access the SAP system to produce a report that lists the hazardous materials stored within the warehouse. The fire department inventory list is a report that shows the quantity of materials in each fire containment area, by storage class. The fire department can review the potential hazards and offer advice on storage changes.

The fire department requires information on hazardous materials in warehouses

You can produce the fire department inventory list using Transaction LX06, or you can access it through the menu path SAP • LOGISTICS • LOGISTICS EXECUTION • INFORMATION SYSTEM • WAREHOUSE • STOCK • HAZARDOUS MATERIAL • FIRE DEPARTMENT INVENTORY LIST.

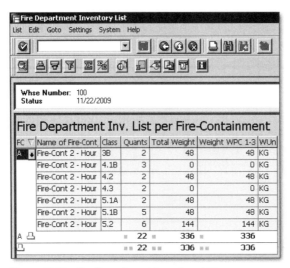

Figure 10.12 Fire Department Inventory List

The fire department inventory list, shown in Figure 10.12, identifies each fire containment area and the hazardous storage classes currently stored inside. The weights and quantities of the materials show the fire department the level of potential hazard within each containment area. If the fire department calculates that there is too much stock of a certain hazardous storage class in a containment area, then the warehouse staff have to move quants to other suitable storage bins.

10.2.6 Check Goods Storage

This report shows that hazardous material in your warehouse has been stored correctly

You use the check goods storage report to ensure that the hazardous materials in your warehouse have been stored correctly. The report analyzes all of the quants of material to see where they are stored and checks against the configuration entered for hazardous materials. It checks the following.

▶ Checks that hazardous materials aren't stored in storage types managed specifically for nonhazardous materials

▶ Checks that materials are stored in the correct storage types based on water pollution class

▶ Checks that materials are stored in the correct storage types based on storage class

If any of these checks produce an error, the report will create an error log showing how many errors occurred for each storage type.

You can execute the check goods storage list using Transaction LX07, or you can follow the menu path SAP • LOGISTICS • LOGISTICS EXECUTION • INFORMATION SYSTEM • WAREHOUSE • STOCK • HAZARDOUS MATERIAL • CHECK GOODS STORAGE.

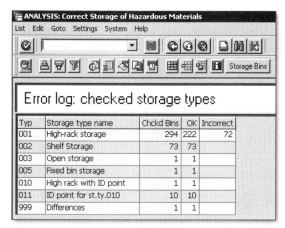

Figure 10.13 Error Log Produced by the Check Goods Storage Report

Figure 10.13 shows that for storage type 001 there are 72 instances where hazardous materials are incorrectly stored, whereas the other storage types have no errors.

10.2.7 Hazardous Substance List

The hazardous substance list produces a report of all of the hazardous materials stored in a particular warehouse, storage type, or fire containment area. This is of particular importance to any safety organization for reviewing the hazardous materials totals in your warehouse.

The hazardous substance list produces a report of all hazardous materials in a specific location

You can process the hazardous substance list via Transaction LX08 or the menu path SAP • LOGISTICS • LOGISTICS EXECUTION • INFORMATION SYSTEM • WAREHOUSE • STOCK • HAZARDOUS MATERIAL • HAZARDOUS SUBSTANCE LIST.

Figure 10.14 shows the hazardous materials stored in the warehouse. In this example the hazardous materials are in storage type 006.

You should use the range of reports available for hazardous materials in combination so that you're aware of the hazardous materials in your warehouse. It's management's responsibility to keep warehouse employees safe by ensuring that hazardous materials are stored in the appropriate storage types.

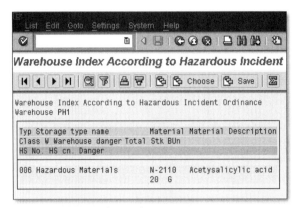

Figure 10.14 Hazardous Substance List

10.3   Business Example – Successful Handling of Hazardous Materials

In your effort to achieve an efficient warehouse by maximizing the warehouse management functionality of SAP ERP, you need to remember that the successful management of hazardous materials is equally important because your employees require a safe working environment.

10.3.1   Hazardous Material Records

To ensure that all of the relevant safety documentation is assigned to your materials, you should create a hazardous material record. It should contain all of the necessary warnings, water pollution class, and composition.

Example

A U.S.-based furniture manufacturer had three locations across the U.S., in North Carolina, Georgia, and Los Angeles. As a cost-saving exercise, the production was rationalized and moved to the North Carolina location. The items produced in North Carolina assembled from mostly imported components. With the components that were used in the production process from Georgia and Los Angeles were brought to the warehouse in North Carolina, the warehouse manager found that a lot of chemicals needed to be stored. The chemicals were used in the production process and needed to be stored in the warehouse until they were used on the production line.

Before the chemicals arrived at the North Carolina plant, the warehouse manager wasn't fully aware of the hazardous nature of some of the items. When he received a full list of items, along with the relevant material safety data sheets (MSDSs), the warehouse manager became aware that the current warehouse layout might not be adequate. The plant management brought in a consulting firm to ascertain the issues that might arise with the chemicals they'd have to store and to examine the existing warehouse facility to see if they had the sufficient fire containment.

The consulting firm recommended some structural changes to the warehouse based on the chemicals to be stored and changes in drainage to avoid water pollution. The firm also recommended that the company expand their use of the warehouse management functionality of SAP ERP to create hazardous material records for the chemicals and to modify the storage type search strategies to ensure that the materials were placed in the correct storage bins.

10.3.2 Hazardous Material Reporting

Several reports are available to warehouse managers to help identify where issues have occurred and incorrect storage has taken place.

Example

A Canadian manufacturer of after-market automotive parts had been using their stand-alone warehouse management system for over a decade and had customized it to take into account their specific processes. The system did hold some information on hazardous materials, but based on consultations with the local fire department, the information was insufficient. The fire department cited that they could not identify what hazardous material was in what location and that no water pollution information was available. The company decided to increase the customization of their existing warehouse system, but the decision was put on hold because a migration to an SAP system had been proposed at the corporate level.

The SAP implementation was completed a few months later, and the warehouse management functionality of SAP ERP was included as part of the project. Hazardous materials information was loaded after the go-live, and existing material master records were amended to add the new hazardous material numbers.

With the entry of the hazardous material information, the company was able to produce reports on storage and water pollution that were required by the fire department.

10.4   Summary

Hazardous materials are used in the production of finished goods in thousands of companies every day. Laws and regulations at different levels of government in every country govern the storage of hazardous materials. In the U.S. federal and state laws determine what is a hazardous material and how that material should be stored. Safety is crucial when working with hazardous materials, and the best safety methods are often the most efficient.

The efficient method for managing hazardous materials in the warehouse allows hazardous materials to be stored in the correct storage bins in the correct storage types. Any error in the storage of hazardous materials is not only potentially dangerous, but can result in financial penalties levied against the warehouse owner.

In the next chapter we'll look at the most efficient way to manage radio frequency (RF) and radio frequency identification (RFID) in your warehouse.

RFID technology has been available for many years, but recently there has been investment in using RFID to track inventory. Large companies and government agencies expect RFID to eventually reduce warehouse costs and improve warehouse efficiency.

11 Using Radio Frequency Identification Effectively

Radio frequency identification (RFID) has been available for commercial applications for the past 25 years, although the technology was developed in the UK during World War II.

RFID has been available for many years

RFID is known today as the reading of physical tags on single products, cases, pallets, or reusable containers that emit radio signals to be picked up by RFID reader devices. Industries see this technology as a way of identifying materials more accurately than traditional means. Many companies and government agencies are assessing whether RFID is suitable for their operations and if the technology is cost effective. However, as the technology improves and the cost falls, RFID will be as commonplace in the warehouse as traditional radio frequency (RF) products.

The current SAP ERP functionality allows the use of RFID technology, and the efficiencies that can be gained from its use are something to consider for companies that want to maximize their use of the system.

RFID is an example of how customers can maximize their SAP ERP functionality

11.1 Introduction to RF and RFID

To increase productivity in the warehouse, many companies use RF devices and RFID tags. By using an RF device to collect data from bar codes, warehouse operators can save time and reduce data entry errors. Although RF devices can be used with many software products, SAP offers the ability to connect devices to SAP ERP without middleware. SAP customers can execute transactions on RF devices that are either handheld or forklift-mounted. One of the benefits is that the functionality in SAP ERP is real-time, so scans entered into a transaction can be immediately accessed.

However, RF technology does have limitations that are being overcome by the developing RFID technology.

11.1.1   RF Devices

RF devices are used to read bar codes

RF devices in the warehouse are bar code readers that read information that is printed on bar code labels affixed to products, pallets, or documents.

A bar code is a series of varying-width vertical lines, called bars, and spaces. The bars and spaces are called elements. Different combinations of bars and spaces represent different characters.

As the laser from an RF device is passed over the bar code, the scanner creates a low electrical signal for the spaces, which is the reflected light, and a high electrical signal for the bars, where nothing is reflected. The duration of the electrical signal determines whether the scanner has detected a wide or a narrow element. The bar code reader's decoder then interprets the signal. The decoder converts this into the characters the bar code represents. The decoded data is then passed to the system in a traditional data format.

11.1.2   Bar Code Functionality

Bar Codes were first developed for grocery stores

The bar code was developed in the 1950s and first used by grocery stores. The first standard was the Universal Product Code (UPC), which was adopted in 1973 as the industry standard, and any bar code on any product could be read and understood by any bar code reader. Standardization made it cost effective for manufacturers to put bar codes on their packages and for printer manufacturers to develop new types of technology to reproduce bar code with the exact tolerances they required.

Bar Code Format

A bar code is made up of the manufacturer's code and the product code

The UPC bar code is split into two parts of six digits each. The first character is always zero, except for some materials that have variable weight or special materials. The next five characters are the manufacturer's code, followed by a five-digit product code and a check digit. In addition, hidden cues in the structure of the bar code inform the scanner which end of the bar code is the start and which is the end. This allows the bar code to be scanned in any direction.

Manufacturer's Code

Manufacturers register with the Uniform Code Council (UCC) to obtain an identifier code for their company. All materials produced by a given company will use the same manufacturer code. These codes are called variable-length manufacturer codes. Assigning fixed-length five-digit manufacturer codes means that each manufacturer can have up to 99,999 product codes, although most manufacturers don't have that many products. If a manufacturer knows it will produce a small number of products for bar coding, the UCC may issue it a longer manufacturer code, leaving less space for the product code. This results in more efficient use of the available manufacturer and product codes.

Manufacturers receive a code from Uniform Code Council (UCC)

Product Code

The product code is a unique code assigned by the manufacturer. Unlike the manufacturer code, which must be assigned by the UCC, the manufacturer is free to assign product codes to each of its materials that require bar coding. Because the UCC will already have guaranteed that the manufacturer code is unique, the manufacturer needs to ensure that they don't duplicate product codes.

The product code is assigned by the manufacturer

Check Digit

The check digit is an additional digit used to verify that a bar code has been scanned correctly. Because a scan can produce incorrect data owing to inconsistent scanning speeds, print imperfections, or environmental issues, it's important to verify that the preceding digits in the bar code have been correctly interpreted. The check digit is calculated based on the other digits of the bar code. Normally, if the check digit is the same as the value of the check digit based on the data that has been scanned, there is a high level of confidence that the bar code was scanned correctly.

The check digit ensures the scan is correct

International Article Numbering Association (EAN)

After the UPC was adopted in 1973, the global interest in bar coding, especially in retailing, led to the adoption of the International Article Numbering Association (EAN) code in December of 1976.

The EAN code has 13 characters, including country code

The EAN code has 13 characters, but is identical to the UPC code in that the actual unique code is 10 digits long. In a UPC code the first digit is for the product and the last is a check digit. An EAN code has three characters that aren't used for the unique code. The three flag digits are used for the check digit and the country that issued the bar code, not the country of origin of the product. Each country has a numbering authority that assigns manufacturer codes to companies within its jurisdiction. The manufacturer code is still five digits long, as is the product code, and the check digit is calculated in exactly the same way as the UPC code.

For the UPC and EAN to be compatible, the U.S. was issued country flags 00, 01, 03, 04, and 06 through 13.

Because the EAN, sometimes called EAN-13, is a superset of the UPC, any software or hardware capable of reading an EAN-13 symbol will automatically be able to read a UPC code.

11.1.3 RFID

RFID tags can be passive or active

RFID is a means of identifying an object, whether a pallet, case, or individual item, using a radio frequency transmission. Communication takes place between a reader and a tag.

Tags can either be active, which means they're powered by battery, or passive, which are powered by the reader field. The communication frequencies used depend to a large extent on the application and range from 125 KHz to 2.45 GHz. Most countries impose regulations to control emissions and prevent interference with other industrial, scientific, and medical equipment. Currently, passive tags are cheaper to produce and therefore more cost effective, but this may change as the technology matures and manufacturing costs fall.

An RFID tag has some memory for name of material and quantity

In a typical system, RFID tags are attached to objects. Each tag has a certain amount of internal memory that stores information about the object, such as its unique ID number, or in some cases more details including manufacturing date and material information. When a tag passes through a field generated by a reader, it transmits this information back to the reader, which identifies the object. Initially, pilot RFID projects reflected small volumes of data, but as RFID becomes more widely used in the supply chain, the volumes of data will increase, which will then have to be filtered and routed to ERP systems. To deal with the huge volume of data, companies have developed special middleware software packages, sometimes known as savants, which act as buffers between the RFID frontend and the ERP backend.

11.1.4 Differences Between RF and RFID

Several differences between RF and RFID can help warehouse management decide what system will be more efficient for warehouse operations.

When we compare RF and RFID, we're examining the source of the information. With RF devices, the source of the information is the bar code, whereas with RFID the source of the information is the RFID Tag.

There are several differences between RF and RFID

RF	RFID
Bar codes not reusable	Reusable
Read only	Read or read/write
Line of sight required	No line of sight required
Requires operator to read	Unattended reading
Product-level identification	Object-level identification
Susceptible to the environment	Less susceptible to environment

Table 11.1 Comparing RF and RFID

Although RF is a mature product and has been implemented in warehouses all over the world, it does have some limitations. The information is on a bar code that has to be read with an RF device and can only be read when the RF device is able to see the bar code. This limitation has been overcome by the RFID tag, because it can be read by a reader when the tag passes near the reader.

RF has a number of limitations

11.2 How You Can Use RF in Your Warehouse

Most warehouses use some kind of RF device to read bar codes. It's important for the efficiency of the warehouse to have the RF functionality fully integrated with the SAP system. Transactions can be executed on RF devices such as handheld or forklift-mounted devices and can connect to the SAP system without the need of middleware.

A major benefit to efficiency is that the each scan from an RF device is handled in real-time in the SAP transaction. Conversely, it's important to be able to collect information from the RF devices when the SAP system is not available, for example, during a power outage, so that materials can still be processed in the warehouse.

Two standard radio frequency devices can be used with SAP systems: graphical user interface (GUI) devices and character-based devices. The

RF devices can be GUI or character based

main difference is that the character-based device uses terminal emulation and the GUI devices use a Windows-based operating system.

11.2.1   GUI Devices

GUI-based devices are the most commonly produced today

The GUI RF device can use a small keypad, touch screen, or some other method, and the data is displayed to the user in a graphical manner, like you would expect to see with a device such as Smartphone. The device is connected to the SAP system like any other stand-alone computer would be. Most new devices use this method.

11.2.2   Character-Based Devices

Character-based devices are connected to the SAP system via the SAPConsole

The character-based device is not connected directly to the SAP system but communicates via an interface called SAPConsole. The communication between the SAPConsole and the RF device can be achieved via a Telnet server or a web server.

SAP supports two industry standards for screen sizes:

▸ RF devices for forklifts: 8 lines by 40 characters

▸ Portable RF devices: 16 lines by 20 characters

11.2.3   SAPConsole

SAPConsole is a stand-alone product

SAP developed SAPConsole to support different types of output devices. SAPConsole supports character-cell terminals, including RF devices. Its primary function is to manage, connect, and exchange information with the SAP system, providing the backbone for interfacing with mobile devices. The latest version of SAPConsole, 7.10, is a stand-alone product, and it doesn't require SAP GUI to be installed. SAPConsole exchanges information by two methods:

▸ **Telnet**
Telnet is used for character-based terminals. During a Telnet connection, the Telnet client connects to the Telnet server and starts a command interpreter.

▸ **Web server**
During a browser-based session, the browser connects to the web server.

SAPConsole can use Telnet or a web server

SAPConsole translates GUI screens to character-based screens that are used on a variety of data collection devices. SAPConsole doesn't contain business logic, databases, or external functionality. Its sole function is to translate SAP GUI screens in the SAP environment to the character-based equivalent. A SAPConsole session allows connection to an SAP system in real time, exactly like an SAP GUI session. All of the functionality and business logic resides within the SAP application. The SAPConsole attaches the user to that business logic.

In SAP ECC 6.0 many transactions are now deemed mobile data entry and are available for use with RF devices. These include:

Many SAP transactions are available

- Goods receipt
- Goods issue
- Material putaway
- Material picking
- Packing and unpacking
- Physical inventory
- Loading and unloading
- Serial number capture
- Stock overview

11.2.4 RF Monitor

Warehouse managers can use the RF monitor to review the queues that are being worked on in the warehouse. The user with a RF device can only see the items in his queue; only users of the RF monitor have the overall picture of the RF operations in the warehouse.

The RF monitor is a great tool for warehouse managers

There are three benefits to using the RF monitor:

- Monitor the queues and review the number of assigned transfer orders, the number of users, and the ratio of workload to users
- Assign transfer orders and users to other queues
- Change the processing priorities of transfer orders in the queues

You can access the RF monitor using the Transaction LRF1, or you can follow the menu path SAP • LOGISTICS • LOGISTICS EXECUTION • INTERNAL WHSE PROCESSES • MOBILE DATA ENTRY • MONITOR MOBILE DATA ENTRY.

Figure 11.1 shows the major components of the RF monitor. The navigation area is the section on the left of the screen that shows the number of users along with the number of transfer orders. In this example there is only one user and one transfer order in the queue. The right-hand side of the screen is the ALV, or the SAP List Viewer. It shows the details from the transfer order, and below that there are the details on the user and the queue he's assigned to.

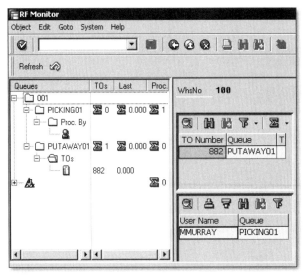

Figure 11.1 RF Monitor Screen

Warehouse managers can move transfer orders to other queues

The RF monitor gives the warehouse manager the opportunity to move transfer orders to other queues by simply identifying the transfer order in the navigation area and dragging it to another queue folder.

Assigning users to other queues follows a similar process, where you highlight the user in the navigation area and drag and drop it into the queue required. You can keep the RF monitor updated by refreshing the transaction by pressing the $\boxed{F5}$ function key.

The RF functionality in SAP ERP is effective in the warehouse. The benefits of fast and error-free data entry ensure that warehouse operations are performed efficiently.

11.3   How You Can Use RFID in Your Warehouse

The SAP solution for RFID is SAP Auto-ID Infrastructure

SAP currently offers an RFID solution called SAP Auto-ID Infrastructure (SAP AII). This is part of the SAP Business Suite, and it integrates RFID with current SAP functionality.

There are two ways to implement SAP AII: as a stand-alone system or integrated in the supply chain function. The latest release of SAP AII is 5.1. As more companies require their vendors to supply products with RFID tags, the SAP AII solution will be an efficient way to comply with your customer's requirements.

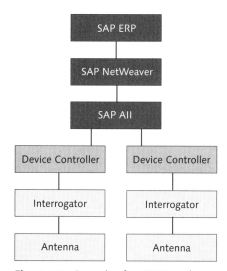

Figure 11.2 Example of an RFID Landscape

Figure 11.2 shows an example of how the RFID solution can be implemented in a warehouse. Device controllers are software components that link SAP Auto-ID with the interrogator hardware components. One device controller can manage many interrogators, which are hardware devices that read RFID tags. Each interrogator can have one or more antennae plus additional equipment, such as light sensors, that can determine the direction in which the goods are moving.

SAP ERP is linked to SAP AII and the device readers by SAP NetWeaver

11.3.1 Supported Functions in SAP AII

The following processes are available and supported by SAP AII. Mobile and fixed RFID devices support these processes as well as desktop user interfaces.

SAP AII supports several processes

- Outbound processing (slap and ship)
- Flexible delivery processing
- Returnable transport items processing

11.3.2 Outbound Processing (Slap and Ship)

This method is
used for minimum
RFID investment

Slap-and-ship describes an approach to complying with customer require-ments for physical identification of materials shipped through the outbound processes. The main goal of the slap and ship strategy is to invest the mini-mum amount of capital into an RFID implementation to comply with the mandates set forth by both Wal-Mart and the Department of Defense.

11.3.3 Flexible Delivery Processing

The flexible delivery process allows the automation of outbound process-ing and inbound processing. The process allows you to:

- Create outbound deliveries in the SAP ERP system
- Pack and load outbound deliveries in SAP AII
- Post goods issue in the SAP ERP system
- Send advanced shipping notifications
- Create inbound deliveries in the SAP ERP system
- Unload inbound deliveries in SAP AII
- Post goods receipt in the SAP ERP system

11.3.4 Returnable Transport Items (RTI) Processing

Items to be
returned, such as
pallets, benefit
from Global
Returnable Asset
Identifiers (GRAIs)

Returnable transport items are assets that can be identified if they're allo-cated with a tag encoded with Global Returnable Asset Identifiers (GRAI). A returnable transport item or asset is one that the owner delivers to the custody of another business entity, usually for a fee.

RTI processing includes the following functions:

- Manage, load, and unload returnable transport items (RTIs) filled with products or with RTIs
- Track the current location of RTIs and evaluate stocks and cycle times
- Achieve transparency across your stocks of RTIs
- Automate processes, reduce stocks, shorten cycle times, and identify bottlenecks

A GRAI has a
unique number
per asset

The GRAI provides a unique identification of an asset. It uses the UCC-assigned company prefixes to develop, assign, and maintain unique asset numbers for equipment, resources, supplies, and so on to track an item's location. Therefore, the GRAI is a unique code that is specific to the asset. The EAN identification number of a returnable asset, GRAI, is defined as a physical item with no reference to the contents. The EAN ID of a returnable asset enables tracking and recording of all relevant data.

Returnable assets such as pallets, barrels, rail cars, and trailers for further usage in transport and trade processes become increasingly important. The main focus is to manage returnable assets within harmonized business processes and leverage the EAN system in the unique identification of assets.

11.4 Business Example – Successful RFID Processes

Although RFID is not as widely used as RF technology, its use is increasing as companies with specific business issues look to RFID and the SAP AII solution to solve them. The solution is being used in many industries with a variety of problems.

> **Example**
>
> A company involved in the manufacture and management of reusable pallets found that one of the largest issues for their customers was the loss of pallets, either by damage, theft, or mismanagement. A quarter of all customers reported a yearly loss of 10% or more of their pallet inventory. Because this loss represented a large financial burden on their customers, the company looked for solutions that would reduce this loss. One possible solution was the introduction of RFID technology to track pallets. The pilot project was to use RFID with SAP ERP in a single country to test the feasibility of rolling RFID out worldwide. The company used reusable tags attached to each pallet so that when a pallet left their warehouse to a customer, the pallet tags were read by an interrogator, and the information was stored against that customer on the outbound delivery. This was a much faster method than having to scan bar codes on the pallets with an RF device. The inbound scan of the pallets also increased efficiency because the pallets were automatically identified when they were returned, saving a manual counting effort, and the project gave the company the benefits of using GRAIs. The company was able to use the RFID on the return of the pallets to inform their customers when the pallets were returned.

The use of RFID can also be implemented inside the warehouse to improve operations and the increase the efficient movement of materials.

RFID doesn't need to be outward looking; it can be used internally

A German automaker had modified their business operations to increase efficiency in the warehouse and the production facility. One area where they felt improvements could be made was in the use of kanban. In traditional kanban a card is used to trigger the demand for more materials to be moved from the warehouse to the production line. However, there was a time delay, and production was slowed from time to time owing to a lack of materials on the production line. To remedy this, the company used RFID tags and RFID gate readers to make the process more efficient. Each kanban trolley was fitted with an RFID tag so that when the trolley was filled with materials from the warehouse, it passed through an RFIG gate reader at the production supply area that identified incoming material. When the trolley was emptied and materials used on the production line, the trolley was moved through another gate reader, which processed an automatic kanban status change and identified the trolley as empty. The creation of a replenishment element was processed, and the materials were then ready for the trolley when it arrived in the warehouse.

RFID can also be used between different facilities in the same company to ensure that shipments are correctly sent and received.

A U.S. paper goods company had an issue with shipments between the manufacturing plant and the regional distribution centers. The major problem was that often the distribution centers didn't receive the items they requested, and after manually counting the trailer that arrived from the manufacturing plant, they found they didn't have items for customers. The level of customer satisfaction began to fall, and management initiated a project to help reduce instances of this situation and to inform the distribution centers ahead of time of the items in their shipments. If the distribution centers knew ahead of time that a shipment was missing certain items, they had a much longer lead time to deal with the situation, either by reordering from the manufacturing plant or moving items from another distribution center.

The project involved one manufacturing plant and one distribution center that were fitted RFID gate readers, and the products were RFID tagged at the case level. When a shipment left the manufacturing plant, the RFID gate reader scanned the cases, and the system transmitted the accurate delivery details to the distribution center via an advance shipping notice (ASN). The distribution center then had the correct information so they could make alternative arrangements for items not being shipped.

When the items were received at the distribution center they were passed through the RFID gate reader, and the system sent the information back to the manufacturing plant in the form of a proof of delivery.

11.5 Summary

Radio frequency identification (RFID) technology has become commercially and technologically viable. RFID tags are microchips that act as transponders constantly listening for a radio signal sent by RFID readers. When a transponder receives a certain radio query, it responds by transmitting its unique ID code back to the transceiver. Most RFID tags don't have batteries; instead, they're powered by the radio signal requesting a reply.

RFID can be used in the warehouse, and since large companies such as Wal-Mart mandated the used of RFID, many companies have been investigating RFID for tracking the movement of materials at a level that can improve their visibility through the supply chain and improve efficiencies in the warehouse.

The SAP Auto-ID Infrastructure (SAP AII) solution is available for companies that want to use RFID with their SAP ERP system. The SAP AII system requires configuration for the interaction of the RFID processes with the SAP ERP functions. As the cost of RFID tags and readers is reduced, RFID will become more widely.

The next chapter will examine the use of data and reports that can improve efficiency in the warehouse.

The warehouse activity monitor and other key reports in the warehouse management functionality of SAP ERP help warehouse managers identify and correct problems in the warehouse as soon as they occur.

12   Effective Use of Warehouse Data and Reporting

To maximize the efficiency of the warehouse you should use all of the functionality available to you in warehouse management in SAP ERP. Several reports and monitors are available to warehouse managers that will give them the information they need to reassign resources, reschedule picking, and plan outbound deliveries. We've seen some of these transactions in the previous chapters, such as the outbound delivery monitor, the cross-docking monitor, and the wave pick monitor.

Warehouse reports can help improve efficiency

In this chapter we'll look at several transactions that will further enhance your staff's ability to make warehouse processes more efficient. The first transaction we'll look at is the warehouse activity monitor.

12.1   Warehouse Activity Monitor

Warehouse managers have to oversee the business in the warehouse and plan the work of warehouse operators so that the warehouse runs at its most efficient. The warehouse activity monitor is available to help them perform those tasks but is also a useful tool when there are delays and errors in warehouse transactions. The warehouse activity monitor helps warehouse managers identify and correct problems in the warehouse as soon as they occur. Without a swift resolution to a problem, the knock-on effect can cause major disruption to picking and subsequently to the delivery of customers' orders.

The warehouse activity monitor displays critical processes

The warehouse activity monitor displays the critical processes in the warehouse. For each of the process functions, the warehouse activity monitor offers functionality that helps the warehouse manager analyze and correct errors. The warehouse activity monitor covers the following areas:

▸ Unconfirmed transfer orders

▸ Open transfer requirements

▸ Open posting change notices

▸ Open deliveries

▸ Negative stock

▸ Stock in interim storage areas

▸ Critical stocks in production

12.1.1 Configuration for the Warehouse Activity Monitor

Configuration is needed for the warehouse activity monitor

Before you can use the warehouse activity monitor, you must complete several configuration steps. The first of these is to activate the warehouse objects for the relevant warehouse.

To activate the object you want to have for each warehouse, follow the menu path IMG • Logistics Execution • Warehouse Management • Planning and Monitoring • Warehouse Activity Monitor • Activate Warehouse Activity Monitor Objects.

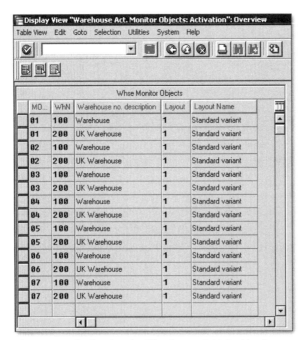

Figure 12.1 Configuring the Warehouse Activity Monitor

Figure 12.1 shows the warehouse objects that have been configured for warehouses 100 and 200. This configuration step allows you to define which objects are relevant for a warehouse. In this example the warehouse activity monitor for both warehouses will feature all of the warehouse objects available. The Layout field allows you to either have the standard screen layout for a particular warehouse object or use a variant layout that show the results in a different format.

The variant layouts are numbered 1 through 6, with 1 being the standard variant. The layouts are described below.

1. Movement type > source storage type > destination storage type

2. Movement type > destination storage type > source storage type

3. Source storage type > destination storage type > movement type

4. Source storage type > movement type > destination storage type

5. Destination storage type > source storage type > movement type

6. Destination storage type > movement type > source storage type

The next configuration step is to define the critical parameters for warehouse monitor objects. This allows you to define when a situation is critical, and the warehouse activity monitor will identify it as such.

To configure the critical parameters for the warehouse activity monitor, follow the menu path IMG • LOGISTICS EXECUTION • WAREHOUSE MANAGEMENT • PLANNING AND MONITORING • WAREHOUSE ACTIVITY MONITOR • DEFINE CRITICAL PARAMETERS.

Unconfirmed Transfer Orders

Figure 12.2 shows the first of the critical parameter screens. You can enter the parameters for the unconfirmed transfer orders so that if a transfer order exists for a period longer than configured, the warehouse monitor will reference it as critical. In this instance the critical duration has been entered so that depending on the movement type the value can be different. The critical duration can be further defined by the source or destination storage type.

In this example for warehouse 100, movement type 91, the critical duration is four hours, but for movement type 101, the critical duration is only one hour.

> You can use variants to personalize the selection

> The configuration of the critical parameter is important for the activity monitor

> You can see unconfirmed transfer orders on the activity monitor

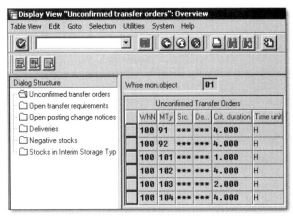

Figure 12.2 Critical Parameters for Unconfirmed Transfer Orders

Open Transfer Requirements

The second critical parameter screen defines the critical durations for open transfer requirements. Like the configuration for the unconfirmed transfer orders, the critical duration is defined for movement types per warehouse.

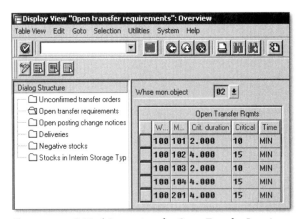

Figure 12.3 Critical Parameters for Open Transfer Requirements

Figure 12.3 shows the critical duration for each movement type for warehouse 100. In addition, a second critical time is used for transfer requirements for which the Immediate TO Creation checkbox is selected. The warehouse activity monitor uses the critical time period entered, which in this case is 10 minutes for movement types 101 and 103, to identify any transfer requirements where the transfer order has not been created within the time period.

Open Post Change Notices

The configuration for open post change notices is the same format as for open transfer requirements. It define the critical duration for each movement type for a warehouse, and if the Immediate TO Creation checkbox is selected, a second critical time period is entered to identify transfer orders not created within the defined time.

Open Deliveries

The warehouse activity monitor displays deliveries where the materials have been picked because either the time requirements for staging weren't met, the time deadline for loading the delivery wasn't met, or the time period for the goods issue for the delivery was exceeded.

Deliveries that are still open after the critical duration are displayed

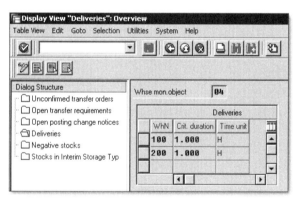

Figure 12.4 Critical Parameters for Open Deliveries

Figure 12.4 shows the configuration for open deliveries. In this example the critical duration of one hour has been entered for warehouses 100 and 200. The warehouse activity monitor identifies deliveries that haven't been completed within the critical duration entered.

Negative Stocks

The warehouse activity monitor shows all negative stock that has exceeded the critical time period entered in configuration.

Negative stocks can cause problems in the warehouse

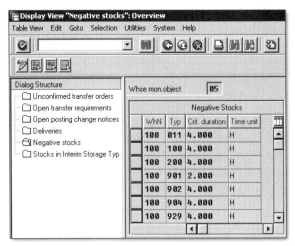

Figure 12.5 Critical Parameters for Negative Stock

Figure 12.5 shows the critical duration configuration that has been entered for each storage type in warehouse 100. The warehouse activity monitor shows all negative stock in a storage type if the status has exceeded the critical duration entered for that storage type.

Stocks in Interim Storage Type

When materials aren't moved out of the interim areas, a problem may have occurred

The warehouse activity monitor displays stock in interim storage types that hasn't moved within the critical duration entered into the configuration for the specific storage type. The configuration entries are the same as those for negative stock, where the critical duration is entered for each storage type.

The stock in the interim storage types is created as part of a movement. If the stock is still in the interim storage type after the critical period, then an issue is likely to have arisen.

12.1.2 Using the Warehouse Activity Monitor

You can only run the warehouse activity monitor for a single warehouse

The warehouse activity monitor runs for a single warehouse. You can run the transaction with or without a specific variant. Depending on the requirements of the warehouse, you can create a variant to use with the warehouse activity monitor.

You can execute the warehouse activity monitor by using Transaction LL01, or you can follow the menu path SAP • Logistics • Logistics Execution • Information System • Warehouse • Warehouse Activity Monitor.

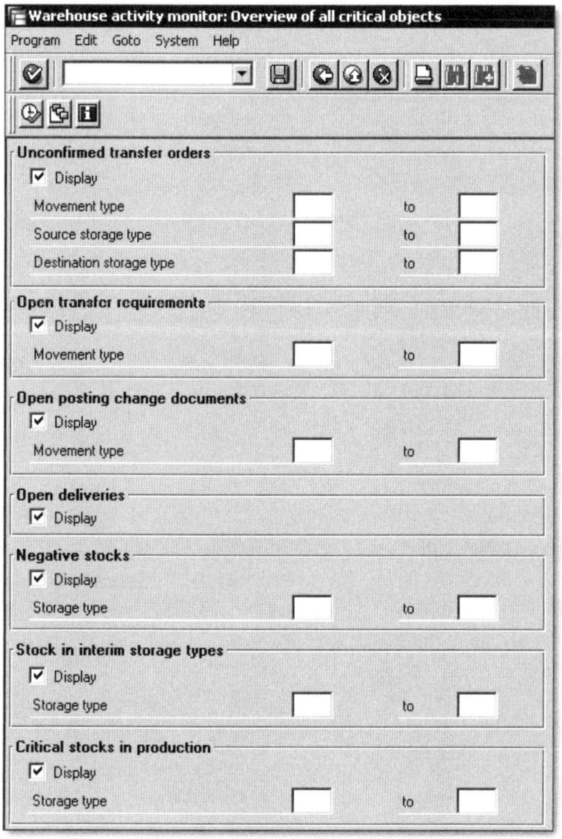

Figure 12.6 Warehouse Activity Monitor Selection Screen

Figure 12.6 shows the selection screen for the warehouse activity monitor, which shows the default selection where all options are selected. If you want to create a variant, select the required options and from the header menu select GOTO • VARIANTS • SAVE AS VARIANT. Then select a variant name and Save.

To execute the warehouse activity monitor, select the options you require.

Figure 12.7 shows the results of the warehouse activity monitor for the selections entered. The screen shows the number of critical processes for each of the selected options.

The traffic light system indicates the status of the processes for each option. A red light indicates that critical processes haven't been processed, a yellow light shows that the critical processes are being corrected but are not yet complete, and a green light indicates that the option has no critical processes.

A variant personalizes the selection options

The traffic light system clearly shows issues on the activity monitor

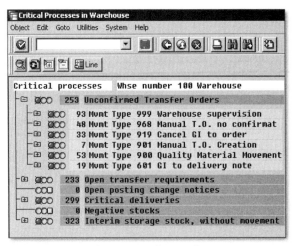

Figure 12.7 Critical Process in the Warehouse

In Figure 12.7 there are no critical processes for negative stocks or post change notices. However, there are 253 critical unconfirmed transfer orders, 233 open transfer requirements, 299 critical deliveries, and 323 critical processes with interim storage types.

In Figure 12.7 the 253 unconfirmed transfer orders have been expanded to show what movement types are affected. It is possible to drill down from the movement type to identify the source and destination storage types associated with the critical process.

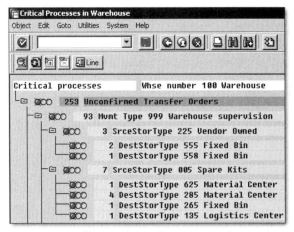

Figure 12.8 Drilldown of Critical Processes in the Warehouse

Figure 12.8 expands on the unconfirmed transfer orders for movement type 999. The drilldown shows three critical processes for source storage type 225 and seven critical processes for source storage type 005. You can drill down on any of the source storage or destination storage types to display the relevant transfer orders.

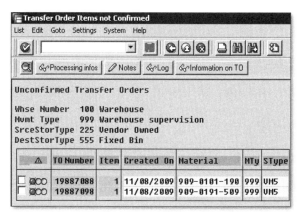

Figure 12.9 Transfer Order Items that Are Not Confirmed

Figure 12.9 shows the two transfer orders that have been identified as critical processes. You can view the processing information and general information on the transfer orders by clicking on the icons. If you need to process the transfer orders, you can use the options in the header menu.

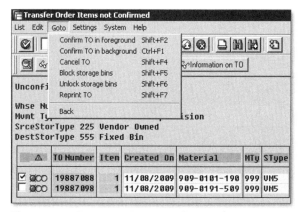

Figure 12.10 Processing Options in the Warehouse Activity Monitor

Figure 12.10 shows the processing options that you can execute. If you've completed the transfer order but not reported it, then you can confirm it.

If it can't be completed, you can cancel it. In addition, it's possible to unblock or block the storage bins if necessary.

> **Note**
>
> If you refresh the screen by selecting EDIT • REFRESH from the header menu, the warehouse activity monitor doesn't retrieve new data, but only refreshes the current data. Select EDIT • DETERMINE DATA AGAIN to retrieve new data.

12.2 Key Warehouse Reports

The standard warehouse reports are important in an efficient warehouse

In addition to the warehouse activity monitor, several standard reports are available to help warehouse staff maintain efficient warehouse operations. This section highlights four key reports that are used each day in collaboration with the warehouse activity monitor to effectively move material around the warehouse.

12.2.1 List of Empty Storage Bins

Warehouse managers sometimes need to know where empty bins are

When materials are placed in the warehouse, they need to be placed into empty bins. Although the system should be configured to provide the optimum storage bin for putaway, a manual intervention is sometimes required. In this instance the warehouse manager can turn to the report that shows the list of empty bins in the warehouse.

You can access the empty bin report by using Transaction LX01, or you can follow the menu path SAP • LOGISTICS • LOGISTICS EXECUTION • INFORMATION SYSTEM • WAREHOUSE • STORAGE BIN • LIST OF EMPTY STORAGE BINS.

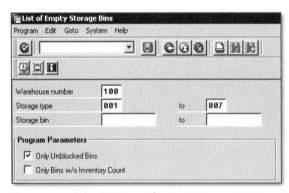

Figure 12.11 Selection Screen for Empty Storage Bin Report

Figure 12.11 shows the selection screen for the empty storage bin report. When you need to find an empty bin, enter a warehouse number and the range of storage types for the area in which the items need to be placed.

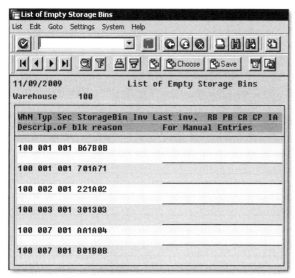

Figure 12.12   List of Empty Storage Bins Report

Figure 12.12 shows the results of the empty storage bin report. You can then select an appropriate storage bin for the transfer order.

12.2.2   Bin Status Report

The bin status report is useful because it gives the warehouse manager an accurate picture of the contents of a storage type and the relevant storage bins.

The bin status report shows warehouse staff what materials are in the storage type

To access the bin status report, use Transaction LX03 or follow the menu path SAP • LOGISTICS • LOGISTICS EXECUTION • INFORMATION SYSTEM • WAREHOUSE • STORAGE BIN • BIN STATUS REPORT.

Figure 12.13 shows the selection screen for the bin status report. You can enter a specific warehouse and storage types to display the relevant storage bins. In this example, the Only Bins with Stock checkbox is selected, which means the report will only show storage bins that actually contain material, and empty bins will not be displayed.

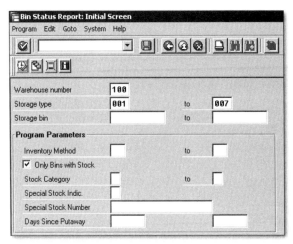

Figure 12.13 Selection Screen for the Bin Status Report

The bin status report shows how long the material has been in the bin

Figure 12.14 shows the results of the bin status report. The line item shows the material that is stored in storage bin and the length of time it has been in the bin, displayed in the TiL field.

If you need more information on a particular bin, you can double-click on the line item or press `Ctrl` + `Shift` + `F3`.

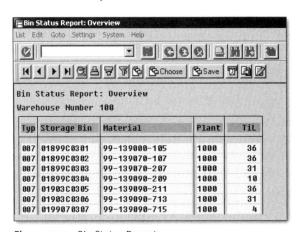

Figure 12.14 Bin Status Report

Figure 12.15 shows the line item detail from the bin status report. The warehouse manager can use this information to decide if materials can be moved to make way for incoming materials or for any other valid reason to identify the details of the storage bin.

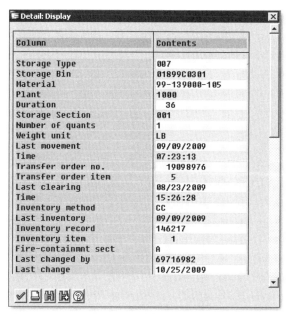

Figure 12.15 Line Item Detail from the Bin Status Report

12.2.3 Capacity Load Utilization

The capacity load utilization report provides an overview of the capacity of the warehouse and specific storage types. If the warehouse manager tries to optimize the use of space in the warehouse, he'll examine the capacity load utilization report and make changes where needed.

The capacity load report is important so managers can distribute material evenly

You can access the capacity load utilization report by using Transaction LX04, or you can follow the navigation path SAP • LOGISTICS • LOGISTICS EXECUTION • INFORMATION SYSTEM • WAREHOUSE • STORAGE BIN • CAPACITY LOAD UTILIZATION.

Figure 12.16 shows the selection screen for the capacity load utilization report. You can selection either a single storage type in the warehouse or a selection. The option to select by storage bin is included if you need to examine loads by bin.

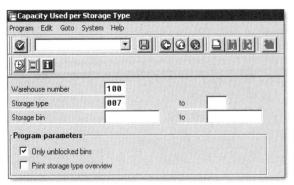

Figure 12.16 Selection Screen for Capacity Load Utilization Report

Figure 12.17 shows the results of the capacity load utilization report. The report shows that for storage type 007, there are five occupied bins and two empty bins, and currently 71.43% of the capacity of the storage type is used.

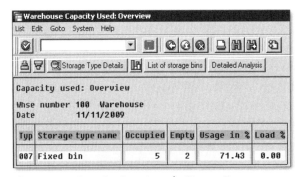

Figure 12.17 Capacity Overview of a Storage Type

12.2.4 Inventory Status

Inventory status shows managers what bins have been counted

The inventory status report helps you assess which storage bins have been through a physical count and if any are planned. Warehouse managers assess whether they want to use a storage bin based on if a storage bin has an upcoming count.

To access the inventory status report, use Transaction LX25 or follow the menu path SAP • Logistics • Logistics Execution • Information System • Warehouse • Physical Inventory • With Bin Inventory Management • Inventory Status.

Figure 12.18 shows the selection screen for the inventory status report. You can enter the warehouse and specific storage type and the inventory time period you want to review.

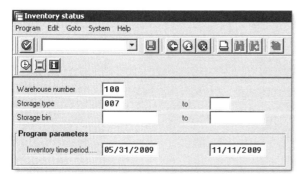

Figure 12.18 Selection Screen for Inventory Status Report

Figure 12.19 shows the inventory status report totals for the selected warehouse and storage type. None of the bins are active, so no current counts are in progress. The report also shows that no inventories are planned for this storage type and none have been performed on this storage type during the period entered in Figure 12.18.

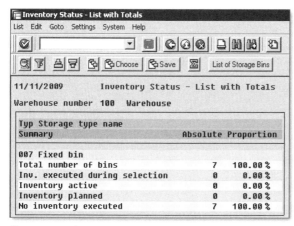

Figure 12.19 Inventory Status Report

Figure 12.20 lists the quants in each of the storage bins in storage type 007. At a glance, the warehouse manager can see the number of quants in the storage type and in which storage bin they're located. The screen

The capacity load report shows the number of quants per storage bin

shows that no count documents were recorded during the count period that was entered.

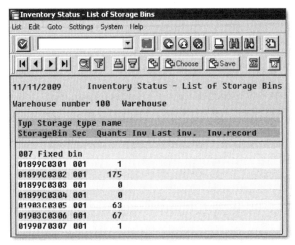

Figure 12.20 List of Storage Bins for the Inventory Status Report

The reports in the warehouse management functionality of SAP ERP offer the warehouse staff a wide range of options to help them manage the warehouse efficiently. You can use the reports shown here with the warehouse activity monitor to overcome any issues that arise.

12.3 Business Examples – Using Warehouse Reports Effectively

The reports and monitors that are available to warehouse management and staff contain the information they need to reassign resources, reschedule picking, and plan outbound deliveries. The combination of the warehouse activity monitor and the standard reports covers all aspects of operations in the warehouse.

> **Example**
>
> A U.S. distributor of automotive parts operated a warehouse in El Paso, Texas, that supplied parts to U.S. and Mexican automotive parts retailers. The company had used an SAP system since the site was opened and was using basic warehouse management functionality. The system automatically assigned storage bins based on a simple storage type search that caused few issues.

After a year of operation, the site moved from a single shift to a two-shift operation. The original warehouse operators were asked to work the first shift, because they were effective at getting deliveries out of the warehouse. A newly trained second shift was mainly responsible for putaway from the trailers that arrived in the afternoon.

Almost immediately the productivity in the warehouse began to fall. The transfer orders for outbound deliveries were not completed because materials weren't in the storage bins assigned by the system. The number of deliveries going out to customers fell, and operators spent more time trying to find materials than moving materials.

The outcome of several weeks of disruption was that the second shift was not always processing the transfer orders correctly. Half the transfer orders were completed correctly, whereas others were confirmed, but the materials weren't moved or were moved without the confirmation being processed. The company decided to take several actions to correct the problems.

The initial response was to move some staff from the first shift to the second shift. This was reinforced with ongoing training of the second shift personnel so that they understood the need to follow the prescribed procedure for putaway and picking. The final response was to introduce the use of the warehouse activity monitor. The plan was for the managers on the first shift to review the warehouse activity monitor for three specific processes: unconfirmed transfer orders, open deliveries, and stock in interim storage areas. The activity monitor was configured so that the processes became critical after eight hours. This meant that when the managers viewed the monitor at the beginning of the first shift, all of the processes from the second shift would be critical if they hadn't been completed. As soon as an item was displayed on the activity monitor, the warehouse manager would then assign an operator to investigate the issue. By using the warehouse activity monitor, the warehouse was able to correct issues before the outbound deliveries needed to be processed.

12.4 Summary

The staff in your warehouse needs information to keep the warehouse operating efficiently. The warehouse activity monitor is a vitally important transaction that management can use to oversee issues and errors as they arise. The configuration of the warehouse activity monitor is important because it controls what is shown. However, it's important to realize that as the efficiency of the warehouse improves, the configuration should be adjusted. If the critical time period for unconfirmed transfer orders had been set at four hours, and after six months, no transfer orders were appearing on the monitor, it may make sense to change the configuration to three hours. This would then encourage further improvement in warehouse efficiency.

The reports contained in the warehouse management functionality of SAP ERP cover all aspects of the warehouse operations. They can help the staff perform their jobs more effectively, and along with the warehouse activity monitor their use should be encouraged.

In the final chapter, we'll summarize the elements discussed in the previous chapters and discuss how your company can adopt the concepts to produce more successful warehouse processes.

13   Conclusion

In the preceding chapters, we've examined how to maximize the warehouse management functionality in SAP ERP to help improve the efficiency of your warehouse operations. In addition, the functionality we've discussed will help you successfully manage some of the complex situations that arise in the warehouse. In this conclusion, we'll examine the lessons learned from this book and make suggestions for further skill development.

13.1   Lessons Learned from This Book

This book is focused on how to maximize the warehouse management functionality in SAP ERP so that companies can deal with their complex warehouse issues. The best way to do this is to have staff and consultants that have a good understanding of the issues and knowledge of the warehouse management functionality to successfully implement the necessary solutions.

In this book we've covered the breadth of this functionality, and in this section we'll recap the major points highlighted in the chapters.

In Chapter 1, we discussed the importance of the warehouse in the supply chain and how it can be used to generate revenue rather than being a drain on resources. The chapter encourages readers to refamiliarize themselves with the key elements on which the warehouse management functionality is built, such as the plant, storage type, and storage bin. In addition to the SAP technical knowledge, the reader to chapter reintroduces warehouse operations such as receiving, deliveries, physical inventory, inspections, and quality.

Chapter 2 looked at the inbound delivery process for the warehouse. There are a number of aspects of inbound delivery that companies decide not to implement such as EDI, IDocs, advance shipping notices, handling units, and the inbound delivery monitor. Without these elements the inbound delivery process can be disjointed and inefficient. The use of the inbound delivery monitor can significantly reduce resource inefficiency because it allows the warehouse manager to plan how to use his staff to receive the inbound deliveries.

Chapter 3 examined the range of options that companies have to improve their putaway process. Not all companies are alike, and their warehouse operations can be significantly different. SAP has developed several putaway strategies that take into account the different ways companies want to place their materials in the warehouse. In addition, this chapter looked at the quality inspection process, which is important so that the unnecessary movement of stock is minimized.

In Chapter 4 we examined internal warehouse movements. These are not only the basic movements from one storage bin to another, but more complex concepts of the configuration of interim storage areas and posting change notices. Quite often companies don't fully understand the concepts of the various warehouse movements, and this can lead to inefficiencies in general warehouse operations.

Chapter 5 covered two major topics. The first topic is the strategies a company uses to pick materials for the outbound process. These picking strategies can make a significant difference in the overall efficiency of that process. Many companies have decided that it's not necessary to use picking strategies in the outbound process, but this lack of functionality can introduce inefficiencies into the picking operation.

The second topic covered in Chapter 5 is storage unit management. Although many companies have decided that this functionality is too complex to implement, many of them would benefit from it. The majority of companies move items in the warehouse on pallets or in cases, and this is the fundamental principal of storage unit management.

Chapter 6 examined the shipping completion functions in the warehouse. The first part of that process is the use of the outbound delivery. Although many companies decide this is an unnecessary step, the outbound delivery benefits the warehouse by allowing the management to plan resources with the use of the outbound delivery monitor. The other major benefit in shipment completion is the use of wave picking. Although this is not suitable for all warehouse operations, warehouses that experience resource issues based on the number of picks can significantly improve their efficiency by introducing wave picks.

The returns process, described in Chapter 7, is an area that most companies wish did not exist, and as such they often have very little in the way of a documented procedure. SAP ERP offers a clear returns process that is only successful if there is commitment from the various departments involved: sales, quality, finance, and warehouse. The interest in creating a value-added process, whereby returned items are restocked or refurbished, should mean that more companies will be reexamining and implementing the defined SAP process.

Chapter 8 examined the alternatives to the traditional annual physical count that companies have been performing for decades. The problem of inaccurate inventory figures affects several areas. Costs are involved in carrying larger safety stocks to offset potential stock outs, which can cause production disruptions or delays in shipments to customers. Different counting methods such as continuous and cycle counting reduce the need for companies to perform a traditional annual count, which increases inventory accuracy.

Cross-docking is not necessary for all warehouses, but if it is, this is a great way to reduce delivery times to customers while reducing costs in the warehouse. Chapter 9 examined the ways in which cross-docking can be planned to optimize the warehouse management functionality so that materials arrive at the warehouse shortly before they're due to be sent to a customer. Two important functions of the SAP solution are the cross-docking monitor and the alert monitor. Warehouse staff reviews these regularly to ensure that each cross-docking decision is successful.

Chapter 10 examined the management of hazardous materials in the warehouse. Not every warehouse contains hazardous material, but if your company does use or handle hazardous materials, it's important to have processes in place that not only comply with safety regulations, but keep your staff and facility safe. Some companies believe that can save money by reducing safety measures, but the opposite is true. Lack of safety procedures can lead to accidents to staff and damage to the warehouse or stock and could lead to fines by authorities. The functionality in SAP ERP for the management of hazardous materials is straightforward and should be considered if your warehouse contains any materials that are deemed as hazardous.

Chapter 11 reviewed how companies can use radio frequency identification (RFID) with their SAP system. Although many warehouses use radio frequency (RF) devices, RFID is becoming more popular because of mandates from companies such as Wal-Mart and government agencies such as the Department of Defense. Many companies have used SAP Auto Identification Infrastructure (SAP AII), and it's ideal for SAP customers who want to implement an RFID solution.

Chapter 12 covered the reporting aspects of the warehouse management functionality in SAP ERP that can increase the efficiency of the warehouse. The many standard reports can help warehouse managers with their daily activities. However, one crucially important function is the warehouse activity monitor. This monitor allows warehouse managers an "at-a-glance" view of the warehouse operations and allows them to react to and deal with issues as they arise. The monitor can be configured so that the unique parameters required in the warehouse can be entered, allowing for a more tailored approach to monitoring the warehouse.

13.2 Applying What You've Learned

Many companies have implemented a simple warehouse system using the warehouse management functionality of SAP ERP. They generally deal with more complex issues, such as hazardous material handling and returns, outside of the SAP system, relying on manual or outdated procedures. The knowledge that you have gained by reading this book will enable you to successfully apply what you have learned to helping these companies. By carefully explaining the concepts and benefits of maximizing the functionality they've already purchased, you may be able to help these companies achieve greater success.

I hope you've found this book a useful and valuable guide to helping your company develop their warehouse processes by maximizing the features of the warehouse management functionality of SAP ERP.

Appendices

A Glossary of Terms

ABC analysis   This analysis is assigned to a material, based on configuration, to indicate how often the material must be counted each year.

Active RFID tag   This battery-powered tag has an active transmitter onboard.

Annual physical   A company performs this inventory counting of assets and stock to start the fiscal year with an accurate financial picture.

Available stock   This is the same as unrestricted stock, that is, material that is free to be sold.

Batch   A batch is a quantity of materials grouped together for various reasons, often because the materials have the same characteristics and values.

Blocked stock   This term refers to material that has arrived at the receiving dock damaged and is not available for sale.

Bulk storage putaway strategy   This strategy is used to place incoming material into bulk storage.

Continuous inventory   This process consists of dividing the annual physical inventory count into several smaller inventory counts that are performed over the year. The goal is to ensure that all material is counted.

Cross-docking   A company performs cross-docking when it takes a finished good from the production plant and delivers it directly to the customer, with little or no material handling in between.

Cross-docking monitor   Warehouse managers use this tool to review the cross-docking situation in the warehouse and make any necessary changes.

Cycle counting   This is a process whereby a company continually checks the accuracy of the inventory in the warehouse by regularly counting a portion, so that every item in the warehouse is counted several times a year.

Distributor cross-docking   This process can include consolidation of inbound materials from different vendors into a mixed-material pallet.

Electronic Product Code (EPC)   The MIT AutoID center developed this RFID standard.

Fire containment section   This area in the warehouse has a specific fire-containment specification.

Fire department inventory list   This report specifies the quantity of material in each fire containment area by storage class. The fire department can then review the potential hazards and offer advice regarding storage changes.

First in, first out (FIFO)   The FIFO picking strategy removes the oldest quant from the storage type defined in the storage-type search.

Fixed bin replenishment   This strategy specifies when the storage bin in the picking area needs to be replenished so that outbound deliveries remain at maximum efficiency.

Fixed bin storage putaway strategy
This strategy for fixed-bin storage takes into account the data that has been entered into the material master record in order for the material to be placed in stock.

Fixed storage bin picking strategy
This is a strategy for using fixed storage bins that relies on the data entered into the material master record for the material to be picked.

Goods issue   Goods issue is the movement of materials from the warehouse to an external source. This source could be a production order or a customer.

Hazardous material   A hazardous material is one capable of producing harmful physical effects such as a fire, sudden release of pressure and explosion, or acute health effects such as burns, convulsions, and chronic injuries such as organ damage and cancer.

Hazardous material warning   This warning is applied to materials to indicate the type and level of hazard.

Hazardous substance list   This report lists all hazardous materials stored in a particular warehouse, storage type, or fire-containment area.

Inbound delivery   An inbound delivery is the process whereby goods are delivered to a receiving area.

Inbound delivery monitor   This tool displays open and completed deliveries, both inbound and outbound.

Inspection stock   Inspection stock is material that has been set aside for a quality inspection or another type of review. This material has been valuated but does not count as available stock.

Internal stock transfer   This process is triggered by the requirement to move materials from one part of the warehouse to another, from storage bin to storage bin.

Last in, first out (LIFO)   The LIFO picking strategy removes the last delivery of material to be received.

Manufacturing cross-docking   This operation involves the receiving of purchased and inbound materials required by manufacturing.

Near picking bin putaway strategy
This strategy is used to place incoming material to an area near the picking bin.

Next empty bin putaway strategy
This strategy determines that the material to be placed in stock is placed in the next empty bin.

Node   This term can refer both to a physical node where material is placed and to a logical node through which resources.

One-step cross-docking   This movement processes the cross-docking movement in one step, directly from the inbound goods-receiving area to the outbound goods-issuing area.

Open-storage putaway strategy   This strategy allows the storage of different materials in the same storage bin.

Opportunistic cross-docking   Applicable in any warehouse, this strategy involves transferring a material directly from the goods-receiving dock to the outbound shipping dock to meet a known demand.

Outbound delivery   This process involves picking goods, reducing the storage quantity, and shipping the goods. The process begins with goods picking and ends when the goods are delivered to the recipient.

Outbound delivery monitor   This tool allows the shipping department of the warehouse to view the deliveries that need to be picked for a variety of criteria entered for the transaction.

Partial quantities picking strategy   Warehouse staff use this picking strategy to reduce the number of storage units with partial quantities.

Passive RFID tag   This tag uses the reader field as a source of energy for the chip and for communication from and to the reader.

Picking area   This term refers to a group of warehouse-management storage bins that are used for picking.

Picking wave profile   Warehouses can us this profile to impose limits on certain criteria when reacting to waves during wave picking.

Posting changes   This warehouse movement changes the stock level of a material because of a change in the status of a material in a storage bin.

Project stock   Project stock is material being stored in the warehouse for a project or a work breakdown structure (WBS) element.

Putaway strategy   This strategy determines the process of deciding where materials received into the warehouse should be stored.

Quant   This term refers to the stock of material stored in a storage bin.

Quantity-relevant picking strategy   Warehouses that have varying sizes of bins and storage types where the same material is stored use this strategy.

Radio frequency (RF) monitor   Warehouse managers use this tool to view the queues that are being worked on in the warehouse.

Radio frequency identification (RFID)   A method of identifying an object using a radio-frequency transmission.

Requirement type   This classifies the origin type, for example, asset, purchase order, cost center, or sales order.

Retail-cross docking   This form of cross docking involves receipt of materials from multiple vendors and sorting onto outbound trucks for a number of retail stores.

Returnable transport packaging (RTP)   These materials arrive on pallets or containers and may need to be returned to the vendor.

Return delivery   A delivery from a customer returning items to the warehouse.

Reverse logistics   An extended returns process where the returns are either restocked or refurbished for resale creating a new revenue stream.

Sales order stock   This is individual customer stock that is managed in a warehouse.

SAP Auto-ID Infrastructure (AII)
AII is the current SAP solution for RFID functionality.

SAPConsole   This SAP tool enables RF devices to be run within SAP applications.

Semi-passive RFID tag   This tag uses built-in batteries and therefore doesn't require energy from the reader field to power the chip.

Shelf life control list   This list shows batches in the warehouse that are actively monitored for shelf-life.

Shelf life expiration date (SLED)   This is the date on which the material is no longer valid for sale.

Shelf life expiration picking strategy
With this strategy, materials are picked based on the shelf life of the quants of material in the warehouse.

Shipment type   The shipment type classifies the movement types in the warehouse, be they stock removal, stock placement, or posting change.

Site   A site can be part of a warehouse, many warehouses, or one warehouse.

Slap and ship   This is a method of complying with customer RFID requirements for physical identification of materials shipped through the outbound processes.

Special stock   This term refers to materials that are managed separately from regular stock.

Split picking   This process involves the splitting of a transfer order, whereby a new transfer order is created when the picking area is changed.

Storage bin   The storage bin is the lowest level of storage defined in the warehouse.

Storage section   A storage section is the part of a storage type that contains storage bins where materials are kept.

Storage type   A storage type is a defined area of the warehouse.

Storage type indicator   This tool allows only certain materials to be picked from storage types. The order can be defined by the storage type search for each storage type indicator.

Storage type search   In this configuration a sequence of storage types is defined, and the sequence is followed in searching for materials that are required for picking.

Storage unit   A storage unit is an identifiable unit in the warehouse containing materials and a container or pallet.

Storage unit management (SUT)   SUT covers the functionality and management of storage units in the warehouse.

Transfer order   A transfer order is the instruction to move materials from a source storage bin to a destination storage bin in a warehouse.

Transfer order print document   This is a printed form of a transfer order, with or without storage unit management.

Transfer requirement   This request covers the transfer of materials from a source storage bin to a destination storage bin in a warehouse.

Two-step cross-docking   This method first moves materials that are to be cross-docked from the goods receipts area to a cross-docking storage type. In a second step, it creates a transfer order from the interim storage type.

Uniform Code Council (UCC)   Manufacturers register with the UCC to obtain an identifier code for their company.

UPC bar code format   This format was adopted in 1973 as the industry standard so that any bar code on any product could be read and understood by any bar code reader.

Wave monitor   This tool enables the selection of waves for certain outbound deliveries.

Wave pick   This is a work package that contains several outbound deliveries.

Zero stock check   This process consists of a stock check on a storage bin after the materials have been removed, to ensure that the storage bin is empty.

B   Bibliography

Robert A Malone, "Chain Reaction: How Today's Best Companies Manage Their Supply Chain for Superior Performance," Kaplan Publishing, 2007.

Stuart Emmett, "Excellence in Warehouse Management: How to Minimize Costs and Maximize Value," John Wiley & Sons, July 2005.

James A. Tompkins, "Warehouse Management Handbook" (2nd Edition), Tompkins Press, October 1998.

Edward Frazelle, "World-Class Warehousing and Material Handling," McGraw-Hill, September 2001.

David E. Mulcahy, "Warehouse Distribution and Operations Handbook," McGraw-Hill, September 1993.

Creed H. Jenkins, "Modern Warehouse Management," McGraw-Hill, 1968.

Wal-Mart Corporation, "Continued Expansion of Radio Frequency Identification (RFID)," Wal-Mart Corporation, November 2006.

Roger B. Brooks & Larry W. Wilson, "Inventory Record Accuracy," John Wiley & Sons, 1995.

Chris Moose, "Make Your Picking Moves in SAP WM Strategically," SCM Expert, Wellesley Information Services, March 2006.

Intermec Technologies Corporation, "Practical Uses for RFID Technology in Manufacturing and Distribution Applications," Intermec Technologies Corporation, 2007.

David H. Williams, "The Strategic Implications of Wal-Mart's RFID Mandate," *Directions Magazine*, July 29, 2004.

Beth Bacheldor, "SAP Introduces Software for Product Tracking," *RFID Journal*, March 20, 2007.

Kevin R. Gue, "Cross Docking: Just in Time for Distribution," Graduate School of Business & Public Policy, Naval Postgraduate School, May 8, 2001.

Maida Napolitano, "Making the Move to Cross Docking," Warehousing Education and Research Council (WERC), 2000.

C   The Author

 A native of London, England, **Martin Murray** entered the computer industry upon his graduation from Middlesex University in 1986. He began working with SAP R/2 in 1991 in the materials management areas for a London-based multinational beverage company. In 1994 he immigrated to the United States and began working as an SAP R/3 consultant. Since then he has been implementing materials management and warehouse management functionalities in projects throughout the world. Martin is employed by IBM Global Business Services.

Martin is the author of the bestselling book *SAP MM – Functionality and Technical Configuration*, now in its second edition, as well as *SAP Warehouse Management: Functionality and Technical Configuration*, *Discover Logistics with SAP ERP*, and *Understanding the SAP Logistics Information System*. Martin lives with his wife in Orange County, California.

Index

T

Gain a detailed and practical understanding of SAP SRM to standardize your processes and lower costs throughout your company

Learn how to integrate SAP SRM with other core SAP components

Uncover key strategies, functionalities, and methodologies

Sachin Sethi

Enhancing Supplier Relationship Management Using SAP SRM

This is a completely updated, second edition that provides a detailed and practical understanding of the essentials of SAP SRM 7.0, including its functionality, new product enhancements, and best practices for optimizing business processes. Throughout the book, the author provides tips and tricks, practical examples, expert analysis on the changes in SAP SRM 7, and information on how SRM integrates with core SAP ERP components. This second edition covers the new SAP SRM 7 release, and includes coverage of Master Data Management, Organizational Structure, and e-Sourcing.

approx. 718 pp., 2. edition, 79,95 Euro / US$ 79.95
ISBN 978-1-59229-312-4, Dec 2009

>> www.sap-press.com

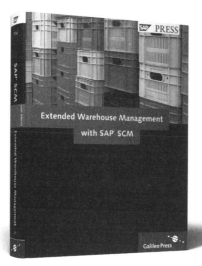

Provides the only complete reference to SAP SCM EWM

Covers everything from a general overview of the capabili-ties to detailed system set-up and configuration guidelines

Explains the difference between ERP EWM and SCM EWM

M. Brian Carter, Frank-Peter Bauer, Joerg Lange, Christoph Persich

Extended Warehouse Management with SAP SCM

This is the definitive guide to SAP EWM with SCM covering everything from a general functional overview to detailed system set-up and configuration guidelines. You'll learn about the key capabilities of the EWM solution; explore the configuration elements available in the standard solution; discover the methods used to solve common business process requirements; and find out how to extend the solution to meet your more complex or unique business requirements.

approx. 560 pp., 79,95 Euro / US$ 79.95
ISBN 978-1-59229-304-9, March 2010

>> www.sap-press.com